# *California*
# STATE PARKS GUIDE

Editor: John McKinney
Book Design: Mary Rose
Additional Cartography: Susan Kuromiya
Typography: Cook/Sundstrom Associates
Cover Design: Cheryl Kline, Pacific Palisades
Cover Photo: McArthur-Burney Falls Memorial
State Park, courtesy of State of California
Department of Parks and Recreation

## Acknowledgements

The editors would like to express their sincere appreciation for the enthusiasm and guidance offered during the preparation of this guide by the California State Department of Parks and Recreation. A special thanks goes to the many helpful park service employees in the Department's Sacramento office, who made available maps, historical data, statistics, brochures, photographs, and most importantly—their personal and collective expertise and enthusiasm.

Particularly helpful was Joseph H. Engbeck, Jr., Publications Director, whose research and writing skills have helped produce many useful publications for the Department, and whose efforts made an important contribution to this guide.

Another heartfelt thank-you goes to the many rangers from Anza-Borrego to Zmudowski, who were unfailingly courteous while conducting the editors through the parks, and who field-and fact-checked the information in this guide.

**Library of Congress Cataloging in Publication Data**

California state parks guide.
Includes index.
1. Parks—California—Guide-books. 2. Recreation areas—California—Guide-books. 3. Campsites, facilities, etc.—California—Guide-books. 4. California—Description and travel—1981 Guide-books. 5. Historic sites—California—Guide-books. 6. Natural history—California—Guide-books.
I. Title. F859.3.C34 1985    917.94'0453    85-11565
ISBN-0-934161-01-1

Photo Credits:
Cristine Argyrakis: 48, 55, 60; David Frech: 22; John McKinney: 20, 21, 22, 30, 31, 33, 34, 41, 43, 46, 50, 51, 54, 58, 59, 64, 124, 134, 138, 214; Maria Serrao: 13; All other photos courtesy of the State of California Department of Parks and Recreation.

Published by
OLYMPUS PRESS
Post Office Box 2397
Santa Barbara, California 93120

Printed in the United States of America

# *California*

# STATE PARKS GUIDE

By
The Editors of Olympus Press

OLYMPUS PRESS          SANTA BARBARA, CALIFORNIA

"Now you are to hear the most extraordinary thing that was ever heard of in the writings or memory of man... Know that on the right hand of the Indies, there is an island called California, very close to the Terrestrial Paradise..."

*The Deeds of Esplandian*
by Garci Rodriguez Ordóñez de Montalvo
1510

"The purpose of state parks shall be to preserve outstanding natural, scenic, and cultural values, indigenous aquatic and terrestrial flora and fauna, and the most significant examples of such ecological regions as the Sierra Nevada, northeast volcanic, great valley, coastal strip, Klamath-Siskiyou Mountains, southwest mountains and valleys, redwoods, foothills and low coastal mountains, and desert and desert mountains."

*Public Resources Code Section 5019.53*

*Camping, 1893*

# Introduction

In 1902, the California State Park System was born with the establishment of the California Redwood Park at Big Basin in Santa Cruz County. It is only fitting that one of the state's proudest possessions—the magnificent coast redwoods—should have provided the inspiration for the creation of California's first state park.

Other states have high mountains, great deserts, and scenic shorelines, but only California has all of these natural features within its boundaries. California's state park system is the most splendidly diverse of its kind in the nation. Dark, solemn redwoods grow along the mist-covered edge of the continent. The alpine beauty of the Sierra Nevada towers above world famous Lake Tahoe. Warm sandy beaches beckon visitors to southern California. The state's unique history comes alive at the Franciscan mission at La Purisima, the old Customs House in Monterey, Sutter's Fort and Old Town San Diego.

The 250-plus units of today's California State Park System are grouped into several different classifications, each of which is managed to best preserve its values and serve its visitors: State Parks contain outstanding scenic, natural, cultural, or ecological values; Wildernesses retain their primeval character; Reserves have outstanding or unusual natural or scenic values; and Historic Parks preserve places and objects of statewide historic significance. Several kinds of parks are devoted to recreation: Recreation Areas, Vehicular Recreation Areas, Beaches, and Wayside Campgrounds. Any of the parks might contain a Natural Preserve—an area of natural or scientific significance sometimes containing rare or endangered plant species, or unique geological or topographical features.

This guide is your invitation to adventure. You'll learn about the history and natural attractions of each park, and discover the best places for camping, fishing, boating, hiking, and picnicking. State parks preserve many stunning examples of California's varied landscape; they are yours to protect and enjoy.

# Southern Inland

## Table of Contents

# South Coast

6

# Central Valley

# Coastal Mountains

# Central Coast

# Coast Redwoods

# Inland Mountains

# North Coast

# Things to Remember

### SCHOOL VISITS

No entry charge will be made to public or private school groups from kindergarten through high school for day use of any state park unit (except Hearst San Simeon SHM) when advance reservations have been made. For reservations contact the parks directly.

### HUNTING

Some hunting is permitted in certain portions of Providence Mountains, Picacho, and San Luis Reservoirs SRAs. The areas open to hunting are shown on maps in the park offices. Check Fish and Game Regulations for seasons and restrictions on the species of game that may be taken.

At other times in these areas, and at all times in other units of the State Park System, hunting or the possession of loaded firearms is prohibited.

### BOATING

Boaters are expected to operate their boats with regard for the rights and safety of others. Operating a boat under the influence of liquor or narcotics is dangerous and illegal.

Boats must have a muffling device. Speed limits, particularly near water's edge, must be strictly observed. Boats operated between sunset and sunrise must have Coast Guard-approved running lights and waterskiing during this period is prohibited. Boaters should check for special local regulations.

Boats equipped with toilets or showers must be constructed so that waste cannot be dumped into the water.

### MARINE LIFE IN TIDE POOLS

It used to be thought that the tidal pools of the ocean, those rocky pockets that retain water when the tide goes out, were limitless sources of marine life. Unfortunately, this is not true. The marine invertebrates that inhabit these intertidal zones are in serious danger, and in some areas the pools have been stripped clean by indiscriminate collectors who perhaps don't realize that these simple animals will die shortly after removal from their environment. Even the mere act of turning over a rock and exposing the invertebrates to the sun can destroy them, so please follow the simple rule of "Look, but don't touch." With a few exceptions, all tidal invertebrates are protected.

## COLLECTING

Flowers, rocks, plants, animals, artifacts, and other features of the parks' natural and cultural history are protected by state law and may not be disturbed or collected. Collection of driftwood, however, may be allowed, and rockhounding is permitted at some beaches; collectors should inquire at the park office for the regulations in effect at each unit.

## DOGS

You may bring your dog with you; he must be kept in an enclosed vehicle or tent during the night, and on a controlled six-foot leash during the day. Dogs are permitted only in campground and day-use areas; in order to protect wildlife, they are not allowed on trails or on many beaches (check with the ranger).

There is a $1-per-dog-per-night camping fee. If your dog is over five months old, a license or other proof of current rabies inoculation is required.

## FIRES

Fires are permitted in park stoves and fireplaces, and gas-type cooking stoves may be used unless the area is posted otherwise. Fireworks are forbidden because of fire danger. In areas with a high fire hazard smoking may be prohibited. Check with a park ranger for local regulations.

Campers and picnickers must bring their own fuel, or purchase it in the park. Down wood may not be collected for fuel since it is a part of the natural environment, forming a humus that assists the growth of trees and plants.

## LITTER

Please help keep your parks beautiful...don't litter. If you brought it in, take it back out!

## POISON OAK

This infamous plant grows abundantly in many parks up to an elevation of about 5,000 feet. It may lurk under other shrubs or take the form of a vine and climb up a redwood or an oak. Poison oak's three-lobed leaves resemble leaves of the true oak. The leaves are one to four inches long and glossy, as if waxed.

All parts of the plant at all times of the year contain poisonous sap that can severely blister the skin and mucous membranes. Its sap is most toxic during spring and summer. Remember the Boy Scout adage: "Leaflets three, let it be."

*Poison Oak*

*Effects of Poison Oak*

## CAMPING IN THE STATE PARKS

(For detailed Campsite Reservation Information turn to page 224.)

Camping in California's State Park System is very popular—so popular that the Department of Parks and Recreation encourages you to reserve a campsite well in advance of your outing. You can reserve a campsite up to 8 weeks in advance, or as late as 2 days prior to arrival date.

Most of the state park campsites described in the *California State Parks Guide* can be reserved through the MISTIX computerized reservation system; all others are available on a first-come, first-served basis. There is a reservation fee in addition to the campsite fee; both must be paid when the reservation is made. Consult the "Reservations Information" chapter in the back of this guide.

For information on the State Park System, the nearest MISTIX outlet location, or to order reservation forms, call the Department's Reservation Office at 1-800-952-5580 (or TDD 916-324-1891) between 8:00 a.m. and 5:00 p.m. on business days (recording after hours). Or write to: Department of Parks and Recreation, P.O. Box 942896, Sacramento, CA 94296.

### TO MAKE A CAMPSITE RESERVATION

Fill out the Reservation Application that you requested from the Department's Reservation Office (that number again is 1-800-952-5580) or make a photocopy of the forms provided in the Reservation Information section of this guide. When you've filled out the forms, you may:

1. PHONE TOLL FREE: 1-800-446-7275 and charge your reservation to your VISA or MASTERCARD.

Reservations for INDIVIDUAL campsites are placed on sale 8 weeks (56 days) in advance at 10:15 daily.

Reservations for INDIVIDUAL campsites LESS than 8 weeks in advance are on sale from 8:00 a.m. to 9:00 p.m. each day.

2. GO TO A MISTIX OUTLET: They accept CASH, VISA or MASTERCARD as payment. (Outlet hours vary: Call 1-800-952-5580 for information on outlet hours and locations.)

3. MAIL THE COMPLETED FORM: With a check or money order made payable to MISTIX or a VISA or MASTERCARD number to MISTIX, P.O. Box 85705, San Diego, CA 92138.

### DIAL (1-800)
# I GO PARK
### (1-800-446-7275)

## ENROUTE CAMPING

If you've ever been frustrated by the "Campground full" signs when you're looking for a place to spend the night, the California State Park System's new Enroute Campsite Program is for you. Most of the enroute campsites, which are one-night-only spots for self-contained RVs, are located along California's scenic coast, in popular areas where campsites are at a premium, and some offer the opportunity to spend the night overlooking the beach in parks that don't have conventional campgrounds.

Enroute campsites are now open at these parks:

Silver Strand SB
4.5 mi. S of Coronado on Hwy 75.

San Onofre SB
3 mi. S of San Clemente on I-15 (Basilone Rd.)

Huntington SB
Hwy 1 at Hwy 39.

Bolsa Chica SB
3 mi. W (upcoast) of Huntington Beach on Hwy 1.

Emma Wood SB
4 mi. N of Ventura on U.S. 101.

El Capitan SB
20 mi. NW of Santa Barbara on U.S. 101

Refugio SB
23 mi. NW of Santa Barbara on U.S. 101

New Brighton SB
4 mi. S of Santa Cruz on Hwy 1.

Half Moon Bay SB
0.5 mi. W of Hwy 1 on Kelly Ave., Half Moon Bay

Mount Tamalpais SP
6 mi. W of Mill Valley on Panoramic Hwy

Samuel P. Taylor SP
15 mi. W of San Rafael on Sir Francis Drake Blvd.

Sonoma Coast SB
Hwy 1, Russian River to Bodega Head

Van Damme SP
3 mi. S of Mendocino on Hwy 1

Westport-Union Landing SB
N of Fort Bragg on Hwy 1 at Abalone Point

Lake Oroville SRA
1 mi. N of Hwy 162 on Hwy 70 (Garden Dr. exit) or 2 mi. N of Hwy 162 on Canyon Dr.

Benbow Lake SRA
2 mi. S of Garberville on U.S. 101.

## NOTE TO CAMPERS WITH DISABILITIES

You can reserve wheelchair accessible campsites now at seventeen parks by contacting the reservation system or by mail on a family campsite reservation form.

Wheelchair accessible campsites may be reserved at the following state parks, listed north to south: (During non-reservation seasons, all campsites are available on a first-come, first-served basis.)

Patrick's Point State Park

MacKerricher State Park

Lake Oroville State Recreation Area

Clear Lake State Park

Bothe-Napa Valley State Park

Folsom Lake State Recreation Area

Calaveras Big Trees State Park

Samuel P. Taylor State Park

Henry Cowell Redwoods State Park

San Luis Reservoir State Recreation Area

Pfeiffer Big Sur State Park

Morro Bay State Park

Carpinteria State Beach

Silverwood Lake State Recreation Area

Lake Perris State Recreation Area

Salton Sea State Recreation Area

South Carlsbad State Beach

## ENVIRONMENTAL CAMPSITES

The park service is reintroducing an old idea—camping as a means of getting away from it all. In one of the new environmental campsites you and your friends and family can feel that you are the only people for miles around.

To achieve this, environmental campsites are placed in settings hand-picked for scenic and natural qualities, separated from each other and from the regular campground. Each site includes a table, stove, and primitive toilet, and some have drinking water and fire pits. Neither vehicles nor other park visitors intrude on these special sites; campers carry their supplies, including fuel and sometimes water, a short distance to their campsites.

Environmental campsites are available at the following: Angel Island, Calaveras Big Trees, Cuyamaca Rancho, Fremont Peak, Salt Point, Humboldt Redwoods, Humboldt Lagoons, Mount Diablo, Mount Tamalpais, Montana de Oro, Julia Pfeiffer Burns, Henry W. Coe, and Sinkyone Wilderness State Parks; Folsom Lake State Recreation Area; and Sonoma Coast State Beach.

You can reserve these sites year-round. Reservations are recommended, but unreserved sites are available on a first-come, first-served basis. To reserve a site, you'll need to receive an application form from: Reservation Office, Department of Parks and Recreation, P.O. Box 2390, Sacramento, CA 95811.

You'll be required to pay both a camping fee plus a reservation fee.

The Reservation Office can supply forms and information at (916) 445-8828. California residents can call 800-952-5580, toll free, 8 A.M. to 5 P.M. weekdays.

14

*View from Mt. Palomar*

# Southern Inland

Many unusual natural features, such as the Joshua tree, can be found in California's hot, dry southern interior parks. Anza-Borrego Desert, with nearly half a million acres the largest of Califonia's State Parks, offers mountains, washes, and oases to delight a wintertime vacationer. And at the higher elevations of Mount San Jacinto and Cuyamaca Rancho SPs, some Southern Californians get their first, unbelieving look at real snow. Relief from summer heat can be found at Providence Mountains SRA; the caverns there are a cool 65° year 'round. Water-oriented recreation is available at Silverwood Lake, Lake Perris, Lake Elsinore, Salton Sea, and Picacho SRAs.

Historic parks tell the story of California's Mexican and early American period.

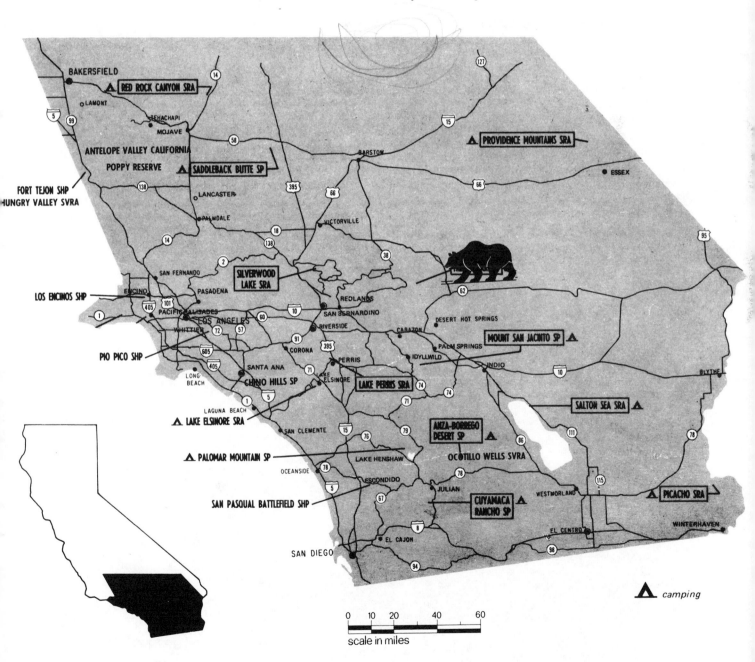

△ camping

scale in miles

16

## ANTELOPE VALLEY CALIFORNIA POPPY RESERVE

The Reserve is known for its spectacular wildflower displays in spring. During favorable years, whole fields may blossom for a duration of four to six weeks. The large bright orange California poppy, the official state flower, carpets the hillsides of the Reserve. Lupine, cream cups, and goldfields also contribute to the show.

March and April are generally the best months to view wildflowers at the Reserve. A state-of-the-art energy conserving Visitor Center has interpretive displays about the poppy and about alternative energy use. The Reserve is located 15 miles west of Lancaster on Avenue I (Lancaster Road).

## INDIAN MUSEUM

Howard Arden Edwards, a self-taught artist, fell in love with the scenery near Piute Butte while visiting the Antelope Valley. He homesteaded the land and in 1928, he and his family began building their dream home.

The chalet architecture has seven separate roof elevations. The interior is a remarkable blend of natural rock formations and man-made structure with painted symbols; large painted Kachina panels in the pitched ceiling of the living room are a prominent decorative feature.

Anthropologist Grace Oliver bought the property in 1938 and converted the home to a museum. Oliver added her own artifacts to those of the Edwards family and operated the museum for forty years. The state purchased it in 1979.

On the lower level is Kachina Hall containing artifacts from several different areas and the Southwest Room, which houses artifacts primarily from the American southwest. A natural passageway through the rocks leads to a California Hall on the upper level, where exhibits focus on California Indians.

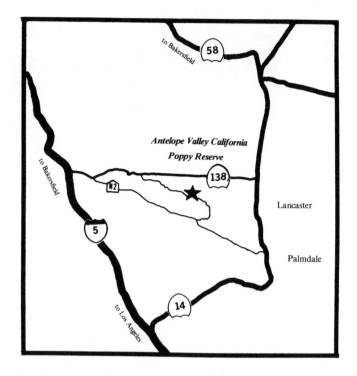

The Museum is situated seventeen miles east of the Antelope Valley Freeway (State Highway 14), located on Avenue M to 150th) or from Pearblossom Highway (138) turn north onto 165th Street East.

Tours are available by appointment only. The Museum is open to the public the second weekend of each month, with the exception of July thru September.

Antelope Valley Indian Museum
C/O High Desert District
4555 West Avenue G
Lancaster, CA 93534
(805) 942-0622

*California poppies*

Anza-Borrego Desert State Park

When Butterfield Overland Mail coaches from St. Louis sped through the desert over the southern route toward Pueblo de Los Angeles in the 1850s, the hot lowlands and rugged mountains that are now part of the half-million-acre Anza-Borrego Desert State Park stood as the final barrier of the vast Colorado Desert. Stagecoach passengers were only too happy to leave this arid wilderness.

Today, this very vastness and desolation are the desert's greatest attraction. Though it is less than three hours from the major metropolitan centers of Southern California, the park's isolation, magnificent vistas, and clear star-studded nights unspoiled by city lights draw nearly one million visitors annually. During the winter and spring, when the park receives its greatest use, the desert wildflowers bloom in a profusion of color and daytime temperatures range in the 70s and 80s.

Narrow, tortuous canyons are exciting places to see by jeep or dune buggy; their sandstone formations—sculptured into fantastic shapes by a million years of wind and rain—meet the eye at every turn.

Ranger-guided nature walks and auto tours, as well as campfire programs, are available on weekends and holidays from October to May; check at park headquarters or with a ranger for the schedule.

The desert is extremely fragile; it needs protection from people rather than the other way around. Proof of this can be seen in the scars left thirty and forty years ago by prospectors and homesteaders—they are as fresh as if made yesterday. Ecologists estimate that it takes about fifteen generations (five hundred years) for nature to restore an area to its original condition, once it has been denuded of vegetation. For this reason vehicles may be driven only on approved routes of travel.

The park contains several self-guided nature trails; self-guided automobile tours also provide an excellent way to become acquainted with the desert. Each tells its own story of geology, of plants, and of history. Brochures describing these tours are available at park headquarters and from the rangers.

# Anza-Borrego Desert State Park

### CAMPING

The park contains two developed family campgrounds, one near park headquarters at Borrego Palm Canyon (117 sites) and one at Tamarisk Grove (25 sites). The sites at these campgrounds contain tables, wood stoves, shade ramadas, and cupboards; water and restrooms with flush toilets and showers are nearby. Wood fuel is sold at the park, or bring your camp stove and fuel. Vacation trailers up to twenty-four feet long and motorhomes up to thirty-one feet can use these sites.

Campers with motorhomes, trailers or pickup campers may prefer to use the trailer area at Borrego Palm canyon; its . fifty-two paved "pull-through" parking spaces have connections for water, electricity, and sewage. This area is not suitable for tent camping.

If you are planning to camp in one of Anza-Borrego's developed or trailer campsites on a weekend or holiday during the winter, reservations are recommended.

Primitive campgrounds are scattered throughout the park (see map). Facilities there include only pit or chemical toilets and trash cans; *you must bring your own water.*

A horse camp is also located in the park. The ten sites include tables, stoves, toilets and showers. Reservations are recommended.

In addition, you are welcome to camp anywhere along park roads or designated routes of travel—for many people, this is the *only* way to camp in the desert. But please remember, when you establish your campsite to minimize your impact, and take out your trash.

There is a group campground located at Borrego Palm Canyon that will accommodate up to 120 campers; for more information, and reservations, contact park headquarters.

Anza-Borrego Desert State Park
Borego Springs, CA 92004
(619) 767-5311

### POINTS OF INTEREST

To list all the major points of interest at Anza-Borrego Desert State Park is impossible. For one thing, they haven't all been discovered yet! Here, however, are some of the scenic highlights. . . .

**Font's Point** (map coordinates E-6)—From the overlook you will see the Borrego Badlands, a maze of barren, steep-sided ravines and flat, dry creek beds almost totally devoid of vegetation. North of the point are the Santa Rosa Mountains.

**Yaqui Well** (G-4)—Many legends of lost gold mines originate at Yaqui Well, a famous old seep in the San Felipe Wash. The seep is on the flyway of many migratory birds. The berries of the mistletoe growing on a large stand of giant desert ironwood here furnish food for the wildlife.

**Split Mountain** (1-8)—This is one of the most breath-taking sights in the park. Perpendicular canyon walls rise more than six hundred feet in places, and during desert downpours the runoff from sixty thousand acres turns the narrow gorge into a torrent of water, sand, boulders, and brush. These flash floods obliterate jeep trails and rearrange creek beds.

**17 Palm Oasis** (D-8)—A desert seep provides sufficient water to enable this small group of palms to survive. Roads to this oasis are recommended only for four-wheel-drive vehicles.

**Elephant Trees** (H-8)—Most of California's puffy-looking elephant trees, a botanical oddity, grow in the park. A large stand of them is on a rocky hillside a short distance from the mouth of Split Mountain, and there are scattered specimens in Indian Canyon and Bow Willow Canyon farther south. A trail leads to the Fish Creek grove from a parking lot 1.5 miles away.

**Mountain Palm Springs** (K-6)—Several groups of palms are hidden from view in the three branches of this canyon. Elephant trees can also be seen on the rocky slopes.

**Box Canyon Historical Area** (1-3)—The famous trail-blazer Kit Carson, the Mormon Battalion, and the Butter-field Overland Mail used this canyon, one of the more difficult portions of the Southern Emigrant Trail.

**Calcite Canyon Scenic Area** (D-8)—This is an out-standing area of unusual sandstone canyons and formations, accessible only to four-wheel-drive vehicles or by foot. The scars left by calcite trench mining operations are still visible.

**Palm Spring** (J-6)—A mesquite oasis with a few native palms, this is a good bird and wildlife area. A marker tells the story of how early travelers used the waterhole.

**Lookout Point** (E-3)—On a clear day, Salton Sea, thirty miles to the east, is visible from this short-hike overlook near the Culp Valley primitive camp area. The 260-square-mile Sea, which lies 235 feet below sea level, is noted for its excellent water sports and corvina and sargo fishing.

**Sandstone Canyon** (I-6)—Four-wheel-drive vehicles, and only narrow ones at that, can negotiate this most spectacular small canyon in the park. Flanked by sheer walls often rising to 200 feet, the canyon winds tortuously into the badlands. Here the brute cutting power of desert thunderstorms is graphically illustrated.

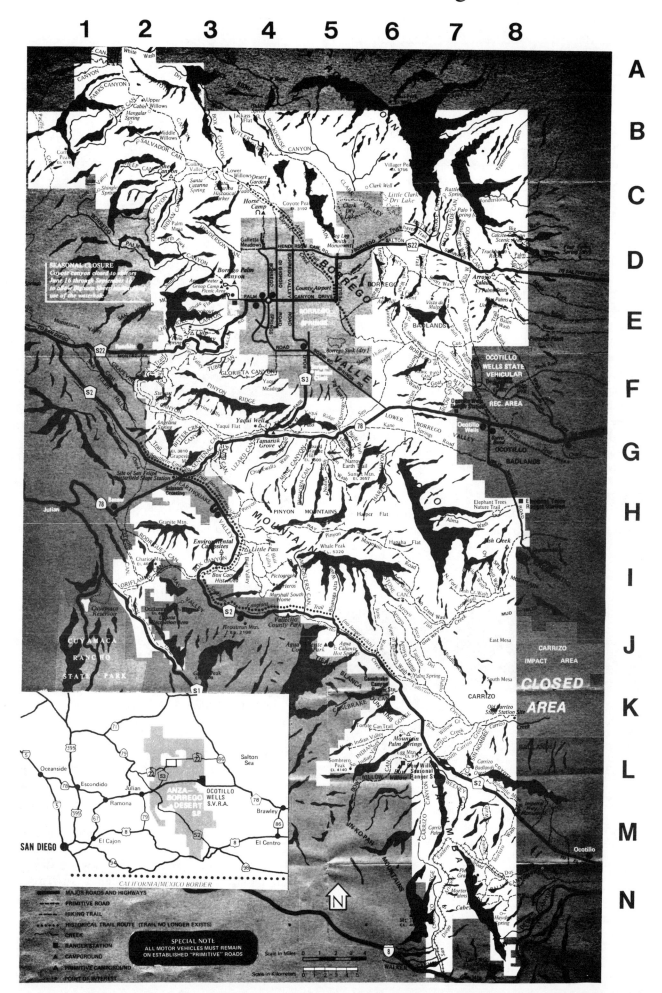

# Chino Hills State Park

Chino Hills State Park, located in Orange, San Bernardino and Riverside counties, preserves some much-needed "breathing room" in this fast-growing area. Nearly three million people live within sight of the Chino Hills and over nine million people live within a 40-mile radius of the park!

When compared with the surrounding urban landscape, the Chino Hills have been relatively unaltered by civilization. On clear days, fine views are available from San Juan Hill, Gilman Peak, and Panorama Point. The grassy hills are brilliant green during spring and golden brown in summer.

The park is the state's most expensive ever, with some $47 million spent by the time it opened for full time use in 1986. Right now, Chino Hills is a park-in-the-making. Few signs or facilities have been installed. Development plans call for 35 miles of hiking trails and 62 miles of riding trails.

The 10,000-acre park is located near the northern end of what geologists call the Peninsular Ranges Geomorphic Province. The Chino Hills are part of a group of hills that also include the Puente Hills to the northwest. These hills form a roughly triangular area of approximately 35 square miles of valleys, canyons, hills, and steep slopes.

Chino Hills State Park experiences a Mediterranean climate, with cool, moist winters and warm, dry summers. Easterly breezes, the Santa Ana winds, bring in dry desert air. Sometimes the strong (35-50 mile per hour) winds may blow for several days and raise temperatures in the park to over 100° Fahrenheit. High temperaturs, often combined with heavy smog, suggest that a summer visit can be something of an ordeal. The park is much more pleasurable in the cooler months, and especially delightful in spring.

*Windmills and rusted farm machinery recall the parkland's ranching history.*

## HISTORY

The land that now comprises the state park was once used by the Gabrielino Indians. The Gabrielino, who situated their villages near dependable water supplies and abundant game, roamed the Chino Hills to seasonal gathering camps in order to collect acorns, walnuts, and wild seeds.

When the Spanish settled southern California, the Chino Hills became part of the extensive grazing lands granted to Mission San Gabriel, established in 1771. During the Mexican-Californian era, the area served as spill-over grazing land for Rancho Santa Ana del Chino to the north, and ranchos Canon de Santa Ana and La Sierra Yorba to the south.

The gold rush brought Americans to the state. Ranchers and cattle companies bought or assumed titles to various parcels of land in the Chino Hills. For more than a century, the land was used exclusively for livestock grazing. The state purchased land from private ranchers and from an oil company, and in 1983 opened the park to limited public use.

## NATURAL HISTORY

Fossils are numerous in the Chino Hills. Most abundant are the microscopic foraminfera contained in layers of marine sandstone. Geologists use these small animal remains as key indicators in order to date strata for possible petroleum exploration. Some larger shell remains from mollusks have been found, as well as shark teeth.

Petroleum has been produced from oil fields in the region since 1885, with the first commercial production of oil in the Los Angeles basin at the old Puente oil field west of the state park. Numerous oil wells have been drilled in the Chino Hills; however, there is no record of commercial production in the park.

Extensive grasslands blanket the slopes. The hills are covered with wild oats, rye, black mustard and wild radish. On south-facing slopes is the soft-leaved shrub community, dominated by aromatic shrubs, including California sagebrush, white sage, purple sage and black sage.

Along the creek bottoms and on north-facing slopes grow cottonwood, coast live oak and sycamore. Of particular interest is one of the state's largest remaining groves of Southern California black walnut trees.

Coastal sage scrub provides important forage for wildlife such as small rodents, rabbits, and seed-eating birds. Chaparral provides the dense cover required by birds such as the California thrasher and wrentit. Mice and squirrels fall prey to numerous raptors such as the American kestrel, red-tailed hawk, and barn and great horned owl. Foxes, coyotes, bobcats, and rattlesnakes are also found in the park.

Aliso Creek, a tributary of the Santa Ana River, supports one of the few remaining populations of the native arroyo chub. Two other native fish, the Santa Ana sucker and the speckled dace, may also use the creek.

One unique aspect of the park is the livestock ponds, which were constructed during the area's ranching era. Some of these ponds still exist, and hold water year-round during most years. McDermont Spring, Windmill, and Panorama ponds provide water for wildlife, and habitat for aquatic plant life.

## FACILITIES

The park's primitive campground has eight sites located in a stand of sycamores. Tables, water, and chemical toilets are provided.

Near the campground is an equestrian staging area (water trough, chemical toilets) for unloading horse trailers. Chino Hills is definitely horse country and horseback riding is one of the most pleasurable ways to enjoy this park. Mounted volunteers patrol the park on weekends and are quite helpful to visitors.

A hikers' trailhead can be found at the park office and ranger station. Hikers will enjoy a 2-mile walk along a creek, returning on an old road through a fine grove of rare Southern California black walnut trees.

Currently, the trail system for the most part is a complicated system of old dirt ranch roads, so hikers (and riders, too) are advised to stop at the ranger station for a good look at the large topographic map that locates trails.

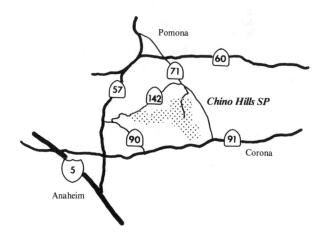

Despite its location so close to the metropolis, Chino Hills State Park can be a bit tricky to find. The park is located east of Highway 71 between the Riverside Freeway (State 91) and the Pomona Freeway (State 60). Traveling south on 71 from 60, visitors should turn right on Los Serranos Road and then make a quick left onto Pomona-Rincon Road. (Visitors heading north on 71 from 91 will spot, before reaching Los Serranos Road, a left turn lane leading directly to Pomona-Rincon Road.) A half mile of travel along Pomona-Rincon Road brings you to a brickyard with a mailbox marked "15838 Rolling M Ranch." Take the dirt road next to the brickyard for 2 miles to the park entrance.

# Cuyamaca Rancho State Park

Cuyamaca Rancho State Park is located high in the Peninsular Range of mountains about forty miles east of San Diego. Several mountain peaks lie within its 26,563 acres, along with a wide range of interesting and scenic natural environments. Beautiful forests of oak and pine and other trees are intermixed with broad upland meadows and little streams that are a special delight in the generally dry Southern California landscape.

Many first-time visitors to the park are surprised to find such a richly forested area in Southern California. Among the magnificent stands of oak trees are some of California's largest specimens of canyon live oak; willows, alders, and sycamores grow along the streams. Perhaps most surprising are the dense stands of tall cone-bearing trees—incense cedar and white fir, and Coulter, sugar, ponderosa and Jeffrey pines.

In 1845, Mexican Governor Pio Pico granted Rancho Cuyamaca—including the area of the present-day park—to Agustin Olverra, who planned to make a fortune by converting the Cuyamaca forests into lumber for Southern California. In 1847 to '48 he sent Cesario Walker into the mountains to build a lumber mill and cut trees. As Olverra later described it, however, the Indians "made a kind of revolution, and Walker abandoned the place."

Then gold was discovered. During the 1860s, Chinese laborers and others worked placer mines in the country north and west of Julian, outside the present-day park boundaries. In the spring of 1870, gold-bearing quartz ledges were discovered in that area and near the southern end of Cuyamaca Lake inside the park area. Within hours a gold rush was under way. Hundreds of miners and prospectors poured into the mountains.

By 1872 the Stonewall Mine was the most extensively developed mine in the region, and the town of Cuyamaca had grown up around it. Before the mine was closed down in 1892 it produced more than two million dollars' worth of gold, with a work force of as many as 200 men. The town of Cuyamaca survived for a time as a summer resort but eventually even this activity faded away, and in later years the town completely disappeared.

There are more than a hundred miles of riding and hiking trails in Cuyamaca Rancho State Park. One of the most spectacular and popular is the 3½-mile-long Cuyamaca Peak Trail which climbs up through a forest of oaks, pines and firs, past Deer Spring to the 6,512-foot-high summit. The view from this peak stretches out to the Pacific Ocean on the west, Desert to the east.

The Harvey Moore Trail, a specially marked riding and hiking trail, begins near the Sweetwater River Bridge a half mile north of Green Valley, goes into the East Mesa country, passes by the Granite Spring Trail Camp and then continues through the scenic Harper Creek Canyon area before coming back to the main road just north of park headquarters.

## CAMPING

*Paso Picacho Campground* and picnic area, located in the northern part of the park, has eighty-five family campsites, each with a table, wood stove, and food locker. Piped drinking water and buildings with restrooms, hot showers, and laundry tubs are nearby. Travel trailers can fit into some sites, but without sewer, water, or electrical hookups. This area also has group camps for up to 160 people.

*Green Valley Campground* in the southern part of the park has eighty-one family campsites with accommodations similar to those at Paso Picacho. The Sweetwater River turns west at this point and descends rapidly through a narrow canyon as the very pretty and popular Green Valley falls. Each spring the river is stocked with trout.

Primitive trail camps for up to forty people are located at *Arroyo Seco* and *Granite Spring*. Registration and other arrangements for their use are handled at Paso Picacho Campground.

A campground for families with horses, *Los Caballos,* found southeast of Cuyamaca lake on the California Riding and Hiking Trail, has sixteen developed sites with two metal corrals each. Additional corrals are available at a nearby equestrian day use area. *Los Vaqueros,* a campground for equestrian groups, will accommodate up to eighty people and fifty horses; it has forty-six metal corrals.

# Cuyamaca Rancho State Park



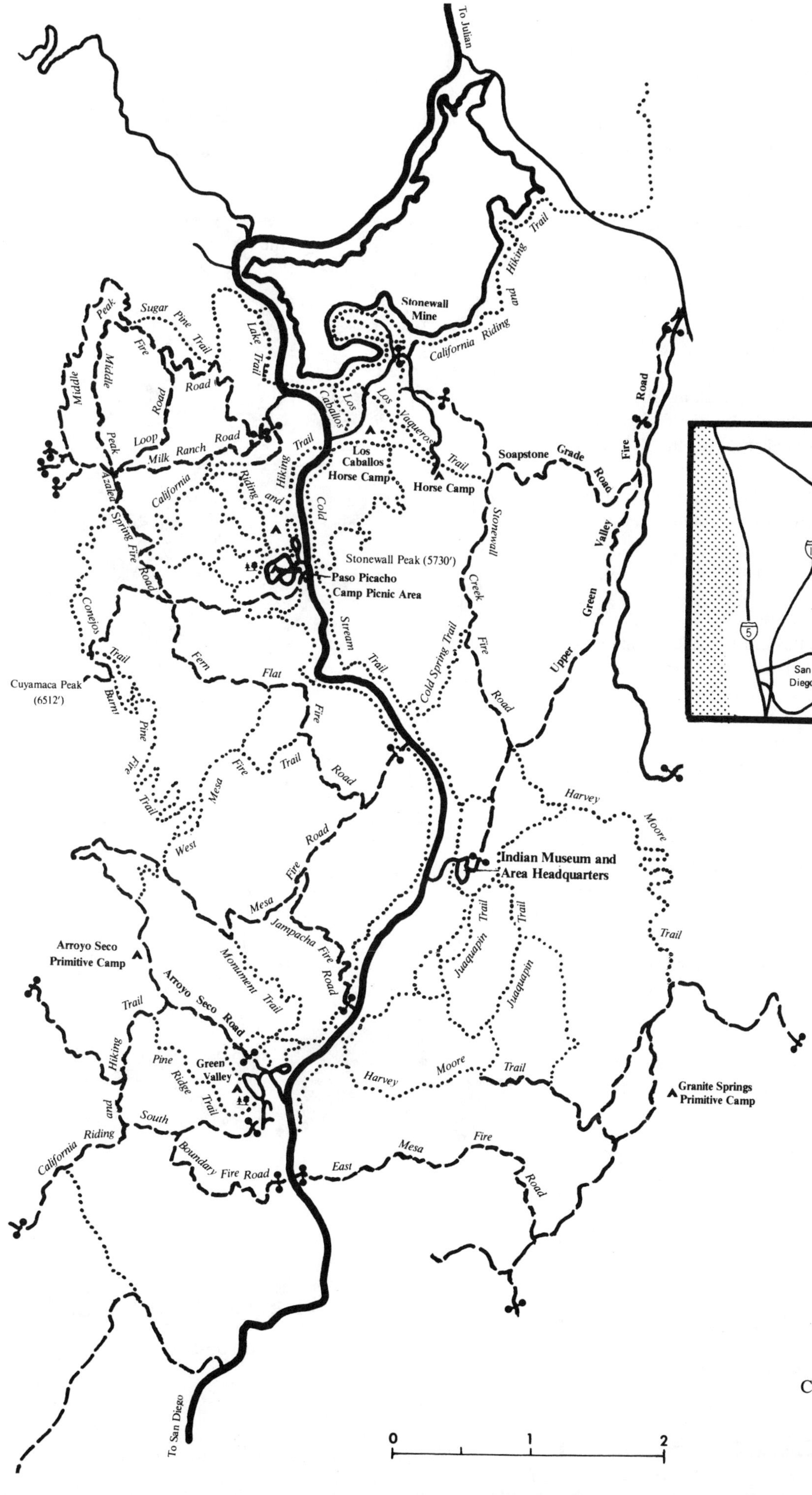

To Julian
Stonewall Mine
California Riding and Hiking Trail
Sugar Pine Trail
Middle Peak Fire Road
Middle Peak Loop
Lake Trail
Los Caballos
Los Vaqueros Trail
Los Caballos Horse Camp
Horse Camp
Milk Ranch Road
Soapstone Grade Road
Fire Road
Azalea Spring Fire Road
Cold Stream Trail
Stonewall Peak (5730′)
Paso Picacho Camp Picnic Area
Stonewall Creek Fire Road
Upper Green Valley Fire Road
Conejos Trail
Fern Flat Fire Road
Cold Spring Trail
Cuyamaca Peak (6512′)
Burnt Pine Fire Trail
West Mesa Fire Trail
Harvey Moore Trail
Indian Museum and Area Headquarters
West Mesa Fire Road
Jampacha Fire Road
Juaquapin Trail
Arroyo Seco Primitive Camp
Arroyo Seco Road
Monument Trail
Pine Ridge Trail
Green Valley
Granite Springs Primitive Camp
South Boundary Fire Road
East Mesa Fire Road
To San Diego
0
1
2


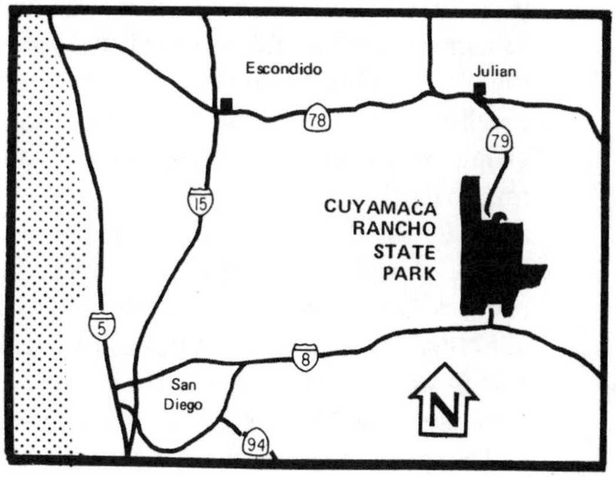

Escondido
Julian
78
79
15
CUYAMACA RANCHO STATE PARK
5
8
San Diego
94
N


Cuyamaca Rancho State Park
12551 Hwy. 79
Descanso, CA 92016
(619) 765-0755

# Fort Tejon State Historic Park

Ignacio del Valle, owner of the original Mexican land grant on which the fort stands, called his land *Tejon,* which in Spanish means badger. Construction of the post began in 1854 by a detachment of Company "A," First U.S. Dragoons under the command of First Lieutenant Thomas Castor.

For a small post, the personnel of Fort Tejon were quite active. Patrols traveled as far east as the Colorado River, penetrated unexplored regions of the Owens Valley, and rode the supply route to and from Los Angeles. The troopers guarded miners, chased bandits and provided law and order for Southern California.

Descriptions of Tejon by visitors in the 1850s include such statements as: "The post of Tejon is on a little plain, entirely surrounded by high mountains, beautifully situated in a grove of old oaks; at this season the frost is most romantic and beautiful. The noble oaks are in full leaf. On the plains and mountain sides, Mother Nature has almost excelled herself, carpeting them with flowers of every hue, giving to the eye one of the most beautiful prospects imaginable."

Under the direction of U.S. Secretary of War Jefferson Davis, camels were imported in 1857 for transporting supplies to isolated posts in the arid southwest. In the fall of 1857, under the direction of Edward F. Beale, twenty-eight camels were used by a wagon road survey party from Fort Defiance, New Mexico to Fort Tejon.

The splendid performance of the camels moved Beale to recommend that the Camel Corps be expanded. One camel was more valuable than four of the best mules—the camels carried water for the mules; they traversed stretches of country covered with sharp volcanic rock without injury to their feet; they climbed with heavy pack over mountains where the unloaded mules found it difficult to go even with assistance from dismounted riders; and they even plunged into rivers without hesitation and swam with ease.

The barracks building and officers' quarter have been restored. A museum interprets the fort's intriguing history. Scattered beneath the big oaks are a number of picnic tables.

Located in Grapevine Canyon on Interstate 5, Fort Tejon is thirty-six miles south of Bakersfield and seventy-seven miles north of Los Angeles near the small community of Lebec.

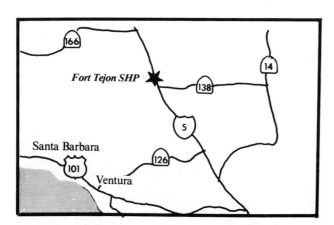

*Camel Corps*

Fort Tejon State Historic Park
35251 Fort Tejon Road
Lebec, CA 93243
(805) 248-6692

# Hungry Valley State Vehicular Recreation Area

Set in the rolling hills of northern Los Angeles and Ventura Counties, the 18,000-plus acres in Hungry Valley SVRA offer a variety of terrains for all levels of motorcycling skill. Four-wheel-drive and dune buggy operators, too, can find challenges in the park's hills, valleys, canyons, and washes. Most of the area's users come on weekends; to have it more or less to yourself, visit during the week.

Just over the hills from Interstate 5 at Gorman, the valley that makes up a third of the park is broad and fairly level, bordered by bluffs for hillclimbs. East of Hungry Valley, rugged badlands in Freeman Canyon offer scenic and challenging off-roading. To the west are connections with motorcycle trails in the Los Padres National Forest.

Much of Hungry Valley SVRA is open to unrestricted off-road vehicle use. Over 15,000 acres are available for trail riding, and the 1,500-acre Quail Canyon area, accessible from Peace Valley road, can be reserved for motorcycle and 4WD club and competitive events. OHVs must be street-legal and licensed or must have current OHV registration (green sticker) and U.S. Forest Service-approved spark arrester.

The State Park Rangers who patrol Hungry Valley SVRA are trained in emergency medical treatment, and they can call in help by radio. The nearest telephones are in Gorman, including a free emergency phone outside the sheriff's station. There are no doctors in Gorman. The hospital nearest to Hungry Valley is Henry Mayo Hospital in Newhall, thirty miles to the south via I-5 and McBean Parkway.

## CAMPING

A 1,600-acre area in Hungry Valley has been set aside for camping; there are chemical toilets, but no water. Primitive camping is also permitted in the Quail Canyon area in connection with special events there.

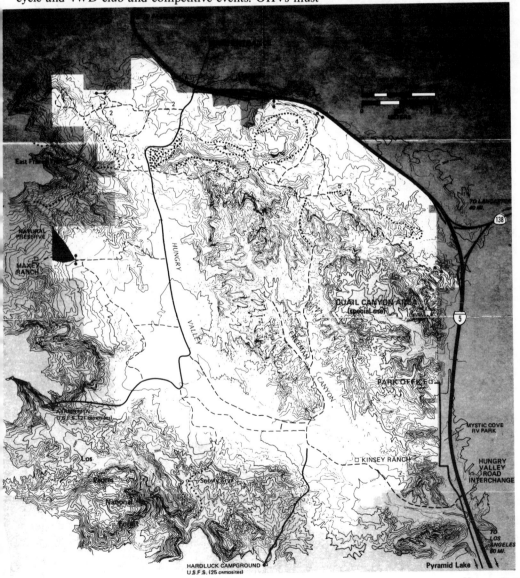

PAVED ROADS

DIRT TRAILS (for motorcycles)

DIRT ROADS

OPEN RIDING AREA

OPEN RIDING/CAMPING AREA

Hungry Valley State Vehicular Recreation Area
P.O. Box 1360
Lebec, CA 93243
(805) 248-6447

# Lake Elsinore State Recreation Area

David A. Frech

*Lake Elsinore*

Lake Elsinore figured prominently in the legends of the Pai-ah-che Indians, who called it "the Little Sea." The lake and surrounding valley provided fish and game, as well as acorns and many edible plants. In the early nineteenth century Spaniards renamed the lake Laguna Grande; it was part of Rancho la Laguna, a land grant embracing the lake.

In 1883, Franklin Heald and two other capitalists purchased Rancho la Laguna and founded the town of Elsinore, which was named after the Danish castle made famous by Shakespeare's *Hamlet*. The town soon gained national recognition as a health and pleasure resort.

By the 1950s Elsinore was a lake in trouble, in danger of completely disappearing by evaporation and seepage through fissures. It was refilled in 1964 and became a State Recreation Area.

Nestled in a little valley between mountain ridges, Lake Elsinore in Riverside County offers a variety of watersports including fishing, boating, and waterskiing. Bicyclists enjoy touring the area. Ultralight and hang gliding events are frequently held at the lake. The record for hang gliding's longest flight was set over Lake Elsinore in 1978. Power boat races and water-skiing competitions are popular attractions.

The lake shore is filled with residences, trailer parks, and motels. Concessionaires offer boating and fishing supplies; other sources of supply are located outside park boundaries.

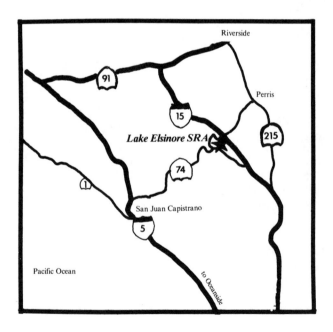

### CAMPING

Lake Elsinore has 176 campsites, many with all the hookups. Near the lake is a large picnic area and a boat launching ramp.

The Recreation Area is located at the north end of the lake and is accessible by both east-west Highway 74 and north-south Interstate Highway 15.

Lake Elsinore State Recreation Area
32040 Riverside Drive
Lake Elsinore, CA 92330
(714) 674-3005

# Lake Perris State Recreation Area

Lake Perris is the end of the California Aqueduct. The lake, filled with water that has traveled over four hundred miles from northern California, is a popular site for such water-oriented activity as swimming, boating and fishing.

## BOATING

Boat launching ramps, with ample parking for boat trailers, are located on the north side of the lake, and a concessionaire operated marina offers boat slips, dry storage, a gas dock, a coffee shop, and boat repair. The marina store carries bait and tackle, boating accessories, camping supplies, and snacks, and you can rent fishing boats, Hobie cats, day sailers, sailboards, jet skis, and waterskis.

Alessandro Island has picnic tables under shade ramadas, and grills are nearby. There's a trail leading to the island's top, where you can get some fine views of the area.

Boaters must keep their speed under five miles per hour within 100 feet of shore, in the area indicated by the five-mile-per-hour buoys. Travel around the lake is counter-clockwise.

## FISHING

Lake Perris was the first lake in Southern California to be stocked with Alabama spotted bass, and anglers also take planted rainbow trout, channel catfish, and Florida bluegill. Though not planted, green sunfish have arrived with the water, along with a tiny shrimp from San Francisco Bay that provides food to the game fish so they grow rapidly to catchable size.

The best areas to fish for catfish are the south corner of the dam or the east end of the lake; the cats go for mackerel or nightcrawlers as bait. Look for bass around Alessandro Island; use water dogs or crawdads. Trout are taken along the dam, and respond to shad; the bluegill, which like mill or red worms, can be taken around the marina or in marshy areas. Fishing from boats is usually preferred during the day; boats must be off the lake by an hour after sunset. Fish-cleaning stations are located throughout the day-use areas.

If you plan to fish past park closing time, and are not camping at Lake Perris, you may park outside at the Bernasconi entrance and walk the short distance to the lake; you may fish from shore all night, but all vehicles must leave the day-use parking lots by the posted closing time.

## PICNICKING

Ramadas, tables, grills, and restrooms are located at Moreno and Perris Beaches and at the Bernasconi Pass area. Pepper, eucalyptus, cypress, palm, and pine trees have been planted for shade, and there is playground equipment and large grassy areas for games.

The six group picnic areas, with ramadas, tables, grills, and restrooms, can accommodate up to 100 people. They are located at the east end of Moreno Beach and can be reserved through the park office.

## ROCK CLIMBING

A rock climbing area just south of the dam provides climbers with a variety of challenges and many spectacular views. Climbers may park at the Bernasconi gate and take the bicycle trail to the Big Rock area.

## CAMPING

The campground has 167 sites for tent campers and 264 paved sites for recreational vehicles up to twenty-seven feet long. Each site has a table, barbecue grill, and parking for two vehicles; water and restrooms with hot showers are nearby. RV sites have hookups for water, electricity, and sink water disposal, and there is a trailer sanitation station.

The group camp has six areas that will accommodate from 25 to 100 people apiece. Each has shade ramadas, tables, restrooms with hot showers, and a campfire ring.

The primitive horse camp with corrals, water troughs, picnic tables, campfire rings, drinking water, and pit toilets will accommodate either families or groups of up to fifty people. It has plenty of parking for vehicles and trailers.

Reservations are recommended during the busy summer season and for spring and fall weekends. The horse camp can be reserved through the park office.

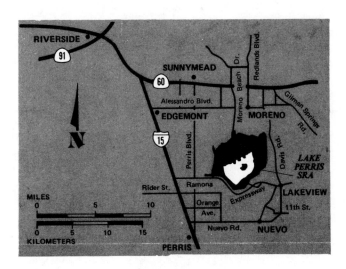

Lake Perris State Recreation Area
17801 Lake Perris Drive
Perris, CA 92370
(714) 657-0676

# Lake Perris State Recreation Area

### HIKING, BICYCLING,
### AND HORSEBACK RIDING

There are nine miles (14.5 km) of hiking-bicycling trail around the lake, all paved except for a short stretch at the south end of the dam.

A trail leads to a scenic overlook at Terri Peak, and another trail, accessible to wheelchairs, leads to a spot near the campfire center that offers a fine view of Moreno Pass; there are also interpretive panels that tell the story of the area before Lake Perris was built.

Horse trails circle the lake, and lead into undeveloped parts of the recreation area; in spring, riders find themselves in the midst of a colorful sea of wildflowers.

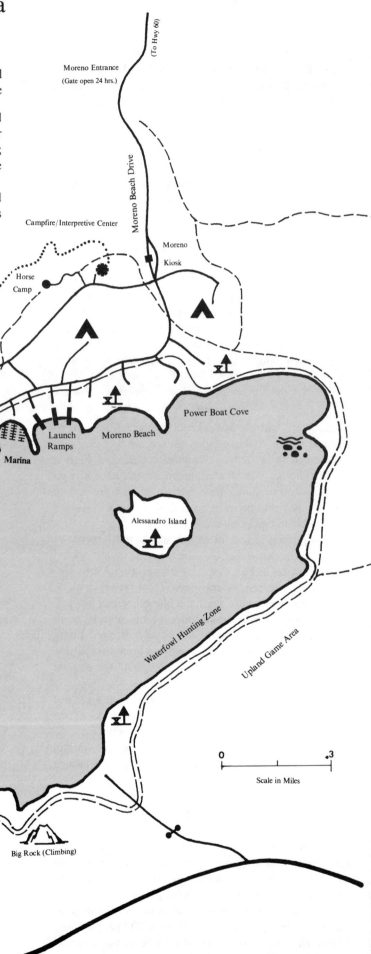

Moreno Entrance
(Gate open 24 hrs.)

(To Hwy 60)

Moreno Beach Drive

Campfire/Interpretive Center

Moreno Kiosk

Horse Camp

Park Office

Sail Cove

Perris Kiosk

Perris Beach

Marina

Launch Ramps

Moreno Beach

Power Boat Cove

Alessandro Island

Perris Drive

Perris Entrance
(Gate open only during day use hours)

(To I-15)

Perris Dam

Waterfowl Hunting Zone

Upland Game Area

Ramona Expressway

Big Rock (Climbing)

0        .3
Scale in Miles

On the afternoon of August 5, 1769, Don Gaspar de Portola's party of discovery arrived at the foot of the Santa Monica Mountains. With Portola was Father Juan Crespi and sixty-three soldiers. No doubt the men were tired from their bushwhacking through Sepulveda Canyon. They rested briefly among the oaks at a point between the present day cities of Sherman Oaks and Encino.

The explorers moved up the valley about a mile and came upon warm springs and a body of water. The springs were the same springs that are now part of Los Encinos State Historic Park. "We reached a very large pool of fresh water where we met two very large villages of very friendly tractable Heathens," reported Father Crespi.

In 1845, Governor Pio Pico gave more than 4,000 acres of valley land to Vincente de la Osa, who built a nine-room adobe in 1849. De la Osa and his wife Rita raised fifteen children in the adobe. The house, with mission-style walls two feet thick, stands today in a fine state of preservation. The rooms have been redone in period furnishings, which reflect the various owners and eras of the adobe.

Two Basque brothers—Eugene and Phillipe Garnier—took over the de la Osa rancho in 1872 and built a limestone house in the style of their native France. The house is closed, pending restoration.

There's a small picnic area, shaded by olive trees, at the park. Tours are conducted 1-4 p.m., Wednesday-Sunday.

Los Encinos State Historic Park
16756 Moorpark Street
Encino, CA 91436
( (818) 784-4849

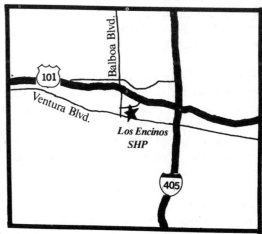

# Mount San Jacinto State Park

Mount San Jacinto State Park with its granite peaks, subalpine forests, and fern-bordered mountain meadows offers the best opportunity south of the Sierra Nevada to enjoy a primitive high-country experience.

The major portion of the park is wilderness, its values to be held inviolate for the use, inspiration, and enjoyment of the people. The park has roads only into the Idyllwild and Stone Creek camp areas, and no motor vehicles are allowed in the back country; however, an excellent system of riding and hiking trails has been developed, and horses are available at Idyllwild. Interpretive programs are also offered to give a better understanding and appreciation of this area's natural magnificence.

The peak of Mount San Jacinto—a giant, often snow-capped crag marked by great upthrusts of weathered granite—rises 10,804 feet above sea level. It is the highest peak in the San Jacinto Range and the second highest point in Southern California. Four other peaks within the park are over 10,000 feet, and much of the rest of the park is more than 6,000 feet in elevation.

The area was at one time the seasonal hunting ground for a large Indian population that lived in its wooded canyons and protected valleys, and on the nearby desert. Their trails still cross the mountain, and several village sites have been located in or near the park. Idyllwild, for intance, was a camping place long before the arrival of the Spaniards or other Europeans. Rocks with carved or painted designs that date back hundreds and perhaps thousands of years also give evidence of long-term human habitation within and outside the park.

The northeast face of the San Jacinto Range plunges down 9,000 feet in less than six miles, making it one of the sheerest and most spectacular escarpments in North America. Directly below the mountain is Palm Springs and the Coachella Valley. The view sweeps on to the desert beyond Palm Springs and extends southeast to the Salton Sea and on into the Imperial Valley with its flanking mountain ranges. The famous landscape architect who directed the first California State Park Survey, Frederick Law Olmsted, said the view was "unmatched in its impressiveness elsewhere in the United States." John Muir called it "the most sublime spectacle to be found anywhere on this earth."

Life zones in the area vary from Upper Sonoran on the desert to Arctic-Alpine atop Mount San Jacinto. Variations in rainfall and temperature account for the presence of some 250 species of plants.

## AERIAL TRAMWAY

The Palm Springs Aerial Tramway is the largest and longest single-lift passenger tramway in the world. Built by the Mount San Jacinto Winter Park Authority, a state agency, the 4-km. (2.5-mi) tramway took over two and a half years to construct and cost more than nine million dollars. It opened to public use in 1963.

Starting in Chino Canyon near Palm Springs, the tram takes passengers from Valley Station, 2,643 feet above sea level, to elevation 8,516 at Mountain Station on the edge of the Mount San Jacinto wilderness area. The two totally enclosed, Swiss-made cars hold eighty passengers each and operate on a fifteen-minute schedule, one car going up as the other comes down. The tram operates daily all year. There are restaurants, coffee shops, gift shops, and lobby facilities at both stations.

## CAMPING

At the Idyllwild Campground each of the thirty-three campsites has a table, stove, and food locker. Piped drinking water and restrooms with showers are nearby. These sites are popular in the summer and remain open, though with fewer facilities, during the winter. There are fifty campsites at Stone Creek.

In keeping with the park's wilderness concept, the campsites in the back country are primitve. Most popular of these areas is the Round Valley Campground, located near a large upland meadow 12 km. (7.5 mi.) by trail from Idyllwild, where rangers are on duty to assist visitors and answer questions during the summer season. Tamarack Valley Campground is only about 0.8 km. (0.5 mi.) away·

Strawberry Junction Camp is located 4 miles from Idyllwild on the Deer Springs Trail. Little Round Valley Campground is situated beside a small stream and meadow just 2.5 km. (1.5 mi.) below San Jacinto Park, and you may also camp in the area immediately surrounding the peak.

## HIKING

An extensive trail system has been developed over the years, much of it built by the Civilian Conservation corps during the 1930s. Among the most popular trails are the Deer Springs Trail and the Devil's Slide Trail, part of which lies outside the park on United States Forest Service land.

Mount San Jacinto State Park
P.O. Box 308
Idyllwild, CA 92349
(714) 659-2607

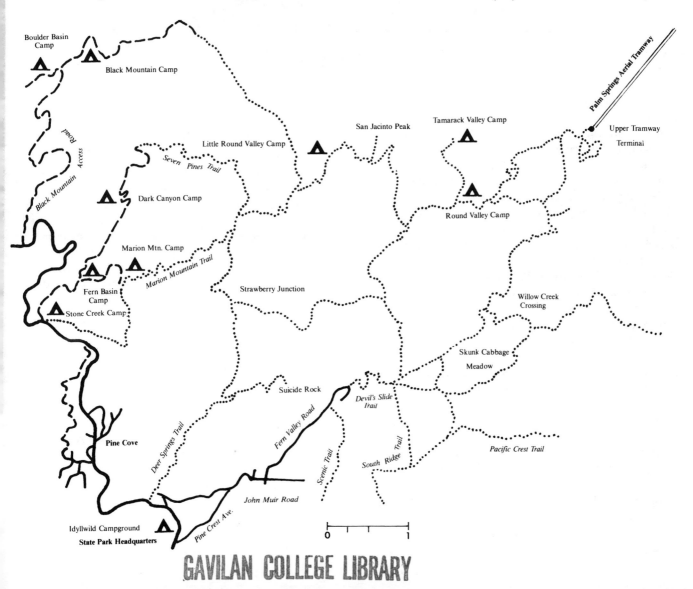

# Ocotillo Wells State Vehicular Recreation Area

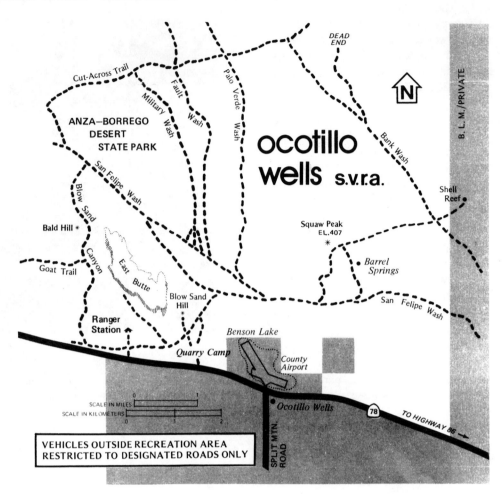

At the request of users, facilities at this 14,000-acre recreation area have been kept to a minimum, so that virtually the entire area is open to off-road recreation. Camping is permitted throughout the area, but no water is available. Vehicle repair shops, fuel, telephones, groceries, and restaurants are available in the town of Ocotillo Wells.

Several points of interest that make good one-day trips for OHVs (remember to stay on designated roads when outside the boundaries of the SVRA—see map):

**Barrel Springs**—Used by the Indians, these springs are surrounded by mesquite sand dunes.

**Squaw Peak (Devil's Slide, Black Butte)**—In the center of the SVRA, this hill boasts good climbs as well as large sand dunes and a spectacular sand bowl.

**Pumpkin Patch**—Though this area has been heavily vandalized, there are still a few pumpkin-shaped sandstone concretions.

**Shell Reef**—A five-foot-thick layer of fossil shells shows that this area was once a sea bottom, thousands of years ago when the climate was wetter.

**17 Palms Oasis**—A desert seep gives enough water to enable these trees to survive.

**Military Wash**—Scene of practice maneuvers of armor during World War II and the Korean conflict, the wash contains concrete bunkers and other military debris.

**Blow Sand Hill**—This huge sand dune, several hundred feet in height, is used for buggy and motorcycle competitions; at night it is often circled and illuminated by headlights.

## IN AN EMERGENCY

Park Rangers and the Anza-Borrego REACT monitor Citizens' Band Channel 9; call "Park Ranger." If CB communication is not available, call 767-5391 or 911.

Since transporting injured persons frequently makes the injury worse, call rangers or REACT for assistance and transportation, particularly for *back* and *neck* injuries. Rangers are trained in emergency first aid procedures and are usually the closest source of help; the nearest hospital is 42 miles from Ocotillo Wells. It is Pioneers' Memorial Hospital in Brawley, phone (619) 344-2120; to reach it, take Highway 78 east to Highway 86, then turn south to Brawley.

Ocotillo Wells State Vehicular Recreation Area
C/O Ocotillo Wells District
5172 Highway 78
Borrego Springs, CA 92004
(619) 767-5391

# Palomar Mountain State Park

The thick forests and rolling mountain meadows of Palomar Mountain State Park are in northern San Diego County on the west side of Palomar Mountain. Large pine, fir, and cedar trees make the park one of the few areas in Southern California with a Sierra Nevada-like atmosphere. Summer evenings are cool (average elevation 5,500 feet) and from several places you can look out over large areas of Southern California ocean and desert.

To the east, beyond the limits of the park, is the world-famous Palomar Observatory and the high point of the 6,100-foot mountain. Many park visitors make the trip—sixteen miles by road—to the observatory which is operated by the California Institute of Technology. A museum and photo gallery are open to the public from 8 A.M. to 5 P.M. daily.

*Mount Palomar Observatory*

## HISTORY

The bedrock mortars and metates in Doane Valley indicate that Indians lived in the area for hundreds, and perhaps thousands, of years. They called the area "Paauw," a Shoshonean word meaning mountain. The Spaniards, however, named it "Palomar," or "place of the pigeons," for the thousands of band-tailed pigeons that nested on its slopes.

Pine and fir trees from Palomar Mountain were harvested for the construction of Mission San Luis Rey, and in 1846 the park area became a part of the famous Warner Ranch. After the Indians drove Warner off the land in 1851, cattle and horse thieves often used the remote mountain meadows of Palomar to shelter their stolen animals until it was safe to take them across the border.

Nathan Harrison, a slave who had followed his Southern master to the gold rush in California, took up residence as a free man near the eastern edge of the present park. He made hay and ran hogs in the Doane Valleys despite frequent trouble with bears and mountain lions. The old road from Pauma Valley is named in his honor.

George Edwin Doane came to the area in the early 1880s and built his shake-roofed log cabin in the little clearing between Upper and Lower Doane Valley, in what is now the Doane Valley Campground. Doane made hay and raised cattle and hogs on his 640 acres of meadowland, and you can still see some of the apple trees he planted.

During the Southern California land boom of the 1880s, many people homesteaded on Palomar Mountain. Four apple orchards within the park date from this period, as does the Scott cabin on Thunder Ridge.

## CAMPING

There are thirty campsites in the Doane Valley Campground that will accommodate trailers and motorhomes up to twenty-one feet.

Each has a table, stove, and food locker; piped drinking water and combination buildings with restrooms, hot showers, and laundry tubs are nearby.

## FISHING

Doane Pond is stocked with trout and fishing is especially good during the winter, spring, and early summer. There is also an informal picnic area near the pond with several tables and stoves, a modern restroom and parking lot.

Palomar Mountain State Park
Montane District
C/O Cuyamaca Rancho SP
12551 Hwy. 79
Descanso, CA 92016

# Picacho State Recreation Area

*Canoeing the Lower Colorado*

Picacho State Recreation Area, located in the Lower Colorado River Basin just twenty-five miles north of Yuma, has fifty-five miles of open river and many backwater lakes in the vicinity.

Known for its spectacular desert scenery and rich variety of river wildlife, Picacho also fascinates those who explore the geological and historical background of the great river and the surrounding lower Colorado Desert.

Pavement covers the road to Picacho from Winterhaven only for the first six miles, but cars and vehicles with small trailers can travel the rough dirt surface for the remaining eighteen miles. Summer thunder storms may cause flash flooding in the washes, temporarily making short sections of the road impassable.

From a distance, the rugged mountains and washes of the Colorado Desert look uninviting. The land seems entirely devoid of life, baked dry by the sun's relentless heat. But, you will find living things even in these apparently barren places. Plants seem to sprout from the very rock itself, and in the springtime the delicate beauty of wildflowers is everywhere. Beavertail cactus and ocotillo put on the most consistent display, but an endless variety of smaller flowers adds color. Carrizo cane and marsh tule line the numerous backwater lakes, and feathery-leaved Tamarisk trees, an import from Africa, have taken over many of the oasis-like flats near the river. Desert ironwood, palo verde, cottonwood trees, mesquite, sage, and other shrubs, and many kinds of cactus and succulents are native to this landscape.

In historical times Kwichyana, or Quechen, Indians lived along this part of the river. Their myths and legends, attached to every major feature of the landscape, tend to center around Picacho Peak. The Quechen used logs, rafts, and shallow pottery vessels to cross the river, and they cultivated maize, beans, squash or gourds, and other crops in the moist silt of the river bottoms.

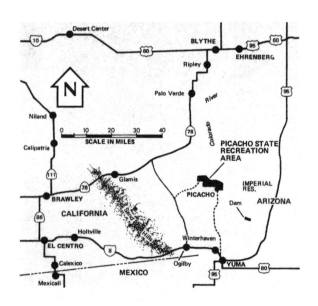

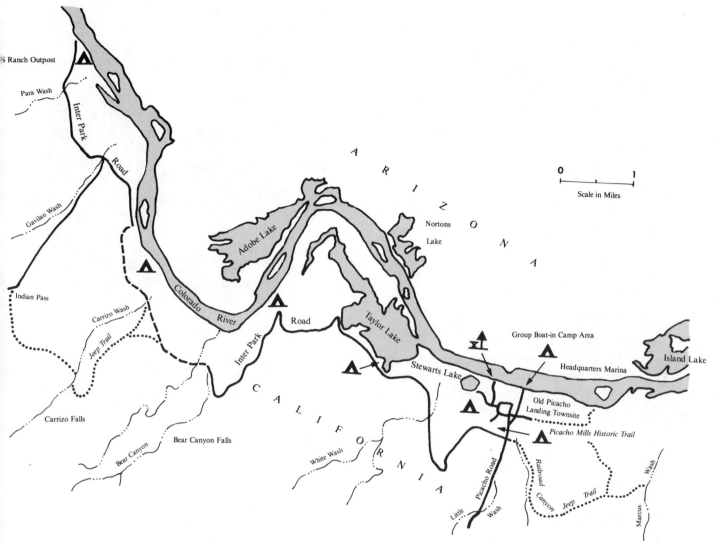

Visitors enjoy exploring the rich geological background of this region. Picacho Peak, a plug-dome volcanic outcropping, and other land features show fairly recent volcanic activity, and other signs—vivid colors, unusual shapes exposed and preserved by desert conditions—tell part of the area's complex geological story.

Temperature extremes at Picacho range from a wintertime low of 20 degrees at night to a summertime high of 120 degrees. Most visitors arrive between mid-October and the end of April, when days are pleasantly cool, but hardy adventurers enjoy the park's remoteness, water sports, and fishing year-round. Desert wildflowers present a magnificent display during the late winter, spring, and early summer. From April on into midsummer mosquitos pester visitors near water areas, especially the relatively quiet backwater lakes. The autumn and early winter months are the most popular time to float down the river. Warm, sun-washed autumn days combine with the strong, gentle current to make cruising down this scenic stretch of water a very peaceful experience. Black bass, channel catfish, crappie and bluegill provide the best fishing.

## CAMPING

Each of the fifty campsites in the main campground has a table and fire ring, with piped drinking water and chemical toilets nearby. You can reserve two group camping areas for large groups—one, for boat-in use, through the Recreation Area Headquarters, and the other, for up to sixty people, through the reservation system.

Headquarters campground also has a day-use area with tables, fire rings, and boat ramp; a boat marina and launching area; and a concessionaire-operated store, open seven days a week during daylight hours, that sells groceries, gas, oil, and boating and fishing supplies.

Picacho State Recreation Area
P.O. Box 1207
Winterhaven, CA 92283
(619) 767-5311

# Pio Pico State Historic Park

Pio Pico is an important figure in California's transition from Mexican to American rule. The last Governor of Mexican California, he was also a leader in the cultural and economic development of American California.

Pio Pico's father and grandfather came to Alta California with the Juan Bautista de Anza trek of 1776. His father served as a mission guard, and Pio was born on May 5, 1801, the second son of ten children, while his father was stationed at the San Gabriel Mission. As Pico states in his memoirs, "I was born in a brush shelter, not even a house."

Pio Pico's political life began in 1826 with his appointment to the *diputacion*, an advisory committe to the governor. In 1829 he received the 8,900-acre Rancho Jamul as his first land grant, the beginning of his empire. In 1834 he married Maria Ignacio Alvarado. They had no children, and when she died in 1860 he did not remarry.

In 1831 Pio Pico was leading his first revolution. At this period of California history, revolutions and counterrevolutions were the accepted mode of political advancement. Governor Alvarado suspended the *diputacion* and tried to restore military rule; Pico was successful in his revolt against another governor, Victoria, who was forced to resign. Pico became governor and although his term lasted little more than a month—he was relieved of office on February 16, 1832—this successful revolution put him on the road to wealth and power.

In 1838 Pico led an unsuccessful revolution against Governor Alvarado. His political conflict with the governors continued until 1845 when he again led a resistance movement, this time against Governor Micheltorena at the battle of Cahuenga Pass. The revolution was successful, and Pico assumed the governorship in February 1845. He was formally sworn in as the Governor of California on April 12, 1845, and served until August 1846. While he was Governor, Pico moved the capital of California to Los Angeles and stepped up the secularization of the mission lands.

Pico's term of office was cut short by the American invasion. He went to Mexico to seek aid and money to fight against the American Army, but the Mexican government failed to give him the help he needed, paving the way for the takeover of all of California by Kearny, Stockton, and Fremont.

Pico returned to California in 1848, and caught the American spirit. A staunch supporter of law and order, he used his wealth and influence for development of education, banking, and townsites. He served as a Los Angeles Councilman; he built the Pico House; he founded Picoville; and he invested in California's first oil venture.

It is in the American Period that Pio Pico's Mansion came into being. In 1850 he bought 9,000-acre Paso de Bartola for $4,600, and affectionately named it "El Ranchito."

In 1852 Pico built a home on El Ranchito. A flood destroyed the mansion in 1883. At the time of its rebuilding, Pico found himself temporarily short of funds and had to borrow $62,000. Through fraud in foreclosure on this loan, for which he had to put up all his property as security, he

*Pio Pico, last governor of Mexican California*

lost all of his properties. He took the case to court but, in 1892, the California Supreme Court decided against him.

Pico died on September 11, 1894. He was buried at Calvary Cemetery on North Broadway in Los Angeles, and later his remains were moved to the "Walter P. Temple Memorial" mausoleum in La Puente.

The social center of the area while Pio Pico lived there, from 1894 until 1907 the Mansion deteriorated. In 1907 Harriett Russell Strong worked to save the Pico property when the buildings were being used for road fill during the repaving of Whittier Boulevard; the property was purchased and restored, and in 1917 the Mansion was given to the State of California.

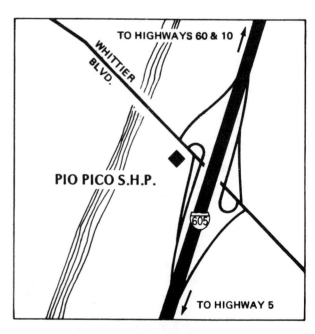

Pio Pico State Historic Park
6003 Pioneer Boulevard
Whittier, CA 90606
(213) 695-1217

# Providence Mountains State Recreation Area (Mitchell Caverns)

Providence Mountains SRA, which includes Mitchell Caverns Natural Preserve, is located about eighty air miles east of Barstow in the center of a vast, arid, sparsely populated portion of the eastern Mojave Desert. This area, from Barstow on the west to the Colorado River on the east and including all the land between the two major east-west highways (interstate 15 and 40) is known to local residents as the "lonesome triangle." It is a sun-scorched land of broad valleys filled with creosote bush and cactus, sand dunes, cinder cones, and dramatic piñon-clad mountain ranges. The 5,900 acre recreation area is situated on the eastern slope of the Providence mountains where the land sweeps up from Clipper Valley to high, heavily weathered, rhyolite crags ranging to 7,171 feet in elevation.

Park headquarters at 4,300 feet overlooks some 300 square miles of desert valleys and mountains. At times it is even possible to see the Hualapai Mountains in Arizona about 100 miles to the east. Due in a large part to the elevation, temperatures in the park are relatively moderate the year around though the months from October to May are most favored by visitors. The caverns are filled with intricate limestone formations and remain at a very nearly constant sixty-five degrees in all seasons. Mitchell Caverns is open to the public and has been equipped with stairs, railings, and special lighting to facilitate the guided tours that are conducted on a daily basis by the park staff. Entry to Winding Stair Cave, on the other hand, is restricted to experienced caving groups that have first obtained a special permit. This cavern goes down 311 feet in a series of free-fall drops that vary in height from 50 to 140 feet.

## HISTORY

Archeological work in the caverns turned up the bones of a Pleistocene ground sloth, one of the prehistoric animals that apparently ranged this territory and used the cavens during the late Pleistocene Epoch some ten to fifteen thousand years ago. Indian artifacts indicate that human beings have been using the caverns for at least 500 years. The smoke-blackened walls, hidden caches of food, tools, and other artifacts show that the Chemehuevi Indians used the caverns at least on a seasonal basis while hunting for game. They also collected the nuts of the piñon pine and used many other desert plants for food or medicine.

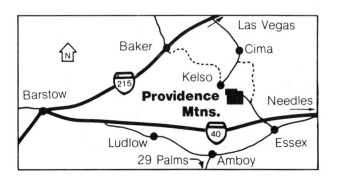

# Providence Mountains State Recreation Area (Mitchell Caverns)

The early 1860s the U.S. Army built a wagon road, the Mojave Road, from the port of Wilmington to Fort Mojave on the Colorado River. Camps were established at springs that were approximately one day's travel apart. Remnants of some of these camps are still visible a few miles north of the park. Then after the Civil War silver was discovered in the vicinity and prospectors and miners began to arrive. Numerous diggings were begun, and a number of mines established that continued to operate until the silver market crash of 1893.

In 1929 while prospecting for silver, Jack Mitchell became fascinated with what were then called the "Providence" or "Crystal" caves. In 1932 he decided to close down his depression-haunted business in Los Angeles and move to the desert. For a time he worked at various silver mining projects, but his real interest was in the caverns and their tourist potential.

Until his retirement in 1954 Mitchell and his wife, Ida, provided food, lodging, and guided tours of the caverns to a small but steadily increasing number of visitors. Famous for his highly entertaining tall tales, Jack Mitchell also gave the caverns their present names: El Pakiva, the Devil's House; and Tecopa after a Shoshonean chieftain.

## NATURAL HISTORY

Near the visitor center the Mary Beal Nature Trail offers visitors a wonderful opportunity to become acquainted with some of the plants and other natural features of this desert landscape. The trail is self-guiding and forms a loop about a half-mile long. Because of the trail's favorable location, a good sample of the region's plant life and other natural features can be seen. For those who would explore further there is a trail up into the Providence Mountains by way of Crystal Spring Canyon. Above the spring the slopes are steep and rugged, and the view spectacular. Along with the drought-resistant single-leaf piñon pines there are junipers and scrub oaks. Perennials such as mormon tea, cliff rose, squawberry, and blue sage share the upland areas with barrel cactus, Mojave and banana yucca, cholla (pronounced choh-yah) and others. In the spring and early summer the wildflower display is likely to be delightfully rich and varied.

Wildlife includes numerous antelope, ground squirrels, cottontail rabbits, and various rodents as well as badgers, lizards, snakes and other small animals. Bighorn sheep are seen occasionally as are the extremely shy wild burros. Coyotes, gray foxes, bobcats and other small predators also live here. Gamble's quail, piñon jays, white-crowned sparrows, roadrunners and cactus wrens are just a few of the many birds in the area.

## CAMPING

There are only six designated camping sites on the flat below area headquarters, and the water supply is limited. Much of the surrounding area is within the Bureau of Land Management's Piute Planning Area and is therefore open to camping. The area staff will be happy to tell you about the back roads, and some of the natural and historic features that can be explored. Visitors are advised to bring a supply of water for themselves, as well as extra food and gasoline as a normal precaution when traveling in the desert.

*Mitchell Caverns*

Providence Mountains State Recreation Area
C/O Mojave River District
Star Route Box 7A
Hesperia, CA 92345
(619) 389-2281

# Red Rock Canyon State Recreation Area

Red Rock Canyon State Recreation Area, with its scenic desert cliffs and natural preserve area, is located about 125 miles north of Los Angeles and 25 miles north of Mojave on State Highway 14. The canyon has been an established route of travel from time immemorial—from long before the arrival of European immigrants—because it is located just at the point where the western edge of the El Paso Range joins the southernmost tip of the Sierra Nevada. The canyon, and the surrounding desert mountains, are of special interest both for their geologic and archeological history, and for their unusual scenic qualities, flora, and fauna.

The most popular activities in the park include camping, picnicking, hiking, desert exploration, photography, and other desert nature studies.

The spectacular rock formations in Red Rock Canyon and in the nearby El Paso Range have been used as settings in countless motion picture and television productions. Each tributary canyon is unique, with colors ranging dramatically from stark white to vivid reds and dark chocolate browns. Most of the relatively soft, deeply eroded cliff formations are made up of sedimentary materials that accumulated in a very deep lake bed during the Pliocene times (about ten million years ago). Relatively hard basalt, sandstone, and tuff materials form a protective caprock over much of these deposits and the most scenic cliffs, buttes, and other landforms occur where this caprock has been cut away by erosion to expose the multi-layered and often very colorful sedimentary materials.

The Pliocene sediments of Red Rock Canyon have provided paleontologists with a great deal of information about the evolution of life in this part of the world. Fossilized remains have indicated, for instance, that a few million years ago Red Rock and Last Chance Canyons were portions of the shoreline of a large freshwater lake. Living on grassy plains and chaparral or forest-covered mountains near this lake in the gentle, moist climate of that time were many plants and animals including pines and cedars, locust, oak and even some fig trees. Numerous small animals such as mice and lizards, as well as some larger ones including horses, camels, antelopes, sabre-toothed cats, wolves, mastodons, and two kinds of rhinoceroses, lived here.

# Red Rock Canyon State Recreation Area

## HISTORY

Indian use of Red Rock Canyon is indicated by a few rock mortars that were used to grind seeds and other plant parts. Just prior to the arrival of European man this area was occupied by the Kawaiisu branch of the Chemehuevi, generally referred to as the Mojave Indians—a nomadic people whose Shoshonean-speaking relatives occupied the Great Basin and southwestern deserts as well as the south coastal Channel Islands and Los Angeles area.

Before the arrival of the Kawaiisu, however, the area was apparently inhabited for as much as 15,000 to 20,000 years by a population known today only as the "Old People." Little is known about them, though it is thought that some of the petroglyphs in the El Paso Range may represent their work.

Mining in this area began in the 1870s, but it was not until the 1890s—when news of the gold strikes in Garlock and Randsburg encouraged prospecting in all the canyons and gulches of the El Paso Range—that gold mining became an important activity. It is reported that several million dollars in gold, including a fourteen ounce nugget, were removed from this area. Scattered mining activities resumed during the Depression years did not prove profitable.

One of the leading figures in the Red Rock Canyon gold rush was Rudolph Hagen, who later acquired much of the land in this vicinity. He named the little town of Ricardo in memory of his son Richard, who died at an early age. After the excitement of the gold rush was over, Ricardo continued to serve as an important stage stop on the main route of travel between Los Angeles and the Owens Valley. The Ricardo Ranger Station (park headquarters) is located on the site of this once bustling community.

## CAMPING

Spring is the most popular season at Red Rock Canyon, but the State Recreation Area remains open the year around. Summer can be very hot, although at night temperatures are almost always moderate enough for comfortable sleeping. Winter is quite cool with nighttime temperatures often dipping well below the freezing point.

A primitive campground with fifty individual sites with tables and stoves, piped drinking water, and pit toilets is located near park headquarters. Picnic areas have not been formally developed, but visitors may picnic in unoccupied campsites or explore the area, particularly the natural preserves where vehicles are not allowed because scenic and other natural landscape features are particularly spectacular and fragile.

Off-highway vehicles are permitted in the campground at Red Rock Canyon and may also use the primitive roads designated by the State Park Commission, some of which provide access to popular areas such as Dove Springs and Jawbone Canyon outside the State Recreation Area.

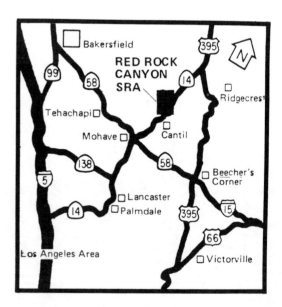

Redrock Canyon State Recreation Area
RRC Box 26
Cantil, CA 93519
High Desert Dist.: (805) 942-0662

Saddleback Butte, elevation 3,651 feet, is a granite mountain top that stands up some 1,000 feet above the broad alluvial bottomland of the Antelope Valley about twenty miles east of Lancaster on the western edge of the Mojave Desert. The 2,875-acre state park surrounding Saddleback Butte was created in 1960 in order to protect the butte (one of many similar land features in the Antelope Valley) and, even more importantly, to preserve a representative example of the native Joshua tree woodland and other plants and animals that were once common throughout this high desert area. Principal activites in the park include camping, picnicking, hiking, photography, bird-watching, and other desert nature-studies.

The best time of year to visit this park is in the springtime (February through May) when wildflowers are apt to put on a fine display of color. Autumn (October and November) is also likely to be pleasant, although temperatures may vary widely and rather suddenly. Summer temperatures average 95 degrees, but occasionally range on up to as much as 115 degrees. Average minimum temperature during the winter is 33 degrees. Frost and·subfreezing temperatures are common. Snow occurs occasionally.

Many small forms of native wildlife still survive in Antelope Valley, and can be seen from time to time in Saddleback Butte State Park: coyotes and kit foxes, jack rabbits, cottontail rabbits, ground squirrels and kangaroo rats. One special highlight of the park is the desert tortoise, which is often seen by those park visitors who have curiosity and patience enough to learn the quiet, unhurried ways of this age-old desert landscape.

## CAMPING

On the flatland about one mile south of park headquarters a primitive fifty-unit family campground offers tables, stoves, water, and pit toilets. Some campsites have shade ramadas.

Also located in this part of the park is a group camp suitable for organized youth groups of up to thirty-two people. It can be reserved up to ninety days in advance.

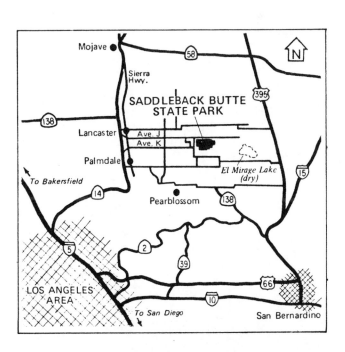

Saddleback Butte State Park
17102 Avenue J East
Lancaster, CA 93534
High Desert Dist.: (805) 942-0662

# Salton Sea State Recreation Area

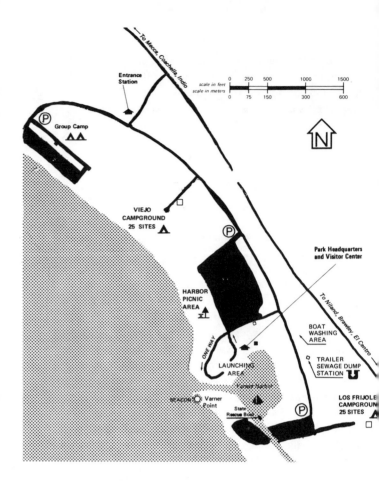

Salton Sea State Recreation Area, one of Southern California's most popular boating parks, is on the northeast shoreline of the Salton Sea about ninety miles northeast of San Diego.

The Sea is 230 feet below sea level; although it is one of the world's largest inland bodies of salt water, it is only a fraction of its ancient size. Ten miles west of the Sea on the sides of the Santa Rosa Mountains are indications that as recently as a thousand years ago an immense body of water filled the desert basin to over sea level. Then, over a period of hundreds of years, the desert heat reduced the Sea to a vast expanse of gleaming white salt flats that remained until 1905, when the floodwaters of the Colorado River broke an irrigation diversion dam near Yuma. River water flowed freely into the basin for two years; when it was finally cut off, a lake forty-five miles long and twenty miles wide had been formed. Further evaporation reduced the Sea to its present size (thirty-five miles by fifteen miles), where it has nearly stabilized because of drainage from Imperial Valley irrigation systems.

Around the Sea is a hot, dry, desert landscape marked by sharp contrasts. Rising directly above the desert floor the Santa Rosa Mountains stand more than 6,000 feet high. After winter storms they are often snowcapped, while temperatures at the Sea remain in the 70s and 80s throughout the winter.

### FISHING

Early in the century, when the Salton Sea had only recently refilled, its water was fresh. But, in dissolving the salt flats that had been left by its predecessors, the lake turned saline—a fact that has led to successful plants of ocean fish. Today it is slightly saltier than the ocean.

The orangemouth corvina, sargo and gulf croaker have done well since the California Fish and Game Department planted them in the early 1950s. The most prolific is the gulf croaker, which feeds on marine worms and in turn is preyed upon by the corvina.

Fishing is best June through October when surface water temperatures soar above ninety degrees. Each year anglers catch more than half a million corvina averaging three pounds each, with the largest going to 32½ pounds. The perch-like sargo seldom weighs more than two pounds.

### BOATING

Varner Harbor at the north end of the 18,000-acre park has a wide boat ramp. Boats may not be moored in the harbor overnight.

The average depth of the Salton Sea is eighteen feet. Sudden squalls can make the Sea unsafe for small boats. Spring is the most unsettled time of the year but strong winds can occur at any time and have been known to push the water into five-foot-high waves. For your safety, check all boating regulations and weather forecasts before setting out on long trips away from shore.

Buoys mark swimming zones at Mecca Beach and the Headquarters area. Boats and waterskiers are not permitted inside these buoy markers. Children should be watched carefully since lifeguard service is not available.

### CAMPING

Los Frijoles and Viejo Campground, in the park headquarters area, are classified as "developed." The fifty sites have flush toilets, piped drinking water, hot showers tables and stoves. These campsites and the group camp area, which will hold two groups of 60 or one group of up to 120 persons, can be reserved.

The 110 sites at Mecca Beach Campground, also classified as "developed," have paved parking areas, piped drinking water, hot showers and tables.

Covina Beach, Bombay Beach, and Salt Creek Campgrounds are all classified as "primitive." Only Salt Creek Campground does not have piped-in water.

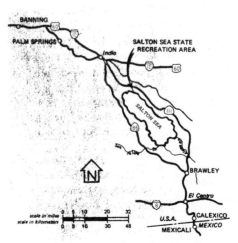

Salton Sea State Recreation Area
P.O. Box 3166
North Shore, CA 92254
(619) 393-3059

# San Pasqual Battlefield State Historic Park

GEN. ANDRES PICO

GEN. STEPHEN W. KEARNY

San Pasqual Battlefield State Historic Park tells the story of the most severe battle of the Mexican-American War fought on California soil. On December 6, 1846, American troops, led by General Stephen Kearney, fought with California forces under the command of General Andres Pico. Historians hold differing opinions regarding the outcome of the battle.

As day dawned on that fateful December morning, General Kearney and his men looked down into the valley through the fog and saw the campfires of the Californians, who were encamped near the Indian village of San Pasqual. Kearney decided to attack. Although the fog may partly have succeeded in hiding the Americans from the Californians, it also hid the Americans from one another and added to the confusion of the battle.

The Americans galloped across the open valley and were met first with gunfire, next with the short heavy-handed lances of the Californians, who were superb horsemen. The miserable condition of General Kearney's men and mounts (they had just endured a long journey from New Mexico) combined with water-soaked firearms gave the advantage to the Californians.

General Pico fought a hand-to-hand duel with Captain Benjamin D. Moore, the best swordsman among the Americans. Pico was armed with a lance and with it he broke Moore's sword. The Captain then reached for his pistol (which probably wouldn't have gone off anyway), but two Californians saw the gesture and lanced the Captain to death.

General Kearney was singled out by a young California lancer, who twice wounded him, but spared his life. General Pico is credited with holding down the American casualties by not pressing his advantage. In all about 20 Americans were killed and about another 20 wounded. Only a few Californians suffered wounds.

The battle of San Pasqual was soon followed by a skirmish on the San Gabriel River and California was soon entirely in American hands. The Battle of San Pasqual was not of great military importance, but has a symbolic significance in illustrating the transfer of California from Mexico to the United States.

The park encompasses a 50 acre area and includes a monument to the men who died in combat, a parking area, amphitheater, and a Visitor Center. The Visitor Center contains displays and panels providing information about the history of the area, the unrest in California at the time of the Mexican-American War, and the events leading up to the conflict. Visitors may watch a video that depicts the battle and walk to a specific observation area for a good view of the battleground.

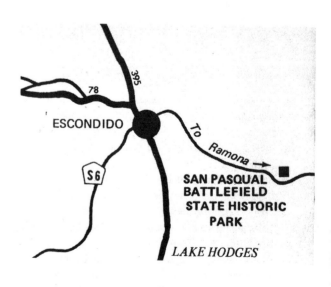

# Silverwood Lake State Recreation Area

Picnicking, fishing, swimming, waterskiing, and boating are among the many recreation possibilities offered at Silverwood Lake State Recreation Area. Located in the San Bernardino National Forest, the park is a scenic thirty-mile drive from the City of San Bernardino on winding State Highway 138.

The higher elevations of the 2,200-acre recreation area are forested with stands of Ponderosa pine, incense cedar, white fir, and black oak; around the shores of the lake these give way to chamise, live oak, manzanita, ceanothus, and mountain mahogany with alders, willows, and sycamores along stream courses.

The creation of Silverwood Lake has provided new territory for water-oriented birds. Great blue herons, snowy egrets, avocets, western grebes and loons have been sighted on the lake. In addition water fowl, including Canadian geese, mergansers, and several varieties of ducks, have used the lake. The diverse habitat of the Sawpit area attracts many different types of birds; these range from birds of prey such as red-tailed and Cooper's hawks, great horned owls, ospreys, and roadrunners to many varieties of song birds including western bluebirds, brown and rufous sided towhees, western tanagers, Bullock's orioles, and many more.

Trout, bass, and catfish have been planted in the lake by the Department of Fish and Game; a fishing license is required.

Silverwood, the highest lake of the State Water Project aqueduct system at 3,353 feet, has a storage capacity of 75,000 acre-feet (25 billion gallons) of water, and a surface area of nearly a thousand acres. It is formed by 249-foot Cedar Springs Dam, which blocks the path through the San Bernardino Mountains cut by the west fork of the Mojave River.

Water for the lake comes more than four hundred miles, boosted from near sea level in the Sacramento-San Joaquin Delta by seven pumping plants, to provide water for Southern California's homes, farms, and businesses as well as for recreation. Released through the four-mile-long San Bernardino Tunnel, water from the lake plunges over a thousand feet through a nearly vertical pipeline to the Devil Canyon Powerplant to generate up to 120,000 kilowatts of electricity. From there, the water flows to the southern terminus of the aqueduct at Lake Perris.

Developed facilities are located on the southern shore of the lake, in the Sawpit Canyon and Cleghorn Cove areas. There are family picnic sites throughout both areas with piped drinking water, barbecue grills, and sanitary facilities; there is parking for over 600 cars in Sawpit Canyon and for 245 in Cleghorn Cove. Lifeguard service is available daily in summer. A concessionaire-operated snack bar is located at the Sawpit swim beach. You can rent paddle boats, kayaks, and beach equipment at both swim beaches.

For boaters, there is a six-lane boat launching ramp at Sawpit Canyon with parking for 185 autos with trailers and boarding docks. A concessionaire in the boat launching area operates a snack bar, rents boats and boat slips, and sells fishing and other supplies.

Additional picnic sites are located at the Chamise, Live Oak, and Sycamore Landing areas. These sites can be reached only by boat and you must bring your own supplies, including drinking water. Open fires, cooking stoves, and barbecues are not permitted in these areas due to the high fire hazard.

## CAMPING

There are 95 family campsites in the Mesa area, each with table, barbecue grill, fire ring, and parking space for a trailer and its towing vehicle; restrooms, showers and laundry facilities are nearby. There are also several campsites for bicyclists.

The three group camps in the West Fork area will accommodate 120 people and 30 cars each; they have barbecues, restrooms, and showers.

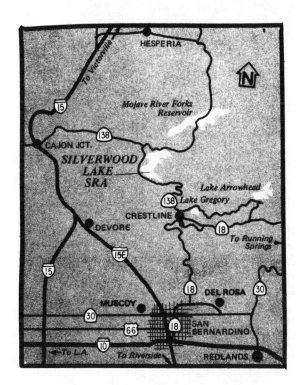

Silverwood Lake State Recreation Area
C/O Mojave River Dist.
Star Route Box 7A
Hesperia, CA 92345
(619) 389-2281

# South Coast

Some of the finest swimming beaches in the world are found along California's South Coast, from Point Conception to the Mexican border. Here warm ocean currents and broad, sandy beaches encourage swimming and surfing almost year 'round.

Historic parks along the South Coast deal with California's Spanish/Mexican heritage.

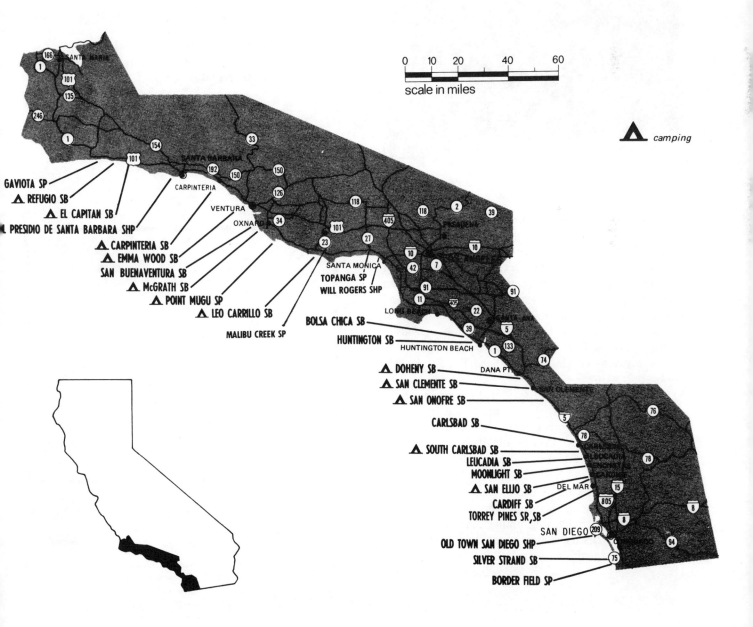

scale in miles

▲ camping

GAVIOTA SP
▲ REFUGIO SB
▲ EL CAPITAN SB
PRESIDIO DE SANTA BARBARA SHP
▲ CARPINTERIA SB
▲ EMMA WOOD SB
SAN BUENAVENTURA SB
▲ McGRATH SB
▲ POINT MUGU SP
▲ LEO CARRILLO SB
MALIBU CREEK SP

SANTA BARBARA
CARPINTERIA
VENTURA
OXNARD
SANTA MONICA
TOPANGA SP
WILL ROGERS SHP
LONG BEACH
PASADENA
SANTA ANA

BOLSA CHICA SB
HUNTINGTON SB
HUNTINGTON BEACH

▲ DOHENY SB
▲ SAN CLEMENTE SB
▲ SAN ONOFRE SB
CARLSBAD SB
▲ SOUTH CARLSBAD SB
LEUCADIA SB
MOONLIGHT SB
▲ SAN ELIJO SB
CARDIFF SB
TORREY PINES SR, SB
OLD TOWN SAN DIEGO SHP
SILVER STRAND SB
BORDER FIELD SP

DANA PT.
DEL MAR
SAN DIEGO

# Border Field State Park

Much of the Tijuana River Estuary, an important wildlife habitat that is one of the last remaining of its type in southern California, is within park boundaries. The typical saltwater marsh vegetation of pickleweed, saltgrass and alkali heath dominates, but colorful sand verbenas and beach primroses are found in the sand dunes. The hillsides, covered with chaparral, turn brilliant shades of orange and yellow when California poppies, sea dahlias, and other wildflowers bloom in spring.

Over 170 species of birds have been seen in and around the park. Commonly sighted are marsh hawks, red-tailed hawks, kestrels, egrets, herons, pelicans, roadrunners, and various shorebirds—gulls, terns, and ducks. Occasionally, an osprey, a golden eagle, or a rare light-footed clapper rail is sighted. Nesting birds include snowy plovers, kildeer, quail, meadowlarks, Beldings Savannah sparrows, red-winged blackbird, and the endangered least tern.

Fishing for perch, corbina, and halibut is good in the surf and estuary mouth.

Border Field is located in the southwest corner of the United States, with Mexico and the Pacific Ocean as its southern and western boundaries. When California became a territory at the end of the Mexican-American War of 1848, an international border became a necessity. American and Mexican survey crews determined the boundary and the monument of Italian marble was placed to mark the original survey site in 1851. Today the monument stands in the shadow of the Tijuana Bull Ring and still delineates the border between the United States and Estados Unidos Mexicanos.

During World War II the Navy used the area as an air field. Combat pilots received gunnery training, learning to hit steam-driven targets that raced over the dunes on rails called Rabbit Tracks. Despite multifarious real estate schemers, the Navy retained control of Border Field until the land was given to the state in the early 70s.

The park includes nearly two miles of ocean beach for hiking and sunning. Other things to do include horseback riding (rentals nearby), hiking, fishing, clamming and bird watching. Facilities include picnic tables, restrooms, barbecues and interpretive displays.

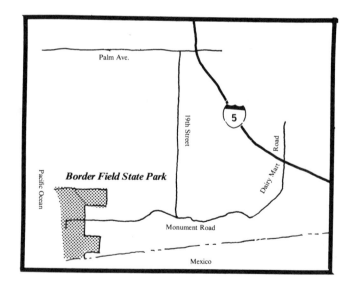

Border Field State Park
C/O Frontera District
3990 Old Town Avenue
Suite 300-C
San Diego, CA 92110
(619) 428-3034

Swimming, surfing, skindiving, beach picnicking, camping, and hiking are among the attractions that draw over a half million visitors each year to Leo Carrillo State Beach, located just twenty-six miles north of Santa Monica on Highway 1.

The park is famous for its beach, which is divided into two separate areas by Sequit Point, a bluff riddled with caves and a sea-carved tunnel. At Canyon Campground is a snack bar, beach equipment rental, and restroom facility with dressing rooms. Summer ocean temperatures here are usually in the high 60s, and lifeguards are on duty in the summer.

Anglers can catch bass, perch, and cabezon, which are especially plentiful in the kelp beds. On rare occasions sea lions and seals can be seen on the offshore rocks, where marine birds—pelicans, gulls, grebes, black brants, and cormorants—search for food; from November to May gray whales, migrating between their breeding grounds off Baja California and Alaska, can often be sighted from the beach.

Though there are few marked trails, hikers enjoy exploring along the creek that runs through the thousand-plus acres of upland, where elevations reach 1500 feet. Some areas are heavily wooded with coast live oak, California sycamore, willow, and sumac.

## CAMPING

The park has three campgrounds. Canyon Campground has 138 family campsites, each with table, stove, food locker, and paved parking space, served by a centrally located shower building and four restrooms. Sites will accommodate trailers or motorhomes up to thirty-one feet long; there is a trailer sanitation station, but no hookups.

The fifty family campsites at the Beach Campground can be used only by self-contained RVs; there are no hookups. Each site has a table and a stove; a restroom with cold showers is nearby. Because of a low underpass on the access road, only vehicles with less than eight feet clearance can reach this campground.

The Group Campground can accommodate up to seventy-five people; it has two barbecues and tables, and the restroom building has hot showers. To use this campground, you might hike in a hundred yards from the parking lot.

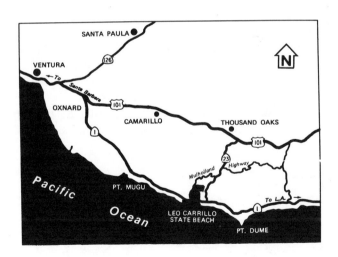

Leo Carrillo State Beach
35000 Pacific Coast Highway
Malibu, CA 90265
District office (818) 706-1310

# Los Angeles County State Beaches

When the summer sun beats down on the metropolis and the smog thickens, half the Southland flees to Los Angeles County's seventy-four miles of coastline. The typical mass-use L.A. beach includes acres of hot sand, waves ranging from the gentle to the inspired, a lifeguard every few hundred feet, and a boardwalk full of roller-skaters, restaurants and raft rental establishments.

L.A. County administers most of the state beaches clustered around Santa Monica Bay: Redondo and Hermosa, Will Rogers and Topanga. The northern part of the county's coastline, beginning about Malibu, is decidedly different from the south. The Santa Monica Mountains veer toward the coast, creating a series of bluffs, rocky points, coves, and sandy beaches. This coastline is the most rural in the county, although there are occasional clusters of homes, built it seems, right over the surfline. The Coastal Commission has been improving access to a number of selected beaches that are far from the maddening crowd. These include El Matador, El Pescador, and La Piedra.

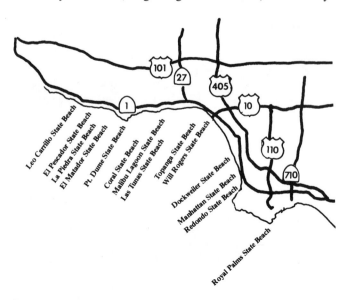

*"The Gorge" on Malibu Creek*

Malibu Creek State Park preserves for public use more than 6,000 acres of rugged, mainly virgin land in the middle of the Santa Monica Mountains and within the largest metropolitan area on the West Coast.

Before Europeans and their descendents explored the Santa Monica Mountains, the park area was inhabited for several thousand years by Indians who were attracted by plentiful water and food sources. The women gathered wild plant foods (edible seeds, roots and shoots) that provided at least 60 percent of the Indians' diet. The yucca plant provided both food and fiber: Young stalks were gathered and stored, the leaves provided needles and fibers for weaving and sewing and the roots were used for soap.

Malibu Creek meanders from west to east through the middle of the park, its elevation dropping from 700 to 500 feet. The creek was dammed at the turn of the century to form the 7-acre Century Lake. Emptying into Malibu Creek from the highlands, particularly in the winter and spring, are numerous smaller creeks.

Some of the best wildflower areas are in the large meadow just south of Mulholland Highway in the northwest part of the park, along the road to Century Lake and westward along Malibu Creek in the northern Liberty Canyon area, and in some of the nearly inaccessible canyons in the highlands to the south. Appearing from mid-May through June are clarkia, golden yarrow, penstemon, Mariposa lily, Humboldt lily, yucca, ceanothus and bush monkeyflower.

From the creek to the northern border of the park, much of the area is sloping grassland dotted with valley oak trees—some of the southernmost of the California valley oaks.

# Malibu Creek State Park

*Touring the Santa Monica Mountains, 1920*

At Century Lake and along Malibu and Las Virgenes Creeks, visitors may see many water-oriented birds such as great blue herons, red-winged blackbirds, violet-green swallows, ducks, and coots. Cooper's hawks, red-shouldered hawks, and woodpeckers inhabit the oak woodlands. In the open grassland and scattered valley oaks are acorn woodpeckers, red-tailed hawks, roadrunners, scrub jays, and an occasional golden eagle.

### HIKING

About fifteen miles of combination hiking and equestrian trails afford visitors many views of the steep, often nearly vertical peaks and rocky outcroppings in the southern part of the park. Some of the peaks rise to elevations of more than 2,000 feet.

One of the more popular trails, the Malibu Creek Trail, follows first High Road then Crags Road to Century Lake. Near the lake are hills of porous lava and topsy-turvy sedimentary rock layers that tell of the violent geologic upheaval that formed Malibu Canyon. The man-made lake was scooped out by members of Crag's Country Club, a group of turn-of-the-century businessmen who had a nearby lodge.

Another interesting trail is the short Gorge Trail. A ⅛-mile stroll off the main trail brings you to The Gorge, one of the most striking sites in the Santa Monica Mountains. The creek makes a hairpin turn through 400 foot volcanic rock cliffs. The "Swiss Family Robinson" TV series was filmed here.

Hikers may also use part of the new Backbone Trail, which when finished will cross the Santa Monica Mountains from Will Rogers State Historic Park to Point Mugu State Park. Currently, hikers may journey as far west as Castro Peak.

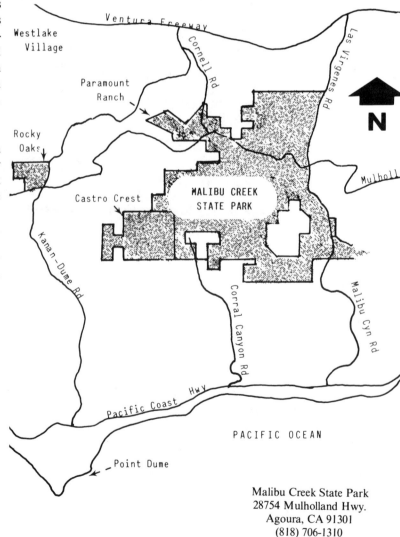

Malibu Creek State Park
28754 Mulholland Hwy.
Agoura, CA 91301
(818) 706-1310

# Old Town San Diego State Historic Park

Estudillo House, Old Town, San Diego, Built 1770.

Old Town San Diego State Historic Park recreates the setting of California life during the Mexican and early American periods. Its displays, historic buildings, and shops and restaurants illustrate the vast changes that have taken place in San Diego since it was first settled in 1769.

Old Town became a state historic park in 1968, and work was begun to restore its buildings, particularly the remaining original adobes. Las Casas de Estudillo, built in 1827 by the commander of the Presidio, and La Casa De Machado Y Silvas, home of the Machado family and now the state park visitor center are two of the restored adobes.

The park also includes the reconstructed Seeley Stable, which features a collection of horse-drawn vehicles and Western memorabilia, and the San Diego Union Building, a wood-frame structure restored to its appearance in 1868 when it was the home to the *San Diego Union* newspaper.

Entrance fees are charged at La Casa de Estudillo and the Seeley Stable; a ticket purchased at either is good for admission to both on the same day and also for a slide show at the Seeley Stable that illustrates San Diego's early history. A guided tour of the park starts in front of La Casa de Machado y Silvas every day at 2 P.M.

Old Town became a state historic park in 1968, and work was begun to restore its buildings, particularly the remaining original adobes. La Casa de Estudillo, built in 1827 by the commander of the Presidio, and La Casa De Machado Y Silvas, home of the Machado family, are two of the restored adobes.

The park also has a large volunteer association that takes pride in dressing in period attire (1821-1872) to lead tours and take part in special events. Twice a year, Living History Days celebrations are presented by the volunteers and park staff. All work together to recreate a day in the history of Old Town, complete with skits and period costumes. Some volunteers belong to a military contingent who, on the fourth Saturday of each month, set up an encampment on park ground for visitors to enjoy.

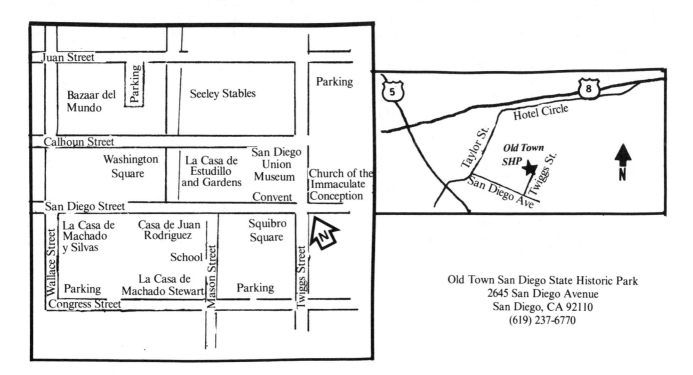

Old Town San Diego State Historic Park
2645 San Diego Avenue
San Diego, CA 92110
(619) 237-6770

# Orange County State Beaches

*Plenty of fire rings on Bolsa Chica State Beach*

### BOLSA CHICA STATE BEACH
### HUNTINGTON STATE BEACH

Bolsa Chica, Spanish for "little pocket," is about four miles upcoast from the City of Huntington Beach on Highway 1. Its 5½ miles of beach have 550 fire rings, toilets, beach showers, parking and drinking water.

Huntington, with two miles of beach, is downcoast from the City of Huntington Beach, just north of the Santa Ana River. It was named for Henry E. Huntington, who promoted electric railroads in southern California before the turn of the century, and endowed a library and art gallery in San Marino. There are 550 fire rings, ten restrooms, outside showers, and parking for 2,500 cars.

These two beaches include seven miles of prime beach frontage within a one-hour drive of the major population centers of Southern California. More than seven million visitors annually come for such activities as swimming, picnicking, fishing, and sunning, and there are surfing areas at the south end of each beach.

Although summer is the most popular time to visit, the climate at the beaches is mild year-round—average winter air temperature is 53 degrees, summer temperature is 68 degrees. Water temperature varies from 56 degrees in winter to 65 degrees in summer.

### DOHENY STATE BEACH

Doheny State Beach has a campground, and large day-use areas, all reached from Del Obispo Street, near the entrance to Dana Point Harbor, in the city of Capistrano Beach on Highway 1.

The campground's 115 developed campsites each have a fire ring and table, with flush toilets, hot showers, and water nearby. The beach south of there has fire rings, chemical toilets, beach showers, and parking. Visitors enjoy swimming, fishing, surfing (at the north end of the beach), and picnicking.

The day-use section has a large developed area by the beach. Around a five-acre lawn are picnic tables and a parking lot. The beach offers fire rings, fishing, swimming surfing (at the north end of the beach), and picnicking, with three restrooms providing flush toilets, changing rooms, and showers. A concessionaire sells food, sundries, and surfing and beach supplies.

## SAN ONOFRE STATE BEACH

Towering bluffs, 3½ miles of sandy beaches, and some of the best surfing in California—these are just some attractions of San Onofre State Beach. Visitors enjoy a wide variety of outdoor activities: swimming, surfing, fishing, observing wildlife along the bluff trails, and relaxing on the beach.

To reach San Onofre, within an hour's drive of the Los Angeles and San Diego metropolitan areas, take the Basilone Road offramp from Interstate 5 just south of the city of San Clemente.

San Onofre actually has three separate beaches, and a large inland section slated for future development of campgrounds and day-use areas. The U.S. Marine Corps leased this land, part of Camp Pendleton, to the State of California in 1971 for fifty years.

The main beach area is undeveloped, with plans to leave it in its primitve, unspoiled state. To reach the beach from the old abandoned highway that serves as day-use parking and camping space, six main trails have been cut into the bluffs. A supply store is open in the summer.

San Onofre Surf Beach, at the north end of the main beach, has a separate access road. This beach is well known for its surfing.

Trestles Beach has no vehicle access; visitors walk in along the beach. This isolated section has a riparian area— where you can observe plant life and migratory birds—at the mouth of San Mateo Creek. Trestles Beach also provides excellent surfing, surf fishing, and clamming.

The abandoned highway along the bluffs above the main beach serves as a camping area with restrooms and outside showers. The area can handle up to 272 campers and trailers. Because of the difficulty of pitching tents on the blacktop and concrete road, tent camping is not practicable in most locations, but about 40 campsites are suitable for tents. The Echo Arch campground, on a terrace between the bluffs and the beach, provides 40 primitive campsites.

## SAN CLEMENTE STATE BEACH

Campgrounds at San Clemente State Beach sit high atop a bluff overlooking the Pacific Ocean; the mile-long beach stretches between the foot of the steep bluff and the curling surf of the ocean. Both camping and day-use areas are reached from Interstate 5 at the Avenida Calafia exit in the city of San Clemente.

The campground has eighty-five units with stoves and cupboards, tables, and nearby water. A separate trailer area has seventy-two spaces with water, electrical, and sewer hookups. Each campground has restroom buildings with hot showers, flush toilets, and laundry tubs. A group camping area can handle fifty people.

The day-use area has picnic sites, each with a stove and table. Visitors enjoy swimming, surfing (at the north end of the beach), picnicking, fishing, skin diving for spiny lobster and abalone, and walking on the trails.

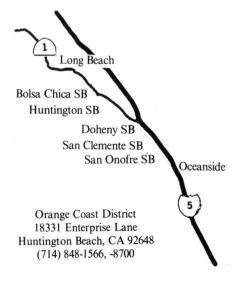

Orange Coast District
18331 Enterprise Lane
Huntington Beach, CA 92648
(714) 848-1566, -8700

# Point Mugu State Park

At the western end of the Santa Monica Mountains, this state park has some five miles of ocean shoreline, with rocky bluffs, sandy beaches; a spectacular sand dune; rugged hills and uplands; two major canyons; and wide grassy valleys dotted with sycamores, oaks, and a few native walnuts.

The park's diversity of environments creates some startling contrasts: along the interior streambeds grow tall sycamores, oaks, and cottonwoods, while on the coast, sand verbena and sea rocket barely poke above the dunes. Inland springs provide cool microclimates where ferns grow under the trees, while on nearby chaparral-covered hillsides summer temperatures may reach over 100 degrees and humidities approach zero.

Birdlife includes the many species associated with these varied habitats, and the same is true for the park's wildlife. Southern mule deer and Beechey ground squirrels are often seen, and there are also gray foxes, striped and spotted skunks, badgers, coyotes, bobcats, and even mountain lions. Seals and sea lions visit the coast, and during the winter and early spring visitors may sight whales on their annual migration between Baja California and Alaska.

The park's sandy beaches provide good swimming, body surfing, beachcombing, and surf fishing. Lifeguards are on duty during the summer, and you are advised to swim only in a guarded area. A picnic area with fifty tables and charcoal-burning stoves is located at Sycamore Cove near park headquarters.

The park's name comes from *muwu,* a word meaning "beach" in the language of the Chumash Indians. They had lived here for over six thousand years when Spanish explorer Juan Cabrillo dropped anchor off this coast in October 1542.

The people that paddled out to meet the Spanish ship in their frameless plank canoes were members of perhaps the most advanced culture in California. The rich and varied marine life along the ocean shores and lagoons assured their food supply so that, instead of migrating in search of food, the Chumash could spend time in developing their crafts and art. Their baskets were among the finest in California, and they also made beautiful soapstone bowls inlaid with mother-of-pearl. Their canoes, up to twenty-five feet long, lashed together with sinew and caulked with asphalt, were unique in North America.

But the coming of the Spanish destroyed this way of life. When Mission San Buenaventura was completed in 1782, the friars began a program that was aimed at making the Indians responsible citizens of the Spanish empire; instead, it decimated them. Crowded together at the mission, most of the Chumash died from epidemics of European diseases to which they had no immunity. Though some runaways from the mission and a few Indians who had never accepted the Spanish way were still living in the wild, inaccessible hills around Point Mugu, by 1850 the culture had been destroyed.

In 1846 Mexican Governor Pio Pico granted 36,000-acre Rancho Guadalasco—including the area of the present-day park—to Isabel Maria Yorba of Los Angeles. She sold 22,000 acres of it to a company that, in turn, sold the land in 1873 to Wiliam R. Broome, an "English gentleman of leisure" from Santa Barbara, who also used it as a cattle ranch. During prohibition, bootleggers with cargos for a "dry" Los Angeles considered its empty beaches next to the new Pacific Coast Highway a "true blessing."

The State purchased the southern part of the park from the Broome family in 1966; the Danielson family donated half the value of the land so that the state could acquire the northern part in 1973.

## CAMPING

At Sycamore Canyon Campground, just across the Pacific Coast Highway from park headquarters, there are 55 family campsites, each with a table and wood- or charcoal-burning stove; piped drinking water and toilets are nearby. There is also an area for campers who reach the park on foot or bicycle. The 102 La Jolla Beach campsites have primitive facilities. Sites will accommodate trailers or motorhomes up to 31 feet long and, while there are no hookups at either campground, a trailer sanitation station is located at La Jolla Beach.

Campers can reach the walk-in campground in La Jolla Valley via either La Jolla Canyon (2 miles or 3.2 km. from the Pacific Coast Highway) or Sycamore Canyon (5 miles or 8 km.). Campsites are primitive, but piped water and restrooms are provided; bring your own stove and fuel. A group camp that will accommodate up to twenty-five people is also located in this area.

The La Jolla Valley walk-in family and group campsites are available on a first-come, first served basis only; register at the La Jolla Beach or Sycamore Canyon entrance station, or at park headquarters, more than an hour before sunset.

## HIKING

Among the more than seventy miles of riding and hiking trails that crisscross the park are the Big Sycamore Canyon Trail, which meanders through the finest example of a sycamore savanna in the State Park System, and the La Jolla Valley Loop Trail, which takes you into an area set aside to preserve a native tall-grass prairie.

From the Overlook Trail on the divide between them, you'll get wider and wider vistas of Big Sycamore Canyon and La Jolla Valley with an occasional view of Serrano Canyon and, beyond it, Boney Mountain to the east; to the west you'll get frequent glimpses of the ocean and, on clear days, perhaps see the Channel Islands in the distance.

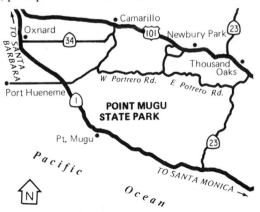

Point Mugu State Park
9000 West Pacific Coast Highway
Malibu, CA 90265
District office (818) 706-1310

# San Diego Coast State Beaches

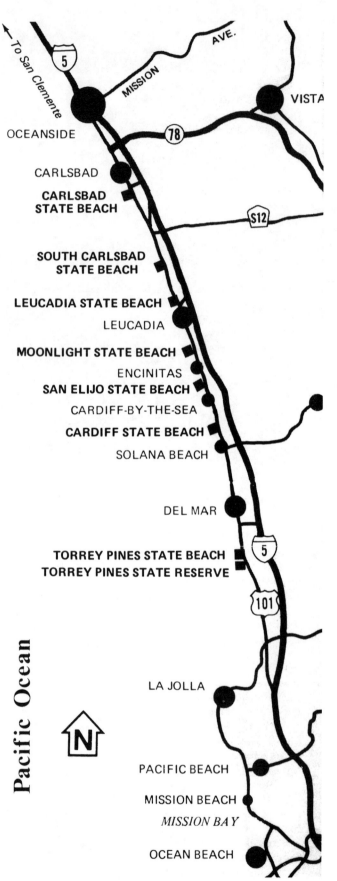

Sun and sea, surf and sand—these are the attractions that put the seven state beaches just north of San Diego among the most popular units of the State Park System. Over four million visitors a year flock to these beaches to enjoy camping, swimming, surfing, fishing, sight-seeing, or just plain loafing in the almost continual sunshine and balmy weather of this area, which has been called the "Riviera of the West."

The beaches dot the coastline between the pleasant seaside communities of Carlsbad and La Jolla. Except for Leucadia, which is reached via Fulvia Avenue, they are all accessible directly from Old Highway 1.

Surfing is popular at all the beaches. Check with lifeguards for suggestions on surfing safely. Surfers and swimmers alike should watch for riptides.

## CAMPING

At South Carlsbad and San Elijo, campgrounds are situated on bluffs overlooking the Pacific. Stairs lead from the campgrounds to the beaches.

South Carlsbad has 226, and San Elijo 171, developed campsites with table, stove, and cupboard; a water supply and restrooms with hot showers are nearby. Concessionaires at each park supply groceries, beach equipment rentals, bait, and laundromat facilities. While there are no trailer hookups, South Carlsbad has a trailer sanitation station, and campsites at both beaches will accommodate trailers or motorhomes up to 28 feet long.

Because these campgrounds are so popular, summer stays must be limited to seven days.

San Diego Coast District
2680 Carlsbad Blvd.
Carlsbad, CA 92008
(619) 729-8947

Silver Strand State Beach occupies the narrow strip of land between San Diego Bay and the Pacific Ocean that connects the City of Coronado with the mainland. The beach, which owes its name to the tiny silver seashells mixed with sand, has been a favorite recreation spot since the 1880s. At that time the newly built Hotel Del Coronado and its accompanying "tent city" enabled visitors to enjoy this ideal recreation area. In 1932 a large part of the Strand acreage was set aside as a state park.

The park's extensive beach frontage on both the bay and the ocean, combined with the area's mild climate, helps make the park one of the finest areas of its kind on the West Coast. Opportunities abound for swimming, fishing, surfing, boating, water skiing, and picnicking. There is overnight camping for self-contained recreational vehicles. During the summer the park remains open for day use until 10 P.M.

Entrance to the park is from State Highway 75, which serves as a divider between the ocean and bay beaches.

The ocean side of the park is favorable for swimming, surfiing, cookouts, and fishing. Perch, corbina, and croaker are caught year-round and grunion spawn on the beach in the summer.

The ocean beach facilities include four large parking lots accommodating nearly two thousand cars. Three pedestrian tunnels lead from the parking lots under the highway to the bay side of the park. Here the calmer, warmer water invites swimming, and picnic areas are provided with cabanas, tables, and fire rings. Crown Cove on this side of the park is the most popular swimming area. The waters outside the cove are a favored overnight spot for local yachtsmen and are also used quite heavily by water skiers.

The park has many family picnic sites and fire rings. Large concrete ramadas are located beside the promenades on the bay side, and each side of the park has its own restrooms, showers, and first aid station. Lifeguard service is available all year around. A snackbar on the beach side also rents beach equipment.

South of the developed area stretches 1½ miles of natural ocean beach, affording the chance for a pleasant stroll and fine beachcombing for horn shells, moonsnails, cockleshells, and an occasional sand dollar.

Marine life of special interest to visitors includes the sea hare and small members of the octopus family, which are found in large numbers in the bay. California sea lions are quite numerous in the ocean, where they feed on the large schools of small fish. An occasional school of porpoises visits the area, and in December and January gray whales can be sighted on their way from the Bering Sea to their breeding ground in Baja California.

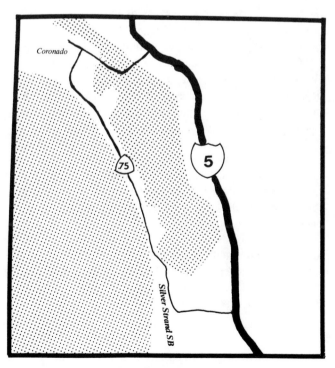

Silver Strand State Beach
5000 Hwy. 75
Coronado, CA 92118
(619) 435-5184

# Santa Barbara County State Beaches

*Carpinteria State Beach*

## CARPINTERIA STATE BEACH

Sheltered inland by the Santa Ynez Mountains and from the sea by the Santa Barbara Islands, Carpinteria, with 4,100 feet of ocean frontage, enjoys a moderate year-round climate with daytime temperatures between 60 and 80 degrees. Ocean temperatures range from around 58 degrees in the winter to 72 degrees during summer and fall. Lifeguards are on duty when beach use is heavy.

The Spanish named this area La Carpinteria, "The Carpenter Shop," because of the woodworking abilities of the Chumash Indians who inhabited the area. Using planks split from driftwood, held together with fiber ropes, and caulked with asphalt from pits that can still be seen in the park, the Indians built canoes seaworthy enough to reach the Channel Islands, across the Santa Barbara Channel, and even Santa Catalina Island.

Channel Coast Area, c/o San Buenaventura State Beach, 901 South San Pedro Street, Ventura, California 93003. Phone: (805) 643-5447.

Carpinteria State Beach
C/O Channel Coast Dist.
24 E. Main Street
Ventura, CA 93001
(805) 684-2811

## EL CAPITAN STATE BEACH

The grove of sycamores on El Capitan Point, visible for miles up and down the coast, is an outstanding feature of this 140-acre State Beach; more sycamores grow with coast live oaks along the banks of El Capitan Creek. Nearly all of the three miles of ocean frontage is sandy beach with a few rocky outcroppings.

Surfing and swimming are popular at El Capitan, and lifeguards are on duty daily from Easter Week through October. Other popular activities are hiking and picnicking; the beach is open for day use from 8 A.M. to sunset.

Reservations are advised for summer and holiday stays at one of the 140 developed family campsites, each with table, stove, and cupboard. Restrooms with hot showers and laundry facilities are nearby, and there is a small snack bar-camping supply store below the campground. Campfire programs are held weekly during the summer, and guided interpretive walks are also given.

The beach is located on Highway 101, 17 miles north of Santa Barbara.

# El Presidio de Santa Barbara State Historic Park

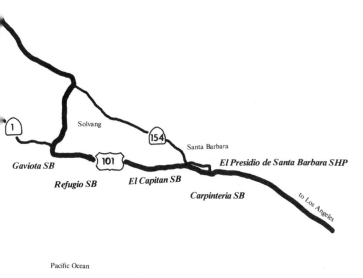

### EL PRESIDIO DE SANTA BARBARA STATE HISTORIC PARK

Founded in 1782, the Santa Barbara Royal Presidio was the last in a chain of military fortresses built by the Spanish along the coast of Alta California. Padre Junipero Serra, founder of the missions, blessed the site of the Santa Barbara Presidio four years prior to the establishment of Mission Santa Barbara in 1786. El Presidio de Santa Barbara State Historic Park encompasses the original Presidio site.

Today you can explore the Presidio's historic structures on a self-guided walking tour. At park headquarters, a scale model and a slide show in the Padre's Quarters will orient you to the site.

Among the items on display is the Presidio's two-century-old chapel bell brought from Peru, handmade tiles, and a padre's rawhide bed. The newly-restored chapel, with decorative wall designs and statuary, is adjacent to park headquarters.

Across the street is El Cuartel, where Presidio soldiers and their families stayed. In the gift shop is a selection of California history books.

Well worth a look is the nearby Santa Barbara History Museum, which displays 200 years of the city's past. Exhibits include everything from a western saddle collection to a Chinese altar from the days when Santa Barbara had a Chinatown. Admission is free.

To reach El Presidio de Santa Barbara, exit U.S. 101 on State Street and go north six blocks to Canon Perdido Street. Presidio buildings are open without charge weekdays from 10:30 A.M. to 4 P.M., weekends from noon to 4 P.M.

Santa Barbara Trust for Historic Preservation, 123 East Canon Perdido Street, Santa Barbara, California 93102. (805) 966-9719.

### REFUGIO STATE BEACH

Many visitors enjoy the 2½-mile walk along the shore from El Capitan to 39-acre Refugio State Beach, 23 miles north of Santa Barbara on Highway 101. This popular beach has about a mile and a half of ocean frontage, with a sandy beach that is popular with swimmers, surfers, and picnickers. Lifeguards are on duty daily from Easter Week through September, and on a limited schedule for the remainder of the year. Day-use hours are from 6 A.M. to sunset.

There are 84 developed family campsites, each with table, stove, cupboard, and nearby restrooms with hot showers and laundry facilities.

### GAVIOTA STATE BEACH

Father Juan Crespi of the 1769 Portola Expedition dubbed the coastline here San Luis in honor of the King of France. However, the soldiers of the expedition thought that La Gaviota, Spanish for "sea gull," was a more apt description of the beach and this name stuck.

Located in a protected cove, Gaviota Beach is a popular year around destination. The surf is gentle, but sometimes the wind whisks around Point Conception and cools down beachgoers.

The park has 39 RV sites and 20 tent sites in a grove of trees. There is a picnic area with barbecue pits near the beach. A small camp store sells snacks, groceries, bait and fishing tackle. A long fishing pier at the north end of the beach has a 3-ton boat launch.

The park also extends inland to the other side of the Highway. (Continue on Highway 101, take the Highway 1 exit, turn right at the stop sign and follow the frontage road to a dirt parking area.) A fire road leads hikers to a hot spring and ultimately to Gaviota Peak (2,458 feet). The road to the peak offers superb views of the Santa Barbara coastline. Day use hours are from 6 A.M. to 10 P.M.

Gaviota District
#10 Refugio Beach Road
Goleta, CA 93117
(805) 968-0019

DE LA GUERRA HOUSE, SANTA BARBARA.

El Presidio de Santa Barbara SHP
Santa Barbara Historic Trust
P.O. Box 388
Santa Barbara, CA 93102
(805) 963-1212

# Topanga State Park

The name Topanga is from the Shoshonean Indian dialect. These Indians and their ancestors occupied the canyon on and off from several thousand years B.C. until the Spanish evicted them and forced them to settle at the San Fernando Mission.

Until the 1880s, there was little permanent habitation in the canyon. Early settlers tended vineyards, orchards and cattle ranches. In the 1920s, the canyon became a popular weekend destination for L.A. residents. Summer cabins were built along Topanga Creek and in subdivisions in the surrounding hills. For a $1 roundtrip fare, tourists could board a Packard Auto Stage in Santa Monica and be driven up Pacific Coast Highway and Topanga Canyon Road to trailheads and picnic spots.

The state park is nestled in quiet and imperturbable Topanga Canyon, surrounded by L.A. sprawl but retaining its wilderness character. Picnicking and hiking are the main attractions here.

To reach the park, turn east onto Entrada Road from Topanga Canyon Boulevard.

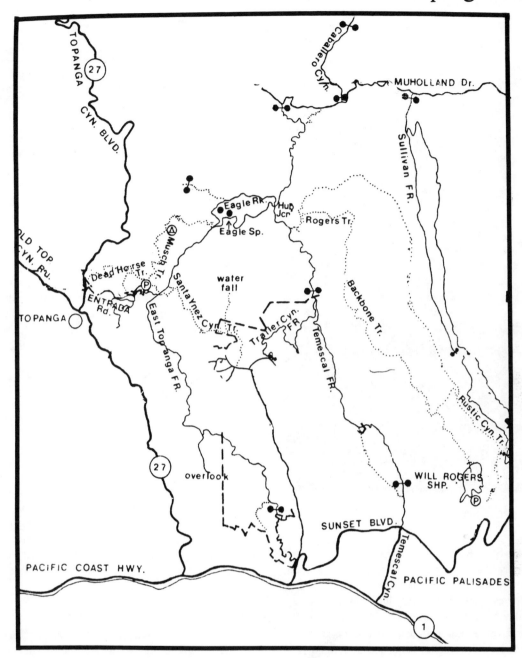

### HIKING

Topanga State Park's 9,177 acres offer an extensive network of trails and fire roads. Musch Ranch Trail (3 miles one way) tours an oak woodland and heads uphill through chaparral to Eagle Junction. Eagle Rock/Eagle Spring Trail (6.5 mile loop) brings the hiker to some impressive sandstone formations and offers fine views of the mountains and the city. Other park trails meander through oak woodland and chaparral, emerging on ridges to provide the hiker with fine views of the ocean to the west and the San Gabriel Mountains to the east.

For many years hikers have promoted the idea of a Backbone Trail following the crest of the Santa Monica Mountains from Will Rogers State Historic Park to Point Mugu State Park. When completed, the trail will link the three large state parks of Topanga, Malibu Creek and Point Mugu, as well as land owned by the National Park Service, and enable visitors to spend days and weekends hiking, backpacking, and horseback riding along the spine of the Santa Monica Mountains.

A 10.5 mile section of the Backbone Trail connects Topanga with Will Rogers State Historic Park. Hikers follow fire roads to the northeast end of the Eagle Rock/Eagle Spring Loop, then follow Fire Road 30, Rogers Road and Rogers Trail, finally entering Will Rogers Park near Inspiration Point.

State and National Park trail crews, as well as volunteers, are working on the Topanga-Malibu Creek State Park Backbone Trail segment. Check at the ranger station in Topanga State Park for the latest trail information.

Topanga State Park
20825 Entrada Road
Topanga, CA 90290
(213) 455-2465

# Torrey Pines State Reserve

Torrey pine, *Pinus Torreyana*

Torrey Pines State Reserve is a majestic wilderness island amidst an increasingly urban area. Its fragile environment is the home of the world's rarest pine tree—*Pinus torreyana*. Ten thousand years ago the tree may have covered a larger part of southern California, but now it grows naturally only here and on Santa Rosa island, 175 miles to the northwest. Of an estimated six thousand or fewer native Torrey pines, an actual count in 1973 showed 3,401 young and mature trees growing within the thousand-acre Reserve.

The Reserve's setting today is much as it was described a hundred years ago: "...a series of high broken cliffs and deeply indented ravines on the bold headlands overlooking the sea with the trees clinging to the face of the crumbling sandstone." The trees themselves take on a variety of shapes as dictated by the elements—bent, twisted, gnarled. Where most exposed to wind and salty air they may grow only ten feet high, as contrasted to a tree planted in Carpinteria in 1890 which is about a hundred feet tall. With a generally poor soil and arid climate, the trees tend to have extensive root systems; a sixty-foot specimen may have roots up to two hundred feet in length. The tree's usual life span is around a hundred years, but the oldest known living trees are over four hundred years old.

About three hundred other species of native plants are protected in Torrey Pines State Reserve, as are about two hundred species of birds. Among them are California quail, scrub jays, brown towhees, and an occasional great horned owl. Brush rabbits and other small rodents are common; a few gray foxes, coyotes, mule deer, and reptiles—including rattlesnakes—are also residents.

Two outstanding areas within the Reserve have been designated as Natural Preserves—Ellen Browning Scripps Natural Preserve, which includes the finest grove of trees, and Penasquitos Marsh Natural Preserve, which forms a part of one of the last remaining salt marsh areas and waterfowl refuges in southern California. The lagoon and marsh offer a home to several rare and endangered species of birds and provide a vital stopping or nesting place for many migratory waterfowl.

Developments in the natural preserves are minimal; they are designed to allow man only as an observer of this unique environment. Various portions of the Reserve may be closed at times to allow the natural features to recuperate from abuse, overuse, or natural disasters; Parry Grove, which was closed for several years, is again open, while the East Grove has been closed since fire destroyed some two hundred trees there in 1972.

## THE BEACH

Both swimmers and surf fishermen find excellent recreation at Torrey Pines State Beach, until 1969 a part of Torrey Pines State Reserve but now a separate park unit. The beach extends 4½ miles, north and south of Los Penasquitos Lagoon, and can be reached by trail from the Reserve and from several points along North Torrey Pines Road.

## TRAILS

The popular Guy Fleming Trail in North Grove is a self-guided nature trail with a guide folder. Unusual forms of the Torrey Pines can be seen on this 0.6-miles (1-km.) loop trail. Two viewpoints overlooking the sea offer a beautiful panorama of the Pacific Ocean and coastal landmarks. On clear days you can see La Jolla to the south and San Clemente and Santa Catalina Islands on the horizon to the west and northwest.

A 0.4-mile (0.67-km.) loop trail through Parry Grove offers views of the more sheltered pines, where trees attain greater size and better form than on the exposed headlands. The grove is named for the botanist who described and named the Torrey pine. Steep stairs form the head of the trail.

The short trail to High Point leads to the location of some of the oldest living trees in the Reserve. Like the trail to Red Butte, it offers a wide view of the Reserve and ocean.

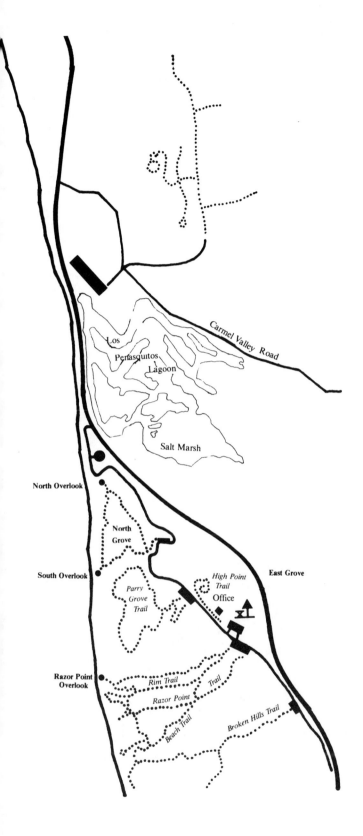

Trails to Razor Point and Yucca Point offer views of spring wildflowers, the beach some 140 to 155 feet below, the sea, and the sandstone sculpturing of the walls to Big Basin, where gnarled trees may be viewed from above.

The D.A.R. Trail and other trails in the Extension Area offer views across the marsh to the main Reserve and the ocean. Many trees are now preserved here, thanks to public donations for land acquisitions.

## INTERPRETIVE SERVICES

When you come to the Reserve, be sure to visit the exhibits at the West Parking Area, the head of the Guy Fleming Trail, and the museum. The Whitaker Memorial Native Plant Garden, under development at the head of the Parry Grove Trail, will aid in plant identification; plant and bird lists are available free at the office/museum, and several other interpretive publications are on sale there. A teacher's guide is available to schools. Check at the museum for programs which may be offered; requests for group programs should be made at least two weeks in advance.

The main Reserve will accommodate only about four hundred people at one time without damage to its delicate ecological systems. Therefore, to protect the natural resources from overuse, you may be asked to check back later or plan to visit another day if the Reserve is full when you arrive. The Reserve is full most weekend afternoons.

Stay on the officially designated trails. The ground cover is fragile, and if it is destroyed soil erosion accelerates. The sandstone cliffs are very soft; climbing mars the spectacular effects created by the elements, and is very hazardous.

Torrey Pines State Reserve
C/O San Diego Coast District
2680 Carlsbad Blvd.
Carlsbad, CA 92008
(619) 755-2063

# Ventura County State Beaches

### EMMA WOOD STATE BEACH

Just outside the western city limits of Ventura, off Highway 101, is Emma Wood State Beach, a narrow strip of land between the Southern Pacific railroad tracks and the ocean. 175 campsites, operated by Ventura County, line an abandoned section of Coast Highway. A bike path extends from Emma Wood State Beach to San Buenaventura State Beach.

The moderate ocean temperatures at Emma Wood assure excellent surfing and swimming, plus surf fishing for perch, bass, cabezon, and corbina.

Emma Wood State Beach Group Camp is located at the west end of Main Street. It has four 30-person sites with restrooms, camp stoves, picnic tables, and showers. There is also a walk in/bicycle camp.

A freshwater marsh at the southwest end of the beach attracts racoons, small rodents, various song birds, and redtailed hawks. Among the coastal shore birds found here are grebes, cormorants, curlews, willets, sandpipers, pelicans, and the ever-present gulls.

### SAN BUENAVENTURA STATE BEACH

Picnicking, swimming and surfing are popular at San Buenaventura State Beach, adjacent to U.S. 101 in the city of Ventura. Two miles of sandy beach, a line of sand dunes, plus plenty of parking and picnic sites make this beach a popular one.

A 1,700-foot pier accommodates a restaurant, snack bar, and bait shop. The most common species fishermen catch from the pier or from shore are bonita, surf perch, shark, bass and corbina. Rock jetties built out from the shoreline to prevent erosion of sand provide shelter for small marine animals such as crabs, marine worms, barnacle, mussels and starfish.

Surfers enjoy San Buenaventura's mild ocean temperatures, which are usually in the mid-sixties. Lifeguards are on duty during the summer season, when the beach is crowded with swimmers and sunbathers.

### MCGRATH STATE BEACH

Located on the western city limits of Oxnard, McGrath State Beach offers two miles of ocean frontage. The park has 174 developed campsites.

A small lake in the southern portion of the park helps to attract more than two hundred species of birds, including white-tailed kites, marsh hawks, owls, and herons. Such rare birds as ospreys, white wagtails, and black skimmers have been sighted here. The Santa Clara River on the northern boundary also offers a haven for birds, weasels, muskrats, skunks, jackrabbits, opossum, squirrels, and mice, plus tortoises and gopher snakes.

Along the beach, visitors enjoy sunbathing or surf fishing for bass, corbina, or perch. Lifeguards are on duty during the summer, but swimming is not recommended because of the strong currents and riptides which can catch a swimmer unaware. A row of sand dunes overlooks the surf between the campsites and the beach.

To reach McGrath State Beach, visitors southbound on U.S. 101 take the Seaward Avenue off-ramp to Harbor Boulevard, turn south on Harbor and travel three fourths of a mile to the park. Northbound visitors take the Victoria Avenue exit left at the light to Olivas Road and then turn right to Harbor Boulevard.

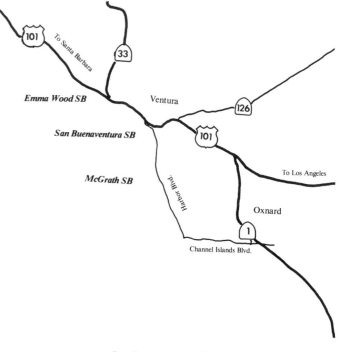

San Buenaventura State Beach
Channel Coast District
24 E. Main Street
Ventura, CA 93001
(805) 654-4611
Emma Wood SB: (805) 643-6037
McGrath SB: (805) 483-8034

*Will Rogers' home*

Will Rogers, often called the "Cowboy Philosopher," carried the mark of the ranching Southwest on him throughout his life. Born on a ranch near what is now Claremore, Oklahoma, he had shown an early interest in show business and while still a young man went around the world as a trick roper in traveling rodeos. Back in the United States he began appearing in shows in New York and worked for many years in the Ziegfeld Follies. His humorous comments on the news of the day soon made him a famous cracker-barrel philosopher, with his roping act as a backdrop.

In 1919 Rogers came to Hollywood at the urging of Samuel Goldwyn. He stayed for three years of only moderate success, then returned to the stage. It wasn't until the "talkies" could display his ready wit and drawling presentation that he became a smash hit. By 1935, he had gained a wide audience as a radio commentator, newspaper columnist, and motion picture star.

On August 15, 1935, on a flight to Alaska, Will Rogers, then 55, was killed in a plane crash with his good friend Wiley Post.

Rogers once said, "You must judge a man by how much he will be missed." By his own criterion, Will Rogers was a great man.

Rogers made his home in Beverly Hills during the early twenties, and in 1922 bought property above Sunset Boulevard commanding a view of western Los Angeles, Santa Monica, and the Pacific Ocean. In 1928 Rogers, his wife Betty, and their three children—Will Jr., Mary, and Jimmy—moved to the ranch, and their weekend cottage was enlarged to its present size of thirty-one rooms.

The grounds and ranch buildings are maintained as they were when the family lived here. The living room—with its comfortable furniture, porch swing in the center of the room, and many Indian rugs and baskets—is most revealing of Rogers' personality. The mounted calf was given to him to rope in place of roping his friends.

The attractive patio was often used for dining. The north wing of the house contains the family's bedrooms, the study, the library, and Betty's favorite, the sunroom.

The ranch became a state park in 1944, after the death of Mrs. Rogers. The park admission charge includes access to the trails as well as admission to the ranch house, a film on Will Rogers' life, and an audio tour of the grounds. The two-mile loop trail to Inspiration Point is particularly popular, and a nature trail and longer hikes are available—check with a ranger. There is also a small picnic area and nature center.

Will Rogers was an enthusiastic horseman and polo player. Polo games were frequently played at his ranch; this tradition continues today, and visitors may occasionally see teams in competition.

The park is open daily except Thanksgiving, Christmas, and New Year's Days, from 8 A.M. to 5 P.M.; the house opens at 10 A.M.

Will Rogers State Historic Park
14253 Sunset Blvd.
Pacific Palisades, CA 90272
(213) 454-8212

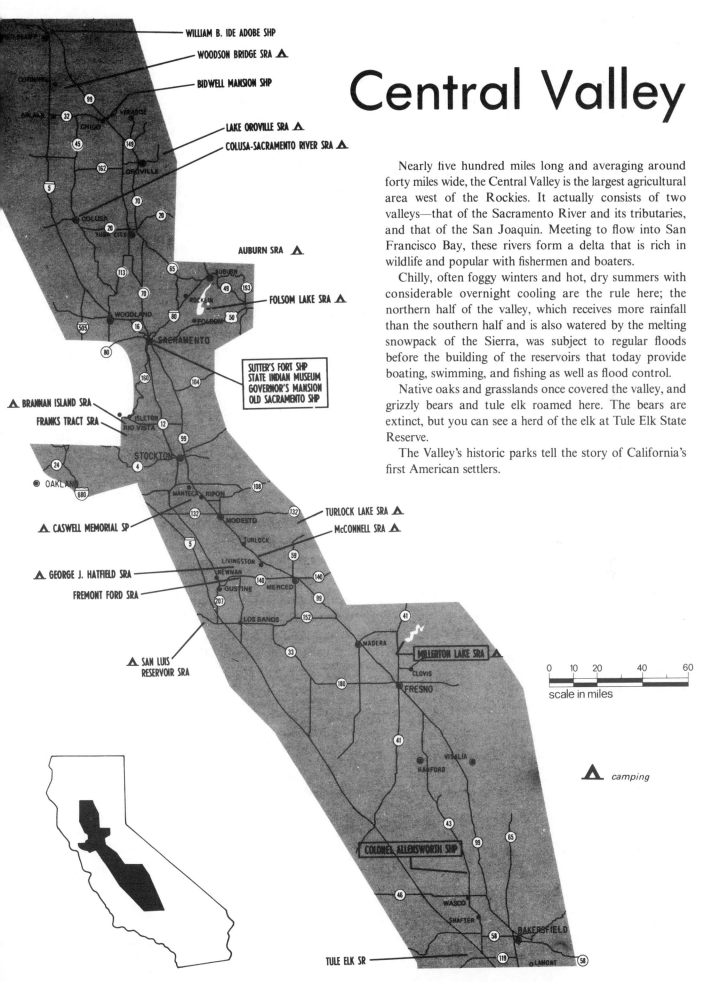

WILLIAM B. IDE ADOBE SHP

WOODSON BRIDGE SRA ⛺

BIDWELL MANSION SHP

LAKE OROVILLE SRA ⛺

COLUSA-SACRAMENTO RIVER SRA ⛺

AUBURN SRA ⛺

FOLSOM LAKE SRA ⛺

SUTTER'S FORT SHP
STATE INDIAN MUSEUM
GOVERNOR'S MANSION
OLD SACRAMENTO SHP

⛺ BRANNAN ISLAND SRA
FRANKS TRACT SRA

⛺ CASWELL MEMORIAL SP

⛺ GEORGE J. HATFIELD SRA
FREMONT FORD SRA

⛺ SAN LUIS
RESERVOIR SRA

TURLOCK LAKE SRA ⛺
McCONNELL SRA ⛺

MILLERTON LAKE SRA ⛺

⛺ camping

COLONEL ALLENSWORTH SHP

TULE ELK SR

scale in miles
0  10  20  40  60

# Central Valley

Nearly five hundred miles long and averaging around forty miles wide, the Central Valley is the largest agricultural area west of the Rockies. It actually consists of two valleys—that of the Sacramento River and its tributaries, and that of the San Joaquin. Meeting to flow into San Francisco Bay, these rivers form a delta that is rich in wildlife and popular with fishermen and boaters.

Chilly, often foggy winters and hot, dry summers with considerable overnight cooling are the rule here; the northern half of the valley, which receives more rainfall than the southern half and is also watered by the melting snowpack of the Sierra, was subject to regular floods before the building of the reservoirs that today provide boating, swimming, and fishing as well as flood control.

Native oaks and grasslands once covered the valley, and grizzly bears and tule elk roamed here. The bears are extinct, but you can see a herd of the elk at Tule Elk State Reserve.

The Valley's historic parks tell the story of California's first American settlers.

69

# Auburn State Recreation Area

The dam builders didn't get their way on the American River. More than a decade ago, construction began on Auburn Dam, which would have turned the gorges and canyons along this stretch of the river into Auburn Lake. But a Montana dam, similar in design to the one under construction at Auburn, collapsed. This incident, along with conservation efforts by such groups as Friends of the River, put a halt to the project. The federal Bureau of Reclamation then allowed the state of California to use a portion of the river as a recreation area.

Since it's possible that the dam project could be revived, no expensive access roads or facilities have been constructed in the recreation area; any such improvements would be covered by water if Auburn Lake came into existence. Fishing, hiking, and camping are the most popular park activities. Rafting excursions on the still untamed American River are offered by various commercial tour groups. Ask for details at park headquarters.

The park straddles the Middle Fork and the North Fork of the American River, the same river where James Marshall found gold in 1848. Today modern-day gold panners try their luck. Scenic Highway 49 winds through the park and offers a glimpse of the sharp canyons and rugged country-side of the Sierra foothills. The park provides an intro-duction to the oak and pine-studded slopes characteristic of the "Gold Country."

*American River*

### HIKING

The Western Pioneer Trail which travels from Sacra-mento to Lake Tahoe passes through the Recreation Area. Endurance horseback rides and marathon runs use this route.

Backpackers may travel to a number of trail camps along the river. Day hikers too enjoy traveling into the river gorge. Early in the season, trout fishing is good. Back-country information and permits are available at the field office, which is located on Highway 49, one half mile south of the Auburn city limits, (916) 885-4528.

### CAMPING

Five primitive campgrounds are available in the area. The sites have picnic tables and chemical toilets are nearby. Campfires are permitted only in provided stoves.

Colfax/Iowa Hill—Camping is permitted on the south side of the river, upstream from the old bridge.

Upper end of Lake Clementine—Camping is permitted on the south side of the river. There is a boat launch area suitable for small boats. Generally closed from October to May. Access is from the Foresthill Road.

Mammoth Bar Upstream to Hoosier Bar—Camping is permitted on the north side of the River (Placer County).

Ruck-A-Chucky—Camping is permitted on the north side of the river (Placer County). Access is either from Drivers Flat Road or McKeon Road, both off of Foresthill Road.

Cherokee Bar—Camping is permitted on the south side of the river (El Dorado County). Access is from Sliger Mine Road.

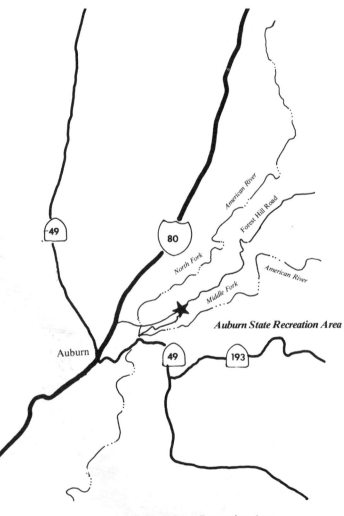

*Auburn State Recreation Area*

Auburn State Recreation Area
P.O. Box 1680
Auburn, CA 95603
(916) 885-4527

California pioneer John Bidwell worked five years for Captain John Sutter and later became a wealthy man after staking out some gold claims on the Feather River in 1848. When California joined the union, Bidwell was elected to the state senate. Soon after he bought the 25,000-acre Rancho de Arroyo Chico.

He was elected U.S. Congressman in 1865. While serving in the legislature, he met and married Annie Ellicott Kennedy. The Bidwell home in Chico became a cultural meeting place for Californians and for visitors from around the world. Many prominent guests were entertained by the Bidwells, who were known both as gracious hosts and promoters of various political and social causes.

John and Annie Bidwell worked for election reform and control of the monopolies, especially in the public service fields of transportation and communication. Together they fought for women's rights—especially the right to vote— and for prohibition. They felt that the use of alcohol in political campaigns was extremely destructive to ideas and idealism. Their activity in these matters brought people such as Francis E. Willard of the temperance movement and Susan B. Anthony of the women's rights movement to Rancho Chico and the Bidwell mansion.

Over the years the Bidwells traveled widely, visiting Europe and Alaska as well as Washington, New York City, and other points on the east coast. Some part of each summer was spent in the Sierra Nevada or on the slopes of Mount Shasta or Lassen Peak. Their interest in natural history ranged from astronomy to wildflowers and brought them lifelong friendships with John Muir, Asa Gray, Sir Joseph Hooker, and other leading scientists of the time.

Their interest in education (especially higher education) as the cornerstone of a free and enlightened society led to friendships with David Starr Jordan of Stanford and Joseph LeConte of the University of California. Gifts of land and money or books were made to various educational institutions. Chico State University, for instance, stands on land donated by the Bidwells, and both John and Annie served as trustees of the school. John Bidwell also served briefly as a regent of the University of California.

In 1890 John Bidwell accepted the Prohibition Party's nomination for governor and though he stood no real chance of winning the election, his uncompromising idealism and eloquence in that campaign led to his nomination for president in 1892 by the National Prohibition Party. His speech, accepting the nomination, was widely read and though he did not campaign in any other way he nevertheless received more votes than any Prohibition candidate for president before or since. Interestingly enough almost all of his ideas—highly controversial at the time—have since been adopted into law and today many of them— particularly women's suffrage and basic election reform measures—are taken for granted.

Bidwell Mansion is open to the public every day from 10 A.M. to 5 P.M. A visitor center in the building itself includes displays and publications about the life and times of the Bidwells, and guided tours of the mansion are conducted at frequent intervals throughout the day. Advance reservations for special group tours can be made by contacting the park headquarters.

*John and Annie Bidwell on the porch of their mansion*

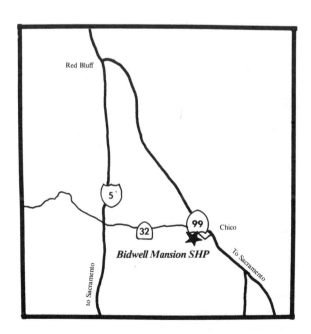

Bidwell Mansion State Historic Park
525 Esplanade
Chico, CA 95926
(916) 895-6144

# Brannan Island/Franks Tract State Recreation Areas

The Sacramento-San Joaquin Delta, a thousand miles of rivers, sloughs, levees, and marshes, has become one of the world's outstanding water recreation areas. At its gateway, Brannan Island State Recreation Area offers year-round camping, picnicking, boating, fishing, and swimming.

The climate in the Delta is mild, but winds up to 25 mph are common, and boaters must be aware of tides, which can vary as much as six feet in a day. The park has a six-lane boat launching ramp with a large parking area.

The park's swimming beach on Seven Mile Slough, which is closed to power boats, has lifeguards on duty during the summer. There is a large picnic area adjacent to the beach with barbecue grills scattered among the picnic tables.

Near the entrance, a visitor center offers interpretive displays as well as publications on the Delta's wildlife and history. Rangers give fishing tips and campfire programs.

## CAMPING

Cottonwood and Willow campgrounds contain 102 developed sites with tables and stoves. The sites can accommodate trailers and RV's up to 31 feet long as well as tents, but there are no utility hookups. A trailer sanitation station is near the park entrance.

There are 32 slips in the Delta Vista Boat Campsite where you can berth your boat overnight. Berths accommodate boats up to 35 feet long and 10 feet wide—wider boats need two berths. The adjoining walk-in campsites have tables, stoves, and cupboards; drinking water and a restroom with hot showers are nearby.

Each of the park's six primitive group campsites will accommodate up to 30 people. The sites offer tables, stoves, chemical toilets and drinking water, and can handle RV's up to 31 feet long.

## FRANKS TRACT

Five miles southeast of Brannan Island, Franks Tract State Recreation Area is accessible only by water. There's a six-slip boat dock on Little Franks Tract across Piper Slough from Bethel Island, the closest access.

All but 300 acres of Franks Tract is under water, and boating and waterskiing are popular here. The lake, created when a break in the levee flooded the island, is an exceptionally productive fishing area, and waterfowl hunting is allowed on part of the open water area, subject to Department of Fish and Game Regulations—check at the Brannan Island park office for details.

Anglers catch striped bass, sturgeon, bluegill, catfish, black bass, crappie, perch, and an occasional salmon or steelhead. There are many marinas, bait shops, and supply stores throughout the Delta to serve boaters and fishermen.

Little Franks Tract, a wetland marsh protected by a levee, is reminiscent of the delta before its settlement. Beaver, muskrats and river otter live here. No hunting is permitted.

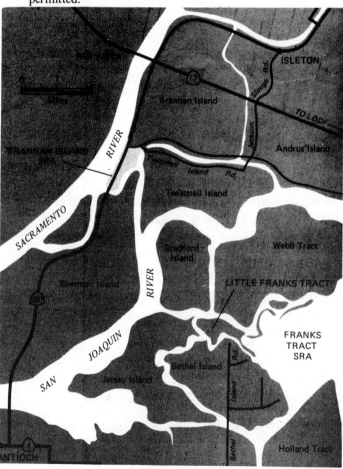

Brannan Island State Recreation Area
Star Route, Box 75A
Rio Vista, CA 94571
(916) 777-6671

# Caswell Memorial State Park

The Stanislaus River, which winds through the park, has a beach and swimming area close to the day-use facilities and campground. Fishing is at its best in the summer when there are striped, largemouth and smallmouth bass; sturgeon, blue gill, catfish, shad, and buffalo carp. In the fall salmon and steelhead are caught.

## HIKING

An interpretive display giving the history of the park is at the head of the Oak Forest Nature Trail. The trail winds through fine stands of valley oak and along the Stanislaus River where a tangle of undergrowth provides protection and food for the wildlife. Outside the oak forest a wide variety of tree and plant life can be found including wild roses, wild currant, and rambling blackberry.

Another trail 100 feet north of the display leads to a point where one can observe a great blue heron rookery on the park's undeveloped west side, a popular field study area. Visitors should not approach within a quarter of a mile of the herons or they will abandon their nest.

## CAMPING

In a pleasant wooded area beside the river there are 66 family campsites, each with a table, stove, and food locker. Piped drinking water and comfort stations with hot showers are nearby. The sites will accommodate trailers up to 21 feet long or motorhomes up to 24 feet, though there are no hookups.

The group campground will accommodate up to 50 people for tent camping only; it may be flooded in spring.

Caswell Memorial State Park is located southwest of Ripon in the San Joaquin Valley. It abounds with wildlife such as opossum, skunk, raccoon, fox, rabbit, muskrat and the beautiful wood duck. The valley oak—*Quercus lobata*—found in the 258-acre park is native only to California and grows best in the low flatlands, although it can also be found in the Coast Range to the west. The park's stand of valley oak is but a remnant of the large hardwood forest that once covered much of the Central Valley's river banks and flood plains. Demand for firewood and efforts to clear the land for agriculture in past years reduced the virgin forest to a few isolated stands. Some of the stands protected in the park contain trees more than 60 feet high with girths of over 17 feet.

Minnie Elizabeth Pope, reflecting on her childhood years here in the late 1800s, said,

> I could ride all over the place. We had many points of interest: a biggest oak tree and a tree that had been burned and had a buzzard's nest in it. I would go to see the young every spring. There was a beaver dam, a woodchopper's cabin, a pen to catch wild hogs, and the Indian burying ground. We cut as much as 300 cord of wood a season.

An area of her pioneering family's ranch is preserved in the park. It remains much as they, and the Caswells who bought the ranch in 1915, knew it.

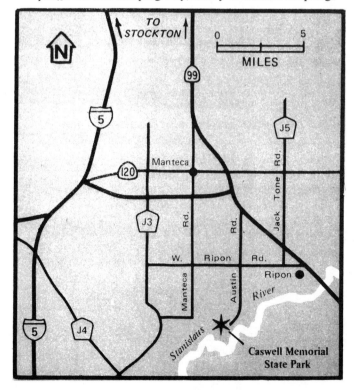

Caswell Memorial State Park
28000 South Austin Road
Ripon, CA 95366
(209) 599-3810

# Colonel Allensworth State Historic Park

This park commemorates black history and the vision of one of California's visionary pioneers, Colonel Allen Allensworth.

Allensworth was born into slavery in 1842 in the deep south. He escaped during the Civil War and joined the Union forces. After the war, he opened two highly successful restaurants in Saint Louis. He became a minister and married Josephine Leavell, a young school teacher. In 1886, Allensworth reentered the U.S. Army, serving with distinction in the Spanish-American War. He retired in 1906 with the rank of Lieutenant-Colonel, the highest rank ever held by a black officer up to that time.

In 1906 Colonel Allensworth and other prominent black leaders decided to establish a black community, free from the discriminatory practices of the time, in order that blacks could achieve their full social and economic potential. Enterprising black people soon migrated to Allensworth, as the new town on the Santa Fe Railroad line in Tulare County came to be known. Farmers worked the fertile land. Shops, homes and schools were built.

Allensworth prospered for about a decade. In 1914, Colonel Allensworth was killed in an accident. The death of their town founder was a tragic loss to the community. Other capable leaders took charge, but one obstacle could not be overcome: lack of water. Groundwater pumping throughout the San Joaquin Valley lowered the water table and impaired the quality and quantity of Allensworth's water. Compounding the town's problems, income from shipping business began to decline as trucks replaced trains in hauling the valley's produce.

The town gradually lost population. Today about thirty families live in the town of Allensworth.

The park visitor center offers a half-hour film about Allen Allensworth and his town. Nearby is the restored Allensworth school and the home of Allen and Josephine Allensworth. The streets of Allensworth are named for important black Americans. Eventually, the California Department of Parks and Recreation plans to restore additional buildings.

The park has 15 semi-improved campsites (no hookups) and a picnic area. Small groups can reserve a dormitory by contacting park headquarters.

Colonel Allensworth State Historic Park
Star Route 1, Box 148
Earlimart, CA 93219
(805) 849-3433

*Colonel Allen Allensworth*

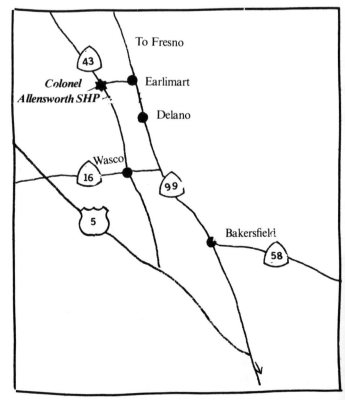

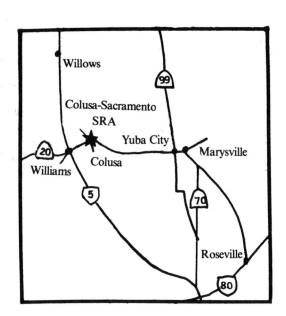

GROUP OF SALMON FROM THE SACRAMENTO RIVER.

The campers, boaters, and fishermen who enjoy this delightful park on the west side of the Sacramento River rarely can guess the previous use of the land now included in the recreation area. It was. . .a dump. Beginning in 1955, the dump was filled, graded, and improved. In 1964 the area was opened as a park.

The banks of the river were once occupied by the River Patwin, who were noted for their fine feather work and basketry. In warfare, the Indians went into battle wearing elk-hide and reed body armor to protect against spears and arrows. The Patwin followed the Ghost Dance Movement, which held that white men would disappear and the land would return to its original pristine state.

But the Patwin were wrong. The Sacramento River lies in a region of Mediterranean climate, with generous winter rains and long hot summers. This climate in combination with a fertile climate attracted farmers. John Bidwell, who was to become the state's leading agriculturalist, explored the Sacramento Valley in 1841. After the Gold Rush, thousands of settlers homesteaded along the banks of the Sacramento.

One nineteenth century writer, Charles Howard Shinn, was very fond of the region: "At Colusa, raisin plantations and stone fruit orchards appear like islands in an ocean of wheat."

By 1850 twenty-eight steamers and 60 or more boats and ships powered by sail and oars were operating on the Sacramento. The river in later years lost much of its commerce to the railroad, but today pleasure boats make extensive use of the waterways extending through the valley. Commercial shipping is also undergoing a renaissance.

The Sacramento, lined by river cottonwoods and willows, wild grapes and figs, may look placid as a lake, but in winter the river often becomes a raging torrent. Great quantities of silt, which is responsible for some of the richest farmland in the nation, is left behind after wet season floods. Sometimes the park's boat ramp and picnic ground gets quite a muddy covering.

The park is a nice place for fishing off the river bank or as a base for fishing expeditions up and downstream. This stretch of California's largest river offers anglers a chance for striped bass and shad in spring, salmon, black bass and catfish in the fall, and sometimes sturgeon and steelhead.

## CAMPING

The park has 22 developed campsites, each with table and barbecue stove. Piped drinking water and restrooms with hot showers are nearby.

Colusa-Sacramento State Recreation Area
P.O. Box 207
Colusa, CA 95932
(916) 458-4927

# Folsom Lake State Recreation Area

Closest to a metropolitan area of all the big state reservoir parks, Folsom Lake attracts four million visitors a year. Situated in the Sierra Nevada foothills, just 25 miles from Sacramento, the lake is popular with those who like to hike, camp, ride horses, waterski, boat and swim. The most popular pastime, though, is fishing. Skillful anglers hook trout, catfish, large- and small-mouth bass, perch and Kokanee.

Folsom Lake, formed by Folsom Dam, has 75 miles of shoreline. The dam is located near the confluence of the North and South forks of the American River; this has created two long arms extending deep into the foothills with a peninsula in between. Downriver is another dam, Nimbus, which creates 500-acre Lake Natoma.

## DAY USE

Hikers and horseback riders will enjoy the park's 80 miles of trail. One stretch is part of the Western States Pioneer Express Trail between Carson City, Nevada and Sacramento. Bicyclists can ride from downtown Sacramento to Folsom Lake via the American River Bike Trail. A hiker-biker campground is located at Beal's Point Campground.

Picnic sites are found at Beal's Point, Granite Bay, Rattlesnake Bar and Dyke 8 on Folsom Lake, and at Negro Bar and Nimbus Flat on Lake Natoma. All have barbecue stoves. Granite Bay group picnic area can accommodate 400 people; contact park headquarters for reservation information.

History buffs will want to visit the little Folsom powerhouse, which in 1895 sent 11,000 volts of electricity to downtown Sacramento; this was the longest transmission of its time. Pacific Gas and Electric Company kept the powerhouse in operation until 1952 when it donated it to the state. The pioneer generating station is located on Riley Street in Folsom; contact park headquarters for hours and tour information.

## BOATING

Around the lake are many launch ramps to handle all sizes of boats. At Brown's Ravine, a concessionaire operates a mammoth marina, which includes a gas dock, tow service, boat slips and a snack bar.

Camping is permitted aboard self-contained sail or power craft. Register for boat camps at the Granite Bay entrance or the marina at Brown's Ravine. A ranger will inspect your boat's sleeping arrangements and sanitary facilities. You will be informed where mooring overnight is permitted. Peninsula Campground is the one place where you may camp ashore.

## CAMPING

Peninsula Campground's 100 sites will accommodate trailers up to 18 feet long and motorhomes up to 24 feet. Located near the end of the peninsula formed by the North and South Forks of the American River, the campground can be reached by boat or by driving over 10 miles of paved and dirt roads from Pilot Hill on Highway 49.

Forty-eight campsites are situated at Beal's Point Campground just north of Folsom Dam. Trailers and motorhomes up to 31 feet long can be accommodated.

Negro Bar Campground on the north side of Lake Natoma has 20 sites for recreation vehicles up to 31 feet long.

Granite Bay is the site of an equestrian camp. Make reservations through the park.

Folsom Lake State Recreation Area
7806 Folsom-Auburn Road
Folsom, CA 95630
(916) 988-0205

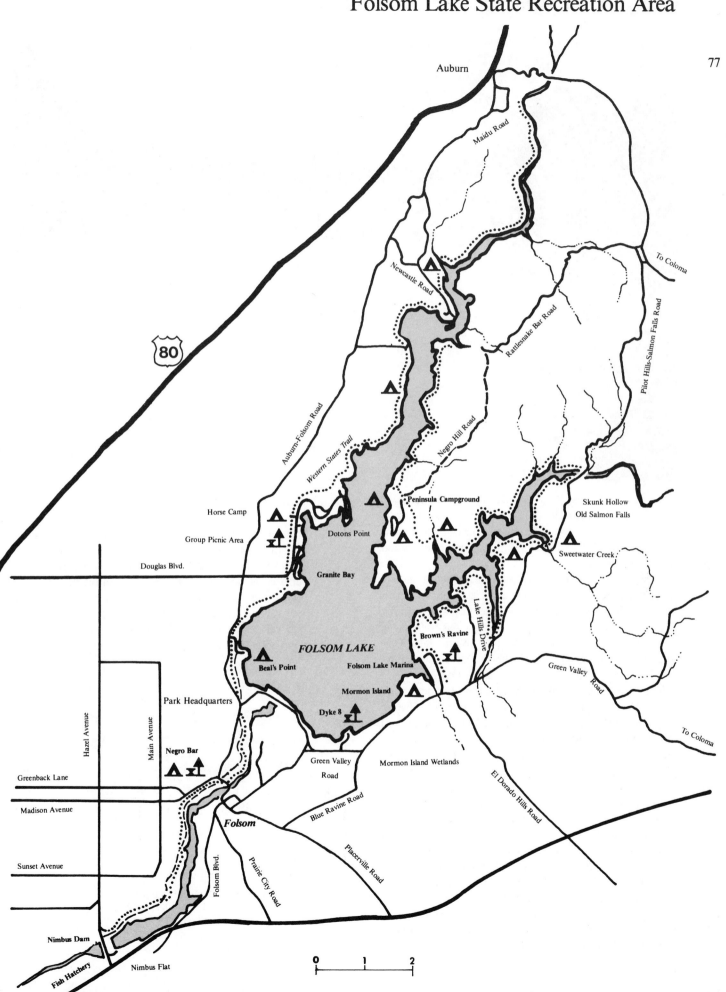

# George J. Hatfield State Recreation Area

George J. Hatfield State Recreation Area is situated in the midst of San Joaquin Valley farmlands on the banks of the Merced River in Merced County. The camp and picnic areas are dotted with valley oak, box elder, cottonwood, and Modesto ash.

Land for the recreation area was donated to the state by the late George J. Hatfield, former Lieutenant Governor and State Senator for California. The area was dedicated September 20, 1953, and a bronze plaque has been placed in a group of oak trees honoring Louisa Jane Cox, grandmother of Mrs. Hatfield, who as a girl came with her family to California in 1849 via the Santa Fe trail.

The recreation area is bordered on three sides by the Merced River, giving it 1¼ miles of river frontage. Visitors may swim and fish in the river (night fishing is permitted), but swimmers should beware of deep holes. No lifeguard service is available. There are several sandy beaches for play.

Groves of valley oak and streamside vegetation make Hatfield a mecca for many kinds of wildlife.

Game birds include ring-necked pheasant, mourning dove and valley quail. Of the larger predators, the most common are crows, yellow-billed magpies, barn owls, Swainson's hawks and bluejays. Other birds include brown and spotted towhees, black phoebes, bewick wrens, western bluebirds, titmice, belted kingfishers and hummingbirds. Transients include the purple finch, Baltimore oriole, hooded oriole, Bullock's oriole, black-headed grosbeak, and several kinds of waterfowl.

Campers may catch an occasional glimpse of a raccoon, opossum, or gray fox at night.

The area contains seven improved family campsites, each with table, grill and food locker. The 27 family picnic sites have tables and grills. Drinking water is piped to the camp and picnic sites. There are two comfort stations.

The group camping area can serve groups up to 200 persons or more, but parking is limited to 40 spaces. The group camp contains a large barbecue pit, sinks, water, serving areas, work area, picnic tables and benches.

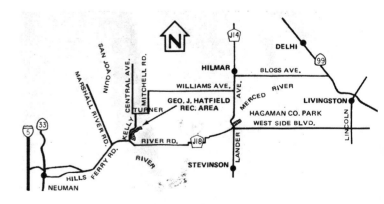

George J. Hatfield State Recreation Area
4394 North Kelly Road
Hilmar, CA 95324
(209) 632-1852

# Lake Oroville State Recreation Area

Lake Oroville State Recreation Area in Butte County offers as wide a variety of outdoor activities as can be found anywhere in California—camping, picnicking, horseback riding, hiking, sail and power boating, waterskiing, fishing, swimming, boat-in camping, and overnight boat camping. The area is located on the Feather River in the chaparral-oak-pine belt of the northern Mother Lode country about seventy-five miles north of Sacramento.

Lake Oroville was created by Oroville Dam, which the State Department of Water Resources completed in 1967 after five years of construction. It conserves water for distribution by the State Water Project to homes, farms, and industries in the San Francisco Bay area, the San Joaquin Valley, and Southern California, and provides flood control and smog-free electric power in addition to recreation.

When full to the 900-foot-elevation mark, the lake offers 15,500 surface acres and 167 miles of shoreline for recreation. Recreation areas are spotted around the lake, and boaters can land at any point to explore; state property extends at least 300 feet, and in some places as much as a mile, from the high water line.

When the lake is at its maximum elevation, you can boat within a quarter of a mile of spectacular Feather Falls on the Fall River. Especially beautiful during the spring runoff, the falls send a cascade of water 640 feet into the river below. There is no trail, but the few rocks in the way are easily climbed.

*Bass Fishing on Lake Oroville*

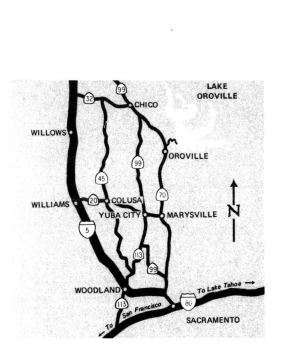

## FISHING

More than a million fish have been planted in Lake Oroville in the last few years, and both shore and boat fishing are popular. Rainbow trout and large- and smallmouth bass are most frequently caught but you might land a German brown, a catfish, a silver salmon, or a lake trout. Fishing is permitted all year long; a valid California sportfishing license is required. Special size and catch limits on the lake, so be sure to check the regulations at a marina or with a park ranger.

# Lake Oroville State Recreation Area

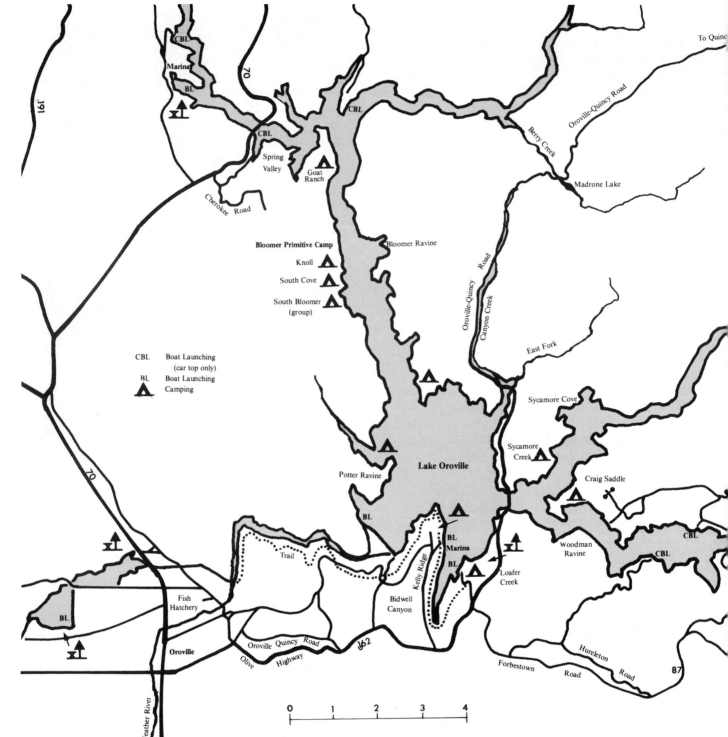

CBL    Boat Launching
(car top only)

BL    Boat Launching

▲    Camping

## CAMPING

**Loafer Creek**—137 developed sites with parking spaces, tables and stoves. Each site will accommodate trailers or motorhomes up to 31 feet long; there are no hookups, but a trailer dump station is located near the entrance. Piped drinking water and restrooms with hot showers and laundry tubs are nearby. Six group areas will accommodate up to 25 persons each and six vehicles per area. Loafer Creek is closed in winter.

**Bidwell Canyon**—82 sites with hookups, sanitation station. Open all year.

Several boat mooring areas have been established on the lake and its tributaries. Located in coves, they offer shelter from the wind and a haven out of the way of other boat traffic, but no facilities. Camping on shore is not permitted except in the designated boat-in campsites; however, you are welcome to go ashore to explore. Overnight mooring is permitted only in the areas identified with buoys; you can tie up to shore or anchor offshore.

Lake Oroville State Recreation Area
400 Glen Drive
Oroville, CA 95965
(916) 534-2409

*A good swimming hole on the Merced River*

McConnell State Recreation Area, named after a pioneer family that once ranched nearby, offers year-round recreation in a shady oasis. The first state park unit in the San Joaquin Valley, this recreation area opened in 1950.

Grassy play areas offer youngsters ample room to romp, and the low, easy flow of the Merced River is great for swimming. Anglers can fish for catfish, black bass and perch; a valid California sportfishing license is required.

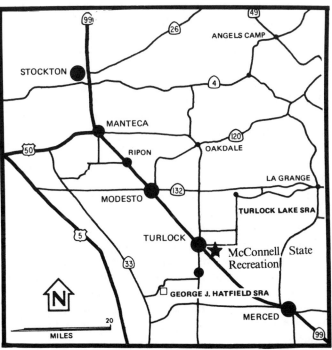

McConnell is a spacious park with lawns and trees. Valley oak, box elder and cottonwood are the primary native trees; sycamore, fruitless mulberry, elm, and Modesto ash have been introduced. There are dense areas of native elderberry, box elder, wild grape and blackberry.

The bottom land along the river consists of a rich, sandy loam. Before the coming of white settlers, this soil supported a luxuriant growth of trees, shrubs, vines and wildflowers that provided abundant food and a place of refuge to Indians and wildlife of the San Joaquin Valley. Today, rich farm lands surrounding the recreation area grow field, row, and nut crops, and there is some poultry and cattle ranching. Only a few isolated spots, as at the recreation area, is the original streamside habitat preserved.

The sandy shore and river bottom are excellent for swimming and beach play, but swimmers should beware of deep holes. No lifeguard service is available.

Because of the high fire hazard there, the wild area on the south side of the Merced River is closed to public use.

### CAMPING

The park's camping and picnic areas contain rock fireplaces, tables, and piped drinking water. The 17 family campsites have food lockers, and the 29-site family picnic area has a few hibachi-like stoves mounted on convenient, waist-level pipestands among the rock fireplaces. The group picnic area has two rock fireplaces and a large barbecue pit. There is also a 40-person group campground. Park personnel offer interpretive programs on Saturday nights during the summer at an outdoor theater next to the group campground.

McConnell State Recreation Area is five miles southeast of Delhi, eleven miles southeast of Turlock, and twenty-five miles northwest of Merced. To reach it from State Highway 99, turn east on El Capitan at Delhi and drive to Pepper Road; turn right and follow the signs.

McConnell State Recreation Area
McConnell Road
Ballico, CA 95303
(209) 394-7755

# Millerton Lake State Recreation Area

Twenty miles northeast of Fresno in almost the exact center of California the San Joaquin River flows out of the Sierra Nevada foothills and into the great central valley. Just at this point Friant Dam was built across the river canyon in 1944, and today Millerton Lake State Recreation Area surrounds the long, narrow lake that has backed up behind the dam.

A mile wide near the damsite, Millerton Lake is three miles wide at its widest point and stretches more than 16 miles back up into the river canyon. With 43 miles of shoreline, and activities ranging from swimming, boating, and waterskiing to hiking, camping, and horseback riding, the lake and the surrounding hills within the recreation area have become extremely popular.

The lake can be enjoyed by as many as 1,500 boats at one time provided everyone follows the rules and is reasonably courteous. Swimming is also very popular and there is a swimming area on the south shore where boats are not allowed. Lifeguards are on duty during the warm weather months.

The hills that surround the lake tend to be steeper and higher toward the eastern end of the park, and are covered by grass or chaparral with occasional trees and wooded areas typical of the Upper Sonoran Life Zone. Digger pines intermingle with valley and live oaks while western sycamore, black willow, and sandbar willow grow alongside the stream.

A surprising variety of birds and other wildlife can be observed within the park including ground squirrels, cottontail rabbits, and California mule deer. Both bald and golden eagles are sighted regularly. Raccoons, muskrats, skunks, badgers, coyotes, and gray foxes also live in the area along with bobcats and even an occasional mountain lion. But wildlife in the area today bears little resemblance to wildlife in the area prior to 1848. Then and for centuries before that time great herds of deer, tule elk, and pronghorn antelope grazed in the valleys. Mink, otter, and beaver were plentiful along the river and streams that every year saw fabulous migrations of salmon and steelhead. Countless millions of migratory waterfowl and other birds filled the air, and even the giant California condor was abundant.

The Indians—Northern Foothill Yokuts—who lived throughout the area of the present park spoke three separate dialects, but for the most part lived a similar kind of life. Fish and acorns were the basic ingredients of their diet, but, like other Indians throughout the state, they made some use of almost every kind of plant or animal in the environment.

Already disrupted by the Spanish missionaries at San Juan Bautista, and ravaged by smallpox and other new diseases, the Indians of this region reacted violently but futilely to the encroachments of the '49ers. The one-sided Mariposa Indian War was finally ended in 1851 when a treaty of peace was signed in what was then Camp Barbour.

Today the blockhouse from old Camp Barbour is preserved in Roeding Park in Fresno. However, its original location is now some 150 feet below the surface of Millerton Lake. Built for the Indian Commissioners in 1850, Camp Barbour was enlarged and became Fort Miller in 1852. Beside the fort a tent city by the name of Rootville sprang up and quickly became the most important town in the area. The town continued to change and grow, and between 1856 and 1874 was the county seat to Fresno County.

The original Millerton County Courthouse, which today stands on Mariner's Point close beside the Friant Dam, was constructed in the town of Millerton in 1867. In 1941 the courthouse was dismantled and saved from the rising waters of Millerton Lake by Fresno County historians who

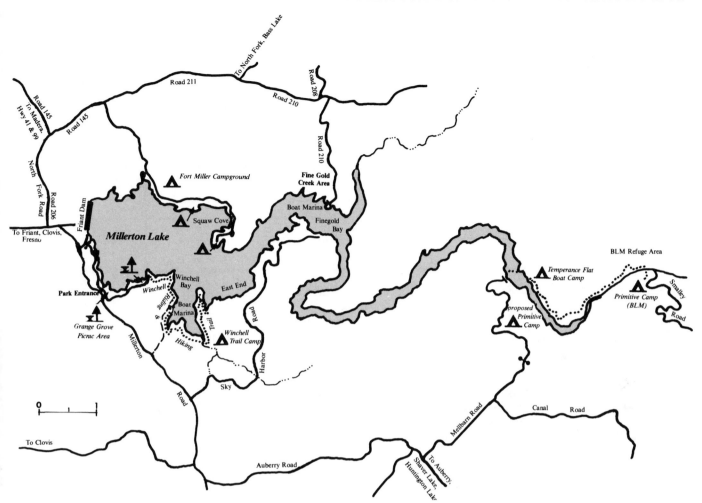

knew that it could be used to tell the colorful story of early-day gold rush times in the region.

Carefully restored by the Department of Parks and Recreation, Millerton Courthouse looks very much the way it did 100 years ago. Various interpretive exhibits and furnishings have also been placed in the building in order to give visitors a fuller appreciation of the region's natural and historical background.

## DAY USE

Hundreds of picnic sites are located in various areas around the lake. Each individual site has a table, and both cooking and sanitary facilities are nearby.

The Finegold area is accessible by both car and boat. This area has tables and wood stoves; piped shelter suitable for group use is also located here and can accommodate up to 150 people.

Boat launching ramps with ample parking lots have been established on both sides of the lake. Fishing supplies, boat rentals, and dock rental space are available at the marina.

## CAMPING

There are three developed campgrounds with a total of 131 family campsites, all of which have individual tables and stoves and are near piped drinking water. The two group camps available in the Meadow Area can accommodate 75 and 40 people respectively.

Boaters can also use the 25 campsites at Temperance Flat, an upstream campground that cannot be reached by car. Tables and wood stoves are provided here along with piped drinking water and pit toilets.

Boat-in campers should register at the south park entrance.

Millerton Lake State Recreation Area
P.O. Box 205
Friant, CA 93626
(209) 822-2332

# Sacramento State Historic Parks

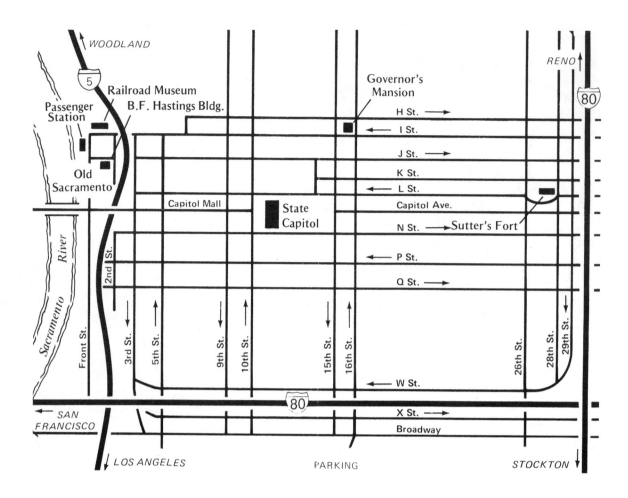

## OLD SACRAMENTO STATE HISTORIC PARK

After the discovery of gold in 1848, a tent city mushroomed on the banks of the Sacramento River. The tents were soon replaced by government and commercial buildings. Sacramento, as state capital and trading center, has been important in the history of California since the Gold Rush; four state historic parks allow visitors to discover this fascinating history.

All the parks are open daily except Thanksgiving, Christmas and New Year's Day from 10 A.M. to 5 P.M. Tours of the Governor's Mansion begin at 9 A.M. The parks are served by the Sacramento Regional Transit buses so visitors may park their cars at a special parking lot (see map) to avoid competing for downtown's scarce parking spaces.

## OLD SACRAMENTO STATE HISTORIC PARK

Admirers of early California urban architecture will enjoy a walking tour of this historic district, which is located in the area along Front Street near the river ends of I and J streets. The Big Four and Bigley Spice buildings are especially well restored. The old Eagle Theatre on Front Street has also been restored and plays from the Gold Rush era to the 1870s are performed.

Some of the early buildings have been reconditioned to house restaurants and shops.

## CALIFORNIA STATE RAILROAD MUSEUM

The museum features locomotives ranging from the 29-foot C.P. Huntington, built in 1863, to the 126-foot SP Cab-forward of 1944, plus a variety of passenger coaches and rolling stock. An authentic waiting room, telegraph office, and baggage room have also been re-created.

In the History building, visitors learn the story of railroading in California—everything from the building of the Southern Pacific network to the demise of the steam locomotive.

## SUTTER'S FORT STATE HISTORIC PARK

John Sutter, an immigrant from Switzerland, established his fort in 1839 and it soon became the center of a vast agricultural and commercial empire. Sutter's adobe-walled fort was a focal point for the flow of covered wagons from other states.

The restored fort illustrates the self-sufficiency of Sutter's enterprise. Restoration was based on a German brochure, containing illustrations and descriptions of the fort, which was designed by Sutter to lure German immigrants to Sacramento.

A self-guided audio tour conveys the sounds as well as the sights of the Fort's daily life.

The Fort's entrance is near 26th and K Streets.

*Sutter's Fort*

### GOVERNOR'S MANSION

California's Executive Mansion, popularly known as the Governor's Mansion, was built in 1877-78 for Albert Gallatin, president of a pioneer Sacramento hardware firm, on land that was once part of the Mexican land grant to John Sutter. It cost more than $75,000.

In 1903 the State bought the house for $32,500 unfurnished. In selecting the 15-room, 5-bathroom Mansion, the Capitol Commissioners were thought to have considered comfort more than style, since the Victorian-Gothic architecture of the home already seemed dated in 1903.

Over a period of 64 years it was the home of 13 of California's governors. Though the State Fire Marshall had declared the building unsuitable for occupancy in 1941, no alternative official residence was provided, and Governors Warren, Knight, and Brown lived there throughout their terms of office. Governor Reagan lived in the Mansion during the first part of 1967.

The Governor's Mansion is located at 16th and "H" Streets, Sacramento. Tours start every half hour.

### CALIFORNIA INDIAN MUSEUM

Displays illustrate the unique heritage of the Indians of California. Several items, ranging from articles hundreds of years old to modern arts and crafts made by today's Indians, are on exhibit. California Indians were outstanding artisans, as evidenced by their clothing and pottery.

Some 104 Indian tribes, representing six distinct cultural regions, lived in California before the coming of Europeans. Museum exhibits tell of these Indians' basketry, featherwork, trade and trails, minerals, dances and ceremonies, houses, boats and much more.

The State Indian Museum building was constructed in 1940. It's located on the grounds of Sutter's Fort. Admission to the fort covers the museum admission.

Sacramento District
111 I Street
Sacramento, CA 95814
(916) 445-7373
California State Capitol Museum (916) 324-0333
Governor's Mansion (916) 323-3047
Sutter's Fort SHP (916) 445-4422

# San Luis Reservoir State Recreation Area

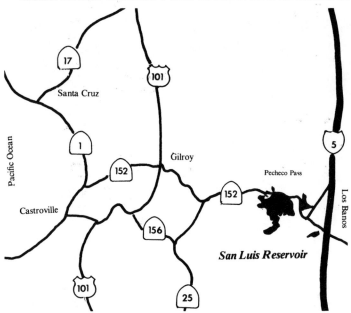

Three lakes invite anglers to this recreation area situated on the west side of the San Joaquin Valley. San Luis, one of the massive reservoirs of the California Aqueduct system, includes three different bodies of water: the main reservoir, O'Neill Forebay and Los Banos Reservoir. A visitor center at Romero Overlook has exhibits which provide information on the water projects. Telescopes are available for a panoramic view of the recreation area.

### BOATING

Boats are allowed on San Luis Reservoir and O'Neill Forebay for an hour before sunrise until sunset, and on Los Banos Reservoir for an hour before sunrise until dark. There is a speed limit of 5 mph on Los Banos Reservoir (boat engines must be 10 hp or less). Rangers keep an ear out to make sure engine noise does not exceed legal levels.

Waterskiing (counterclockwise) is permitted on the main reservoir and O'Neill Forebay. A two-lane boat ramp was recently installed.

### FISHING

Striped and black bass, white and channel catfish, crappie and bluegill come south with the aqueduct and thrive in the ideal environment of O'Neill Forebay and San Luis Reservoir. Los Banos is planted with these same kinds of fish.

Boat and shore fishing is generally good from late February through the summer. Striped bass fishing is best in winter and spring, black bass in spring, bluegill and crappie in spring and summer. Night fishing is permitted all along the shoreline except in the O'Neill Forebay around San Luis Creek and the Dinosaur Point area on the main reservoir.

### CAMPING

Seventy-nine developed campsites with shade ramadas, tables and stoves are set in a young forest of eucalyptus and pine planted when the recreation area was built. All sites have a table and barbecue grill. Restrooms and solar-heated showers are nearby. Some sites will accommodate RV's up to 37 feet in length. No hookups.

At O'Neill Forebay in the Medeiros area, up to 500 campers can use the primitive area between Highways 33 and 152. Drinking water and chemical toilets are available.

Twenty primitive camping/picnicking sites with shade ramadas, tables and stoves are scattered along the shoreline of Los Banos Creek Reservoir. A primitive equestrian campsite is also located here.

San Luis Reservoir State Recreation Area
C/O Four Rivers District
31426 West Hwy. 152
Santa Nella, CA 95322
(209) 826-1196

*San Luis Reservoir*

*The great Central Valley once supported a huge population of tule elk*

Tule elk once ranged as far north as the north-central Sacramento Valley (Shasta County), south to the Tehachapi Mountains, east to the limit of the oak-grassland environment of the Sierra Nevada foothills, and west to the Pacific Ocean from Point Reyes to the vicinity of Santa Barbara. In California's great Central Valley the tule elk was by all accounts the predominant form of animal life, comparable to the bison of the great plains or the antelope of South Africa. Though this particular subspecies of elk normally forms herds of forty to sixty animals, they were so numerous, particularly in the fertile floodplains and low-lands of the northern San Joaquin Valley, that they were sometimes observed in groups of one or even two thousand.

Tule elk dominated the landscape until the California gold rush began to bring thousands of new immigrants to California. Then, overnight, the human demand for food began to double and redouble. Cattle that had been worth two dollars—for their hides—were suddenly worth $35.00 for their food value. Elk and other forms of wild game were free for the taking, and some '49ers found it more profitable (and more pleasant) to hunt than to work in the mines. Within two years the entire tule elk population in the Sacramento Valley had been wiped out. In the San Joaquin Valley where hunting pressure was less severe the elk managed to survive somewhat longer, but even there they very quickly disappeared from the open range. in 1863, market hunters claimed to have killed the last elk cow and calf left in the tules of the San Joaquin Delta, thus restricting the remaining elk range to the willow and tule-filled marsh country between Buena Vista and Tulare Lakes. Even this refuge began to disappear in later years as the area was slowly diked, drained, and cleared for agri-cultural use.

In 1954 management of the elk herd—by then reduced to just 41 animals—was turned over to the State Park System and soon afterward a supplementary feeding pro-gram was devised in order to keep the elk in good health. Artificial ponds were also created to provide opportunities for the elk to cool off during the heat of the summer and otherwise indulge in their favorite sport of "wallowing."

Tule Elk State Reserve is located in the southwestern part of the San Joaquin Valley, 27 miles west of Bakersfield and just four miles west of Interstate Highway 5. Picnic tables, piped drinking water, restrooms, and a tree-shaded grassy area have been provided for visitors to the Reserve along with a number of interpretive exhibits. No camping facilities are available, but a modern campground with some 112 family campsites is open all year at Buena Vista Aquatic Recreation Area about 12 miles south of the Reserve on the north shore of Buena Vista Lake.

Weather conditions at the Reserve are most pleasant during the spring and autumn; however, the elk are in many ways at their most interesting during the hottest part of the summer when daytime high temperatures may range from 100 to 115 degrees. Elk viewing opportunities con-tinue to be good in the autumn and until the first heavy rains of winter; supplemental feedings, when necessary, are done at 2 P.M. Binoculars are always helpful, and don't forget your cameras as the elk can often be photographed quite effectively from the viewing area.

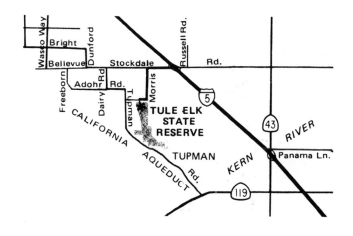

Tule Elk State Reserve
28577 Statron Road
Buttonwillow, CA 93206
(805) 765-5004

# Turlock Lake State Recreation Area

*Good fishing at Turlock Lake*

Nestled in the rolling foothills of eastern Stanislaus County, Turlock Lake State Recreation Area is an ideal place for a day's or week's outing. Open year around and featuring camping, picnicking, fishing, swimming, boating, waterskiing, and clean country air, the area offers visitors an opportunity to see the kind of native plant life that once blessed all the rivers of the San Joaquin Valley, and witness the mark of man as recorded in the dredger tailings and agricultural development of the twentieth century.

The area, bounded on the north by the Tuolumne River and on the south by Turlock Lake, provides an ideal setting for water-oriented outdoor recreation. Comprised of 228 acres of foothill country leased from the Turlock Irrigation District in 1950, the recreation area features the 3,500-surface-acre lake containing some 26 miles of shoreline, where day use and boating facilities are offered, and camping along the Tuolumne River. In summer, the lake may be drawn down to 1,800-surface acres. Impounded by the Turlock Irrigation District in 1913, the lake's greatest depth, when full, is 45 feet.

At elevation 250 feet, the recreation area boasts typical San Joaquin Valley weather, with warm summers and mild winters. During the summer months night temperatures usually drop to the high sixties and are comfortable for sleeping. Quick relief from even the warmest summer day is available in the cool waters of Turlock Lake.

From several lookout points, the visitor can view the surrounding grasslands and some of the dairy farms and cattle ranches nearby. From the highway that separates the campground from the day-use area, an excellent view is offered of the campground, the river and sloughs, and miles of dredger tailing piles, the by-product of a half century of gold mining.

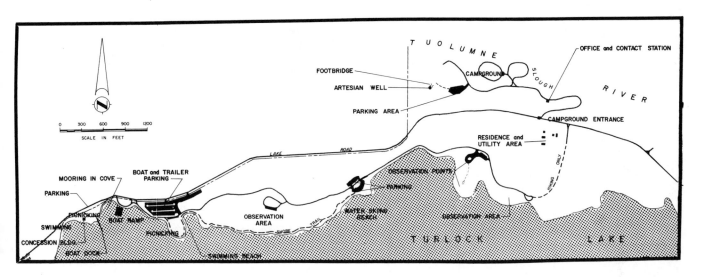

## CAMPING

With a sheer bluff rising on its south boundary and the Tuolumne River on the north, a secluded campground offers 65 improved campsites on level ground that, many years ago, served as the river's natural flood plain. Ample shade is provided by native trees, and the heavy growth of native blackberries entices jam and pie fanciers from mid-July into early September. Trails have been cut through the blackberries to the river's edge.

Each campsite has a stove, table, and food locker, and piped drinking water is within a hundred feet of each. Hot showers and restrooms with flush toilets are nearby.

An artesian well, accessible via a footbridge that crosses a small slough, offers drinking water with a special flavor that perhaps you can identify.

Although no trailer hookups are available, trailers up to 18 feet in length can be accommodated in the campsites. The campground fills daily from mid-June through mid-September, so reservations are advisable.

## FISHING

For the fisherman, black bass, crappie, and bluegill are found in nearby waters. The park rangers can give you directions.

The concessionaire-operated marina, open between April and October, offers boat fuel, boat mooring, prepared food and drinks, groceries, fishing tackle, and other supplies. Wood also is sold, as forest litter in the recreation area should not be picked up.

There is a boat launching ramp and ample parking for boat trailers and cars.

Turlock Lake State Recreation Area is located 21 miles east of Modesto and about the same distance north and east of Turlock. It is a short drive off State Highway 132, and a well-signed intersection tells you where to turn off the highway to reach the area.

Turlock State Recreation Area
22600 Lake Road
LaGrange, CA 95329
(209) 874-2056

# William B. Ide Adobe State Historic Park

William Brown Ide, a farmer from Illinois, became president of the Bear Flag Republic only eight months after he and his family arrived in California in October 1845. But the seeds of the American settlers' revolt against Mexican authority had been planted long before.

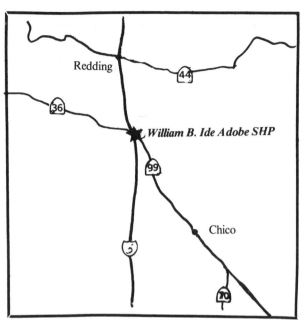

The party rallied around Ide and declared him president of the new republic. They raised their famous flag, which featured the grizzly bear—then common in California—plus a star and the words "California Republic." Later their design was adopted for California's official state flag.

*Bear flag of 1846*

In June 1846, the Americans heard that a Mexican military force under the leadership of General José Castro was on its way to the Sacramento Valley, destroying crops, burning houses, and driving off the cattle of American settlers. Though untrue, this rumor was enough to arouse the settlers to action.

On June 15, 1846, a group of thirty American settlers marched on Sonoma (at that time the center of Mexican authority north of San Francisco), captured the town, and made a prisoner of its leading citizen, former General Mariano Vallejo. They announced the establishment of the Bear Flag Republic and declared themselves independent of Mexican rule.

Then, some of the party had second thoughts. If they were not supported by the United States Army as well as by other Americans living in California, they would be unable to withstand General Castro's forces. Concern spread, and there was a move to abandon Sonoma.

At this critical moment, Ide stepped forward and exclaimed:

> *Saddle no horse for me...I will lay my bones here, before I will take upon myself the ignominy of commencing an honorable work, and then flee like cowards, like thieves, when no enemy is in sight. In vain will you say you had honorable motives; who will believe it: Flee this day, and the longest life cannot wear off your disgrace! Choose ye! Choose ye this day, what you will be! We are robbers, or we must be conquerors!*

Ide's term as president was short; on July 7, only 22 days after the capture of Sonoma, Commodore Sloat raised the American flag at Monterey, and the California Republic became a protectorate of the United States. Two days later the Bear Flag was struck, the Stars and Stripes were raised at Sonoma, and the Bear Flag force merged with Frémont's men to campaign against the Mexican forces in central California.

After taking part in the campaign against the Mexicans, Ide returned to his farm and family. In 1848, he and his sons brought back $25,000 they had earned in the gold fields to purchase part of a Mexican land grant, called Rancho de la Barranca Colorada (Red Bluff Ranch) because of a high red cliff along the west bank of the Sacramento River. Ide built an adobe house overlooking the river and established the Adobe Ferry where the California-Oregon Trail crossed the river to link Sacramento and the Mother Lode with Shasta and the Northern Mines.

The Ide Adobe was sold and resold a number of times over the years until 1951 when it was transferred to the state. Extensive repairs to the adobe house and other construction—a cover over the hand-dug well, an adobe smokehouse, a carriage shed, a small corral, and restoration of a covered wagon—have created a scene typical of Ide's day.

William B. Ide Adobe State Historic Park is open daily from 8 A.M. to 5 P.M.

William B. Ide Adobe State Historic Park
3040 Adobe Road
Red Bluff, CA 96080
(916) 527-5927

# Woodson Bridge State Recreation Area

*Woodson Bridge*

Woodson Bridge State Recreation Area, nestled in beautiful oak woods on the Sacramento River between Chico and Red Bluff, offers year-round camping, fishing, boating, and hiking in an unspoiled, natural setting. Located on South Avenue, the park is just three miles west of Highway 99 at Vina, or six miles east of Interstate 5 at Corning. Mount Lassen, Mount Shasta and the Trinity Alps loom in the distance.

Over a hundred plant species have been identified throughout the park; the most prominent is the large valley oak. The California black walnut, Oregon ash, black cottonwood, blue elderberry, sycamore, and willow are also plentiful. Beneath the oaks and cottonwoods along the river is a profusion of elderberry, wild grape, other shrubs, and wild flowers in season. The fall coloring is spectacular.

Spring and fall are favored seasons at Woodson Bridge, but summer camping can also be delightful here. Summer daytime temperatures generally vary from 85 to just over 100 degrees, but cool nights are the rule. There is a broad sand-and-gravel beach for wading but the water remains chilly even in summer.

A boat-launching ramp, picnic ground, and a cafe are available in Tehama County Park adjoining the state recreation area. A privately operated trailer park with utilities hookups, a small store, fishing bait, a boat dock, and boat rental service are adjacent to the county park. Ice, groceries, and other supplies are available at nearby Vina or at Corning.

## FISHING

Fishing is a year-round activity at Woodson Bridge and there is no closed season on any of the species taken from the river here. Boat and bank fishing are equally popular.

There are three distinct runs of king salmon. Fishing for the fall run is best in October and November, but there are fresh-run salmon arriving through December. A winter run provides good fishing January through March, then a spring run keeps things perking through April and May. Salmon fishing is best done by boat, but good numbers are taken from the bank, particularly off the mouths of tributary streams such as Deer Creek, a few hundred feet upstream from the park. Shad fishing is best in July and August.

Steelhead fishing peaks here in October and November; by January, most of the steelhead have moved into tributary spawning streams. Striped bass fishing is usually best in the early fall.

Catfish are taken virtually year around from the river and from Koptka Slough, which also offers largemouth bass and bluegills. An occasional huge sturgeon is caught in the river.

Favored bank fishing spots are the mouth of Deer Creek on the campground side of the river, and three places across the river via Woodson Bridge—just below the west end of the bridge, a deep hole at the mouth of Koptka Slough, and the west bank of Koptka Slough parallel to the old Gardiner Ferry Road.

## CAMPING

Forty-six well-equippd campsites are spread among huge oaks. Facilities include tables, piped drinking water and restrooms with hot showers. There are no trailer hookups, but travel trailers and motorhomes up to 31 feet long are welcome.

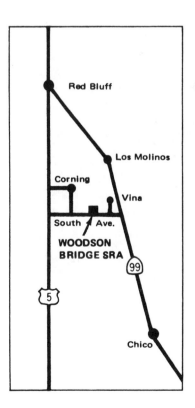

Woodson Bridge State Recreation Area
25340 South Avenue
Corning, CA 96021
(916) 839-2112

*Mount Diablo*

# Coastal Mountains

A range of mountains runs parallel to much of central California's shoreline. Around San Francisco, these mountans reach a height of only three or four thousand feet—on clear days spectacular views can be had from Mount Tamalpais, elevation 2571 feet, or Mount Diablo, elevation 3849 feet—but further north and south heights reach seven and eight thousand feet. The area is underlain with fault zones, the most famous of which—the San Andreas Fault—enters the sea at Thornton SB just south of San Francisco.

Grassland, chaparral, and oak woodland cover much of the coastal mountains, with pine and fir at higher elevations. The valleys are used for dairying and agriculture—some of California's most famed wines come from the valleys north of San Francisco, and in the valleys to the south of the city such crops as artichokes, lettuce, and celery are grown.

Three of California's Spanish missions are among Coastal Mountain historic parks.

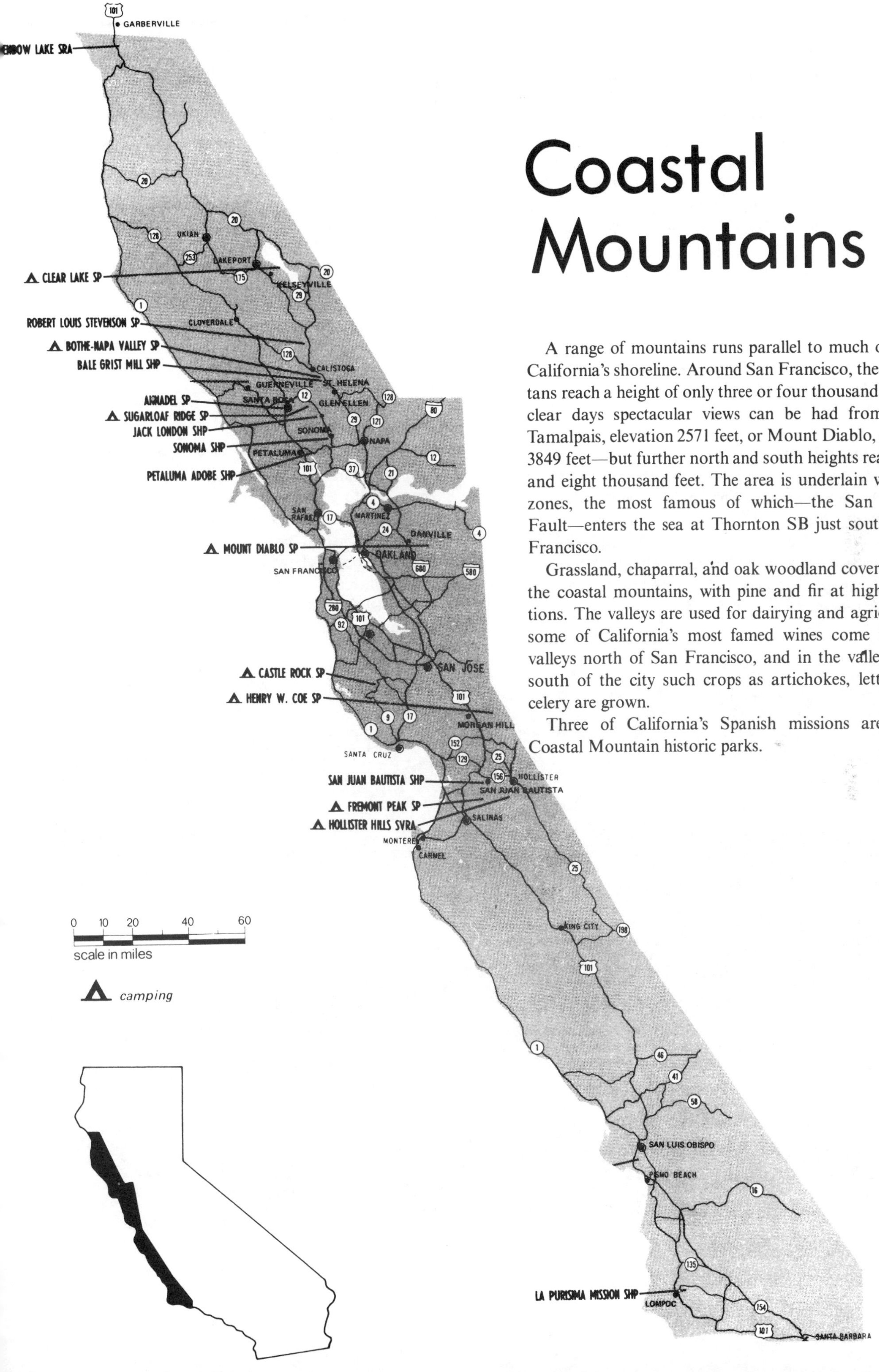

GARBERVILLE

BENBOW LAKE SRA

▲ CLEAR LAKE SP
ROBERT LOUIS STEVENSON SP
▲ BOTHE-NAPA VALLEY SP
BALE GRIST MILL SHP
ANNADEL SP
▲ SUGARLOAF RIDGE SP
JACK LONDON SHP
SONOMA SHP
PETALUMA ADOBE SHP

▲ MOUNT DIABLO SP

▲ CASTLE ROCK SP
▲ HENRY W. COE SP

SAN JUAN BAUTISTA SHP
▲ FREMONT PEAK SP
▲ HOLLISTER HILLS SVRA

UKIAH
LAKEPORT
KELSEYVILLE
CLOVERDALE
CALISTOGA
GUERNEVILLE   ST. HELENA
SANTA ROSA   GLEN ELLEN
SONOMA
PETALUMA
NAPA
SAN RAFAEL
MARTINEZ
DANVILLE
OAKLAND
SAN FRANCISCO
SAN JOSE
SANTA CRUZ
MORGAN HILL
HOLLISTER
SAN JUAN BAUTISTA
SALINAS
MONTEREY
CARMEL
KING CITY
SAN LUIS OBISPO
PISMO BEACH
LA PURISIMA MISSION SHP   LOMPOC
SANTA BARBARA

0  10  20    40      60
scale in miles

▲ camping

# Annadel State Park

Hikers, horsemen, photographers, and anglers will find abundant opportunities for enjoyment at Annadel State Park. Its five thousand acres of hills, streams, woodlands and meadows—only fifty miles north of San Francisco, on the eastern edge of Santa Rosa—include forty miles of hiking and horseback trails uninterrupted by modern intrusions such as the automobile.

Elevations in the park vary from 300 to 1800 feet, but most of the trails—except the steep Steve's S Trail—rise and fall gradually. As you hike, you will pass through woodlands where California black oak, coast live oak, and Oregon oak predominate; large, grassy meadows strewn with wildflowers—buttercups, goldfields, lupine, poppies, mule-ears—in the springtime; and lush canyons with ferns, redwoods, and Douglas fir.

You will also see rubble and pits where basalt was quarried around the turn of the century—much of it to rebuild roads and buildings in San Francisco after the 1906 earthquake. The rock was hauled out of the hills on a narrow-gauge railway.

Lake Ilsanjo, less than a three-mile hike from the parking lot, is a popular destination for fishermen; it offers good shore fishing for black bass (average weight two pounds, though some have been caught weighing eight pounds or more) and scrappy bluegill. The lake's Spanish-sounding name actually comes from the first names of the property's former owners—Ilsa and Joe.

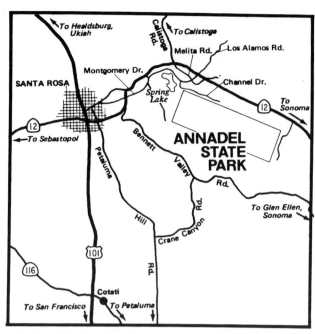

Ledson Marsh, along Bennett Ridge, is an ideal spot from which to observe and photograph the park's wildlife. You will probably see some of the 130 species of birds that have been sighted in the park, among them white-crowned sparrows, Cooper's hawks, great blue herons, screech owls, western bluebirds, and even the rare pileated woodpecker, as well as Columbian black-tail deer, foxes, raccoons, muskrats, skunks and bobcats.

Annadel State Park
6201 Channel Drive
Santa Rosa, CA 95405
(707) 539-3911

# Benbow Lake State Recreation Area

Benbow Lake is a temporary body of water created by a dam on the Eel River. The dam is usually installed about Memorial Day (weather and water level permitting) and removed after Labor Day.

The park receives a lot of day use and is popular with picnickers, sunbathers, swimmers and boaters (non-powered craft). Guided horseback trail rides (nearby horse rental) are offered. The Eel River features steelhead and salmon fishing in season.

Benbow's campground, with 76 improved sites, is located on the wooded slopes above the river bank. It will accommodate trailers up to 24 feet and campers up to 30 feet.

The park is located 2 miles south of Garberville on U.S. 101. It's closed during high water periods in winter.

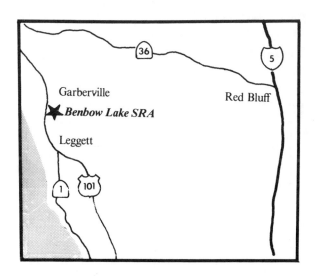

Benbow Lake State Recreation Area
C/O Eel River District
P.O. Box 100
Weott, CA 95571
(707) 946-2311

# Bothe-Napa Valley State Park/Bale Grist Mill SHP

Located in the heart of the beautiful Napa Valley grape country, Bothe-Napa Valley State Park offers camping, picnicking, and a swimming pool with lifeguard on duty throughout the summer season. Hiking trails in the 1,400-acre park go through some of the most easterly stands of coastal redwoods as well as forests of Douglasfir, tan oak, and madrone, and there are beautiful displays of wildflowers in spring and early summer. In addition to the many birds to be seen in the area, there are raccoons, gray squirrels, deer, and foxes. Elevations range from about 400 to 2,000 feet.

In 1872, Dr. Charles Hitchcock bought a thousand acres here and built a home, "Lonely," where the park maintenance building now stands beside Ritchie Creek, which tumbles from the slopes of nearby Diamond Mountain. His unconventional daughter Lillie and her many friends from San Francisco's elite enjoyed lively social gatherings here that helped make the area a popular vacation spot.

An early feminist, Lillie Hitchcock Coit scandalized some by riding horseback astride; she once forced her way into a men's club, and she was noted for playing poker with San Francisco celebrities—and winning. Though she once rode the cowcatcher of a steam engine, she preferred to ride in the cab with the engineer.

Lillie began her legendary interest in firefighting in 1851, at the age of eight. With no playmates her own age near the hotel in which she lived, she made friends of the men of San Francisco's Knickerbocker No. 5, a volunteer fire company housed across the street. To the end of her life, one of her most treasured possessions was the gold and diamond pin in the shape of a fireman's helmet that symbolized her honorary membership in the company. San Francisco's Coit Tower was built with the money Lillie left to the city in her will.

"Lonely" burned down after Reinhold Bothe acquired the property in 1929 for a commercial campground, which became a state park in 1960.

## CAMPING

The park has fifty developed family campsites, each with table and stove; restrooms with hot-water showers are nearby. Though there are no hookups, the campsites will accommodate trailers up to 24 feet in length and motorhomes up to 31 feet long. The park has a group camp for tent camping only.

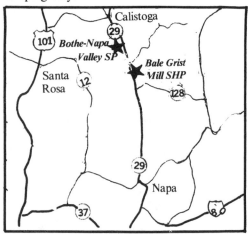

*Bale Grist Mill*

## BALE GRIST MILL STATE HISTORIC PARK

Edward Bale had probably not intended to settle in Mexican California. But when the English ship on which he was serving as surgeon ran aground off the coast of Monterey in 1837, he found that, as a physician, he was welcomed into the community.

Though they respected his professional ability, his new neighbors soon began to gossip about Bale's fondness for the bottle. Nonetheless, he married a niece of Captain Salvador Vallejo's in 1839 and was granted two leagues—nearly nine thousand acres—of land in the upper Napa Valley.

Bale was not interested in large-scale farming or ranching, but newly arrived settlers were planting increasing amounts of grain in the fertile valley, so Bale sold off enough land to finance a large water-powered gristmill.

The slow turning of the old stones and the dampness of the mill's site gave its meal an exceptional quality for making cornbread, yellowbread, shortening bread, and spoon bread. Cornmeal dumplings were designed to use stone-ground cornmeal, fresh from the mill. And as the old-timers put it, "When meal comes to you that way, like the heated underside of a settin' hen, it bakes bread that makes city bread taste like cardboard."

During the Gold Rush, Bale sold his mill and went prospecting. Alas, he caught a sickness from which he never recovered. Back home, he realized that he had not long to live, and sold a large part of his rancho to provide for his family. He died in October 1849 at the age of 38.

Bale Grist Mill is located just off Highway 128, one mile south of Bothe-Napa Valley State Park.

Bothe-Napa Valley State Park
C/O Napa District
3801 St. Helena Hwy., N.
Calistoga, CA 94515
(707) 942-4575

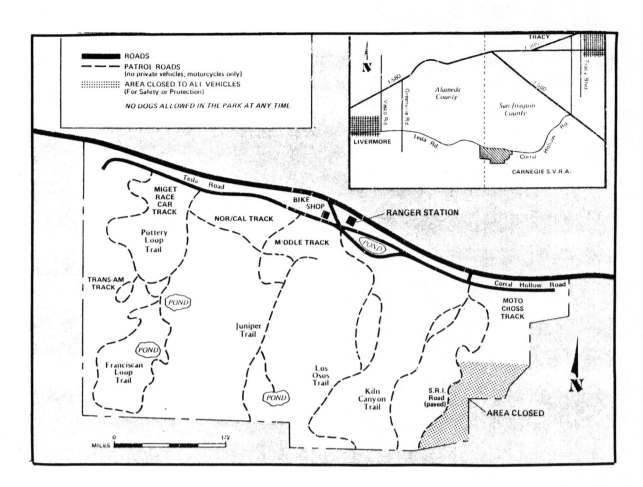

Carnegie SVRA, purchased and operated with money from the Off Highway Vehicle fund from OHV registration, gas taxes, and citation fines, has over 1,500 acres of motorcycle riding area. There are picnic tables, chemical toilets, and drinking water, and a concession bike shop that is open most weekends offers bike parts and service and sells some snacks.

Carnegie is open every day of the year, from 8 A.M. to around sunset (check posted hours), and medical aid and rescue equipment are available at all times.

Areas of the park will occasionally be closed for safety, reseeding, resource protection, and special events; please observe warning signs and fences. Contact the ranger station for information on holding special events and a special-event application.

All OHV laws are strictly enforced, among them:

1. Only 2- and 3-wheeled vehicles are allowed out of the parking areas on the Corral Hollow Creekbed.

2. All vehicles must be registered.

3. All motorcycles must be equipped with a U.S. Forest Service-approved spark arrester and adequate muffler, both in working order. Spark arresters are required at all times.

4. Obey all signs and closed-area fencing.

5. Speed limits on the main roads (those used by other vehicles as well as motorcycles) and within 50 feet of a concentration of people is 15 mph.

6. You may not drive a motor vehicle in a manner that endangers the safety of other persons or their property.

7. Only one person per motorcycle, unless the bike is equipped with 4 foot pegs.

8. For safety: helmets, boots, and eye protection are recommended.

Carnegie State Vehicular Recreation Area
P.O. Box 1105
Tracy, CA 95376
(415) 447-9027

# Castle Rock State Park

Castle Rock State Park perches on the western ridge of the Santa Cruz Mountains that separates San Francisco and Monterey Bays, and is within an hour's drive of either bay. Above the smog and fog, the park is 3,000 acres of semi-wilderness offering visitors an opportunity to picnic in rolling meadows, hike through shady forests, enjoy spectacular vistas, and see an array of wildflowers and wildlife. The park has hiking and equestrian trails, picnic tables, and backpack campsites. No vehicles are allowed beyond the parking areas.

## NATURAL HISTORY

The ridges of Castle Rock State Park began rising from the seabed about 25 million years ago. They started a series of folding, faulting and uplifting that continues today. The park's sandstone caves and honeycombed sandstone surfaces are the result of rainwater's chemical erosion. Steep slopes, springs, erosion and landsliding characterize the Castle Rock landscape. At the 3,000-foot elevation of Castle Rock Ridge, storm clouds cool rapidly, dropping 40-50 inches of rain in an average year.

The rocks, especially Castle Rock and Goat Rock, offer excellent opportunities for rock climbing. Climbing, however, can be dangerous, and should be undertaken only by those with proper equipment and training.

## HISTORY

After the Civil War, the Castle Rock Area was settled by loggers and farmers. Through farming, fishing, hunting, and mutual trading, ridge families were so self-sufficient that they only needed to make two trips a year to town for supplies. In the 1870s the settlers could catch the stagecoach which ran along the Saratoga Toll Road three times a week.

Castle Rock School opened in 1886 with six students. Until her cabin was completed, the first teacher—Ida Jones—lived in the big Castle Rock cave.

By the turn of the century, Castle Rock, owned by Judge J.R. Welch of San Jose, had become a local tourist attraction. People from the Santa Clara Valley would ride a big streetcar—the InterUrban—to Congress Springs above Saratoga, and then hike or hire a rig up to Castle Rock and back.

One young man who visited Castle Rock often in those days was Russell Varian. Through the years, Russell introduced the area to others, hoping and working to preserve the Castle Rock area as a public park for all to enjoy. His dream came true in 1959 when memorial funds donated by friends and associates after his death secured the first 27 acres for the park. Since then acquisitions have greatly expanded the park and created a valuable preserve in the Santa Cruz Mountains.

## HIKING

Castle Rock State Park can only be experienced on foot. The 23 miles of park trails travel through many different plant and animal communities, and pass by rock outcroppings, vista points, a waterfall, and park headquarters.

The main entrance to the park is the parking lot off of Highway 35, 2.5 miles southeast of Saratoga Gap (the intersection of Highways 9 and 35). Hikers can reach the park on trails from the Santa Clara Valley via either Sanborn Skyline County Park or Midpeninsula Regional Open Space Preserves, and from the San Lorenzo Valley via the Skyline to the Sea Trail.

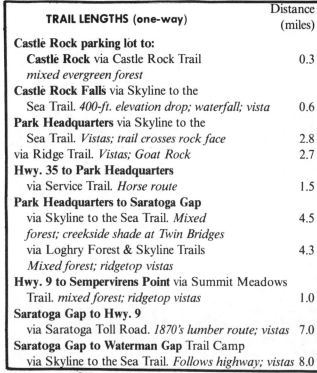

| TRAIL LENGTHS (one-way) | Distance (miles) |
|---|---|
| **Castle Rock parking lot to:** | |
| **Castle Rock** via Castle Rock Trail *mixed evergreen forest* | 0.3 |
| **Castle Rock Falls** via Skyline to the Sea Trail. *400-ft. elevation drop; waterfall; vista* | 0.6 |
| **Park Headquarters** via Skyline to the Sea Trail. *Vistas; trail crosses rock face* | 2.8 |
| via Ridge Trail. *Vistas; Goat Rock* | 2.7 |
| **Hwy. 35 to Park Headquarters** | |
| via Service Trail. *Horse route* | 1.5 |
| **Park Headquarters to Saratoga Gap** | |
| via Skyline to the Sea Trail. *Mixed forest; creekside shade at Twin Bridges* | 4.5 |
| via Loghry Forest & Skyline Trails *Mixed forest; ridgetop vistas* | 4.3 |
| **Hwy. 9 to Sempervirens Point** via Summit Meadows Trail. *mixed forest; ridgetop vistas* | 1.0 |
| **Saratoga Gap to Hwy. 9** | |
| via Saratoga Toll Road. *1870's lumber route; vistas* | 7.0 |
| **Saratoga Gap to Waterman Gap** Trail Camp | |
| via Skyline to the Sea Trail. *Follows highway; vistas* | 8.0 |

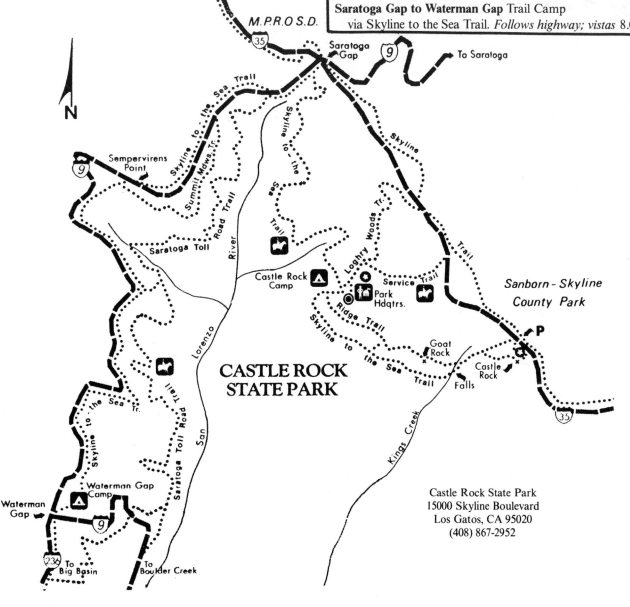

**CASTLE ROCK STATE PARK**

Castle Rock State Park
15000 Skyline Boulevard
Los Gatos, CA 95020
(408) 867-2952

# Clear Lake State Park

*Clear Lake*

Clear Lake is the largest natural body of water entirely within the state. The park includes more than two miles of shoreline on the lake and offers camping, swimming, hiking, waterskiing and fishing.

The area was once occupied by peaceful tribes, the Pomo and the Lile'ek, who were known for their basket weaving. A nature trail, which begins near the park's entrance station, shows how they used the area's plants and trees to supply their everyday needs. They used the park's Moki Beach for canoe landings.

Many names throughout the area bring Indian legends to mind; for instance, nearby Mount Konocti is said to be named after an Indian prince whose spirit is the guardian of the lake.

Fishermen try their luck on the lake's crappie, catfish, perch, black bass, and bluegill. A boat launching ramp is available, with a handy fish-cleaning station nearby. Fishing and waterskiing boats and equipment can be rented within a mile of the park.

The swimming beach is located next to the Lower Bayview Campground on Soda Bay; there is lifeguard service only during the busy season. A picnic area overlooks the lake.

## CAMPING

The park's four campgrounds total 147 campsites, each with stove, table, cupboard, and nearby restrooms with hot showers. A trailer sanitation station is available near the boat launch parking lot. The park also has two Hike and Bike campsites.

## ANDERSON MARSH STATE HISTORIC PARK

Located on the southeast end of the lake between Clear Lake and Lower Lake, the recently opened 1,000 acre Anderson Marsh State Historic Park preserves ancient Indian village sites that date back 10,000 years. Approximately 40 sites have been identified.

The new park also includes a 540 acre Natural Preserve, which protects the habitat of mammals and birds, including some eagles. The park includes an early California ranch that belonged to the Anderson family. One of Lake County's earliest cattle ranches, it dates back to 1855. The park is currently open for day use only Friday-Saturday-Sunday from 10 A.M. to 4 P.M.

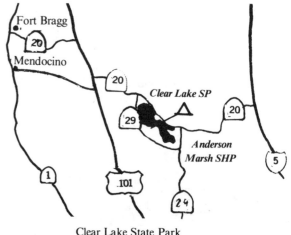

Clear Lake State Park
5300 Soda Bay Road
Kelseyville, CA 95451
(707) 279-4293

# Fremont Peak State Park

*Captain John C. Fremont*

101

Fremont Peak State Park is at the end of an eleven-mile hard-surfaced road that leaves State Highway 156 near San Juan Bautista and winds up through canyons to ridges studded with oak, pine, and madrone.

Here, the view of the surrounding countryside and Monterey Bay is unobstructed, and the clear air makes it a favorite spot for amateur astronomers. Although there is no physical evidence that Indians from the many villages in the vicinity of the San Benito and Salinas Rivers ever ventured to the lofty summit of Fremont Peak, when you are viewing this panorama it is easy to imagine that they may have believed it to be the home of their supreme beings.

There are two distinct life zones in the park. The dense growth on the northern slopes includes scrub oak, manzanita, toyon, and coyote brush. The slopes enjoying southern exposure are open grasslands; when rain is plentiful the wild grasses grow knee high—the slopes turn green in spring and then, in summer, a golden brown.

The upper ridges support a growth of Coulter pine, madrone, and several different types of oak trees. In the deep canyons, where there is more water, laurels and willows are interspersed with poison oak. Wildflowers are abundant during the spring and summer months.

More than a hundred different species of birds have been identified. Hawks and turkey vultures soar across the canyon, and occasionally eagles are seen high above the peak.

### CAMPING

Fremont Peak has 10 primitive family campsites and 40 picnic sites, each with table and stove; pit toilets and water are nearby. During the summer, campers enjoy campfire programs and nature hikes.

Fremont Peak State Park
P.O. Box 1110
San Juan Bautista, CA 95045
(408) 623-4255

### CAPTAIN JOHN C. FRÉMONT

In March of 1846, during his third expedition to explore California and Oregon, Captain John C. Frémont and his party camped near Monterey. Alarmed at the presence of armed men so close to the town, which was then capital of the Mexican province of Alta California, the Mexican military leader demanded that they leave the territory.

Frémont refused, and built a small fort in the vicinity of the peak. He raised a modified version of the flag of the U.S. Army Corps of Engineers, which had crossed peace pipes instead of swords, atop the peak—the first American flag to fly over California.

Finally, he acceded to the requests of Castro and Thomas Larkin, American consul in Monterey, and quietly broke camp. Though there were no immediate consequences of the incident, it does shed some light on the state of affairs in California just before the Bear Flag Revolt and California's entry to the Union.

After the flag-raising, Frémont continued his explorations in Northern California. He returned south in time to head up American forces during the Mexican-American war and, after Mexico ceded California to the United States, he acted as military governor for a short time. But he disagreed with General Kearny, who was appointed to the position, and returned to Washington under court-martial. Pardoned by President Polk, he returned to private life and served as one of the first U.S. Senators from California. He ran for President in 1856, the first presidential nominee of the infant Republican Party. When the Civil War came, he was reinstated in the Army and served as a general of the U.S. Army of the West in Missouri.

After the war, he became territorial Governor of Arizona and eventually returned to California, where he owned the Mariposa Grant, to try his luck at gold mining for a time. He died in New York City in 1890.

In 1926, the Native Sons and Daughters of the Golden West dedicated a plaque at the summit of Fremont Peak, also called Gabilan Peak from the Spanish word for hawk, to commemorate Frémont's visit and the historic rising of the American flag. Ten years later the State of California acquired the peak and the adjacent 244 acres of land in order to preserve this historic site.

# Henry W. Coe State Park

Hiking, camping, and nature studies are the primary activities in this little known and often overlooked coast range park. A small museum and other exhibits near park headquarters tell the story of the cattle ranching business that dominated life in this region throughout the last century.

Spring and fall are the most popular times to visit the park. Temperatures are moderate, and color brightens the landscape. The spring wildflower show is at its best during March, April and May; starting in late September, and throughout October and November, the deciduous trees and shrubs—especially black oaks—bring a different palette.

The park can best be reached via Dunne Avenue which runs due east from its point of intersection with U.S. Highway 101 at Morgan Hill. The 14-mile, 40 minute drive from Morgan Hill takes you up through the hills past Anderson Reservoir on a narrow winding road that offers ever more imposing vistas of the surrounding countryside.

### HIKING

There are more than 100 miles of riding and hiking trails in the park that can be used in all seasons. As a precaution in the case of fire or other possible emergency situations, please contact the park ranger before entering the primitve area for any long or overnight excursions. Drinking water is available at park headquarters, but should be carried into the back country on any long trips.

### CAMPING

Henry W. Coe State Park is essentially a wilderness park—very little developed—and is therefore most enjoyable to those who are willing to do without the conveniences of modern life.

Headquarters Area—There are 20 primitive drive-in family campsites near park headquarters, each with a barbecue-type stove and table; pit toilets and piped water are nearby. These sites are available on a first-come, first-served basis.

Trail Camps—Family groups and individuals are welcome to backpack into the park's primitive trail camps but must obtain a backpacking permit at park headquarters before starting, since the number of people allowed into each area is limited in order to insure a wilderness experience for all. These camps may be closed during the summer because of high fire danger, or restrictions may be placed upon their use.

Group Camps—The ten hike-in group camps at Manzanita Point can accommodate up to 50 people each. Limited toilet facilities are available, and water must be carried in from park headquarters.

*Giant manzanita thrive in the park*

Depending on weather and road conditions, one motor vehicle per group may be allowed into this area to transport supplies and be on hand for emergencies. Reserve the group campsites through park headquarters at least ten days in advance.

Water—Though water is available at many springs and creeks throughout the park during much of the year, these sources may be limited or may disappear during the hot summer months, so water must then be packed in from park headquarters. *All back country water should be purified before use.*

Extreme dryness during the long summer season can result in almost explosive fire conditions throughout the Hamilton Range. Because of this, open fires are permitted only at the Headquarters campground and at designated locations in the Manzanita Point Group Camps.

During the fire season all fires, including stoves, may be prohibited, or the back country may be closed to overnight use.

### FISHING

Bass and bluegill are found in Frog Lake and Manzanita Point Reservoir, and some trout are taken from Coyote Creek during trout season each spring. A valid California fishing license is required.

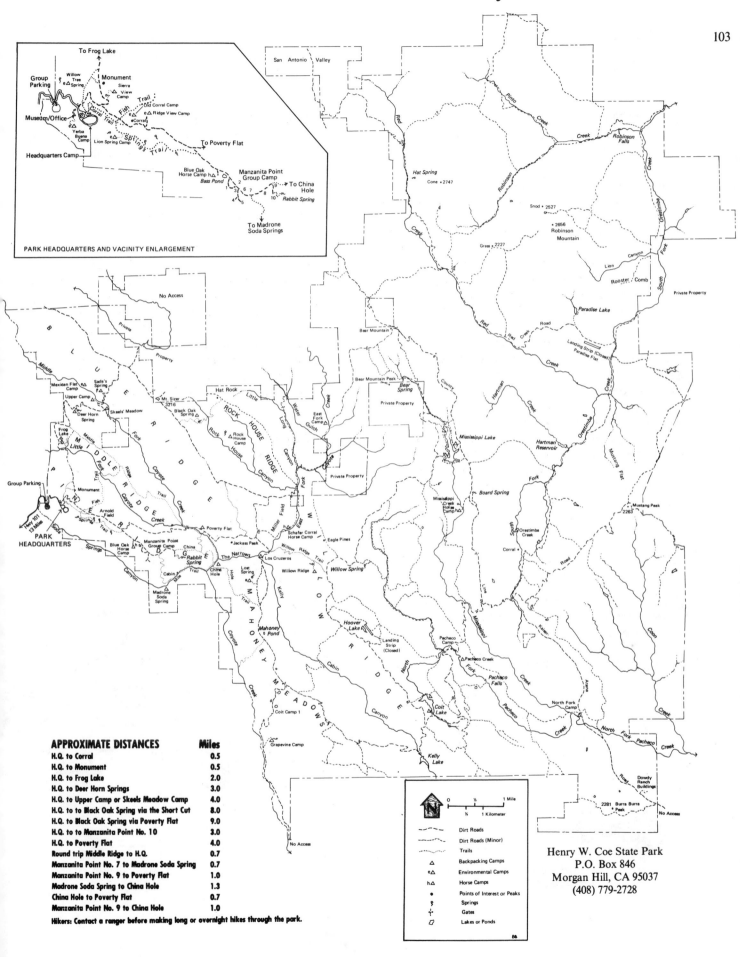

**PARK HEADQUARTERS AND VACINITY ENLARGEMENT**

| APPROXIMATE DISTANCES | Miles |
|---|---|
| H.Q. to Corral | 0.5 |
| H.Q. to Monument | 0.5 |
| H.Q. to Frog Lake | 2.0 |
| H.Q. to Deer Horn Springs | 3.0 |
| H.Q. to Upper Camp or Skeels Meadow Camp | 4.0 |
| H.Q. to to Black Oak Spring via the Short Cut | 8.0 |
| H.Q. to Black Oak Spring via Poverty Flat | 9.0 |
| H.Q. to to Manzanita Point No. 10 | 3.0 |
| H.Q. to Poverty Flat | 4.0 |
| Round trip Middle Ridge to H.Q. | 0.7 |
| Manzanita Point No. 7 to Madrone Soda Spring | 0.7 |
| Manzanita Point No. 9 to Poverty Flat | 1.0 |
| Madrone Soda Spring to China Hole | 1.3 |
| China Hole to Poverty Flat | 0.7 |
| Manzanita Point No. 9 to China Hole | 1.0 |

Hikers: Contact a ranger before making long or overnight hikes through the park.

Legend:
- — — — Dirt Roads
- ········ Dirt Roads (Minor)
- ·······  Trails
- △ Backpacking Camps
- e△ Environmental Camps
- h△ Horse Camps
- • Points of Interest or Peaks
- ¶ Springs
- † Gates
- ◻ Lakes or Ponds

Henry W. Coe State Park
P.O. Box 846
Morgan Hill, CA 95037
(408) 779-2728

# Hollister Hills State Vehicular Recreation Area

Hollister Hills SVRA offers recreation for motorcyclists, 4-wheelers, picnickers, and campers in the Gabilan Mountains less than two hours' drive from San Jose. Elevations here range from 660 feet to 2425 feet.

The park straddles the San Andreas Fault and you can see the rift along Bird Creek—the east side is adobe soil and the west side is granite. The fault moves an average of two inches annually in this area.

Hollister Hills was a family ranch for many years, producing wild oat hay for Wells Fargo express teams and later a variety of other farm products—grain, tomatoes, cattle, garlic, beans, fruit, and melons. Walnut trees planted in 1927 set a world production record of four tons per acre.

In the 1940s the Bird Creek Hunting Club used off-road vehicles here to help control trespassing, and in 1956 there began a series of motorcycle races, hillclimbs, and play days. The ranch was opened to public riding in 1970 and became a state vehicular recreation area in 1975.

### THE UPPER RANCH

This 800-acre area is used for 4-wheel drive recreation and for 4-wheel drive and motorcycle special events; a fenced motocross track is also located here.

Four-wheel drive operators should call before coming, especially on weekends, to make sure that the area isn't reserved for a special event. To use the area for the day, register first at the park office. For safety reasons there must be at least *two* 4-wheel drive vehicles in each registering party. If your vehicle gets stuck or breaks down, you are responsible for removing it. The Upper Ranch is open for day use from 8 A.M. to sunset.

Unless it is reserved for group camping or a special event, the Garner Lake area can be used by small off-road vehicles such as odysseys.

### CAMPING

The Upper Ranch has two group campgrounds—Sycamore, which accommodates about 60 people, and Garner Lake, which accommodates up to 200. Both have water and flush toilets. 4-wheel drive clubs can reserve these campgrounds through the park office unless the area has been reserved for a special event. Call the park office for information regarding required deposit.

### SPECIAL EVENTS

Four-wheel drive and motorcycle clubs can reserve the Upper Ranch for special events. Make the reservation three to twelve months in advance to allow time for processing the required permits and insurance forms. The area will be closed to individual 4-wheelers when a special event is in progress. Contact the park office to obtain forms and amount of deposit required for the type of event being given. The motocross races are held in a separate area and will not close the Upper Ranch to four-wheel use.

### PLEASE NOTE:
- The gates to the Upper Ranch area must be attended or kept locked at all times.
- Remember, others are using the area, so always expect to meet another vehicle.

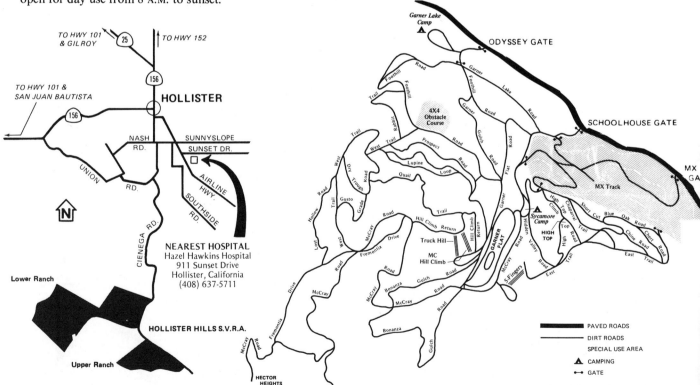

### THE LOWER RANCH

This 2400-acre area, set aside for motorcycle and ATC use only, has about eight miles of trails and several hillclimbs. There are also two picnic areas, a TT track, a mini-bike trail, and a mini-track. A washrack is located in the Lodge Camp. Riding is allowed from sunrise to sunset.

### CAMPING

The Lower Ranch area has three family campgrounds. Campsites have tables and fire rings; flush toilets and drinking water are nearby. Campsites are available on a first-come, first-served basis. The camp store in Lodge Camp (open on weekends) sells motorcycle parts and snacks, but no beer or gas.

In this area you can hike Azalea Canyon self-guided nature trail and several miles of hiking trails, enjoying cool canyons where it's damp enough for ferns and azaleas to grow. This relatively undisturbed area is also a good place to see the park's wildlife—quail, ground squirrels, jack-rabbits, deer, wild pigs, and raccoons.

The park's two environmental campsites, which offer the peace and solitude of an old-fashioned camping trip, are located in this restricted use area. Each site has a table, fire pit, and primitive toilet; campers must bring in water. It's about a half-mile hike to Hidden Springs Camp from the parking area, and about a mile to the Azalea Camp. It's a good idea to make reservations for the use of these camps.

### RESTRICTED USE AREA

A small area in the southwest corner of the Lower Ranch is closed to vehicle use to avoid disturbing the sensitive equipment of the San Andreas Geological Observatory located there.

### PLEASE NOTE

- Your motorcycle must be registered and its license or off-highway green sticker displayed on the motorcycle.
- Your motorcycle must be equipped with a legal spark arrester at all times.

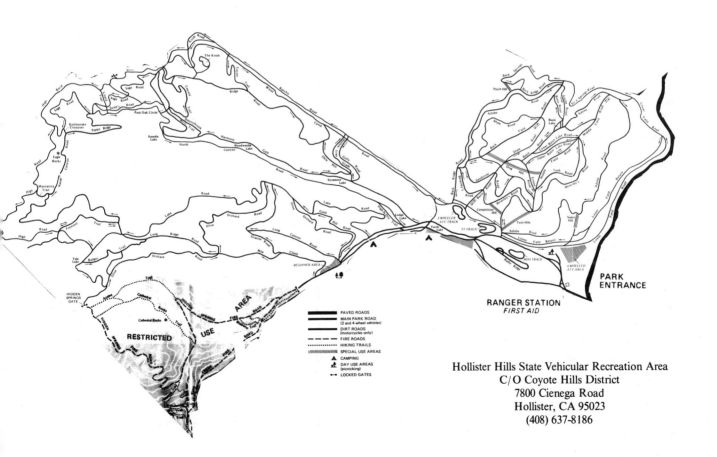

Hollister Hills State Vehicular Recreation Area
C/O Coyote Hills District
7800 Cienega Road
Hollister, CA 95023
(408) 637-8186

# Jack London State Historic Park

*I am the sailor on horseback! Watch my dust! Oh, I shall make mistakes a-many; but watch my dream come true. Try to dream with me my dreams of fruitful acres. Do not be a slave to an old conception. Try to realize what I am after.*
— *Jack London*

Jack London fought his way out of the factories and waterfront dives of Oakland to become the highest paid, most popular novelist and short story writer of his day. He wrote about the struggle to survive with dignity and integrity and he wove this elemental idea into stories of high adventure based on his own first-hand experience at sea or in Alaska or in the fields and factories of California. As a result, books such as *Call of the Wild* and *The Sea Wolf* appealed not to the few, but to millions of people around the world.

Along with his books and stories, Jack London was widely known for his personal exploits. He was a celebrity, a colorful and controversial personality who was often in the news. Generally fun-loving and playful, he could also be combative, and was quick to side with the underdog against injustice or oppression of any kind. Strikingly handsome, full of laughter, restless and courageous to a fault, always eager for adventure on land or sea, he was one of the most attractive and romantic figures of his time.

The beautiful natural landscape with all of its liveliness and diversity is what first attracted Jack London to Sonoma Valley. He didn't care that the farm was badly run down. Instead, he revelled in its deep canyons and forests, its year-round springs and streams. "All I wanted," he said later, "was a quiet place in the country to write and loaf in and get out of Nature that something which we all need, only most of us don't know it."

Jack London called his writer's retreat, "Beauty Ranch," and at one time it included about 1,400 acres. Between 1905 and his death in 1916, he raised a variety of crops and kept pure-bred livestock. His goal was to achieve a scentifically-operated ranch where new ideas and techniques could be developed and shared with all farmers.

Jack London State Historic Park was created in 1959 when a small portion of London's original Beauty Ranch was acquired by the State of California partly through a gift from Irving Shephard (London's nephew and heir to the London estate). A 1-kilometer (.6 mile) trail leads through the heart of the ranch. Among the highlights are several buildings London purchased from the Kohler and Frohling Winery and the "Cottage," where London wrote many of his later stories and novels. Other interesting buildings include the "Manure Pit" and the "Pig Palace," a deluxe piggery designed by London.

The park now has over 800 acres and includes 9 miles of riding and hiking trails. The park opens daily at 8 A.M. Visitors are asked to observe closing hours posted at the park entrance. The House of Happy Walls Museum is open daily from 10 A.M. to 5 P.M.

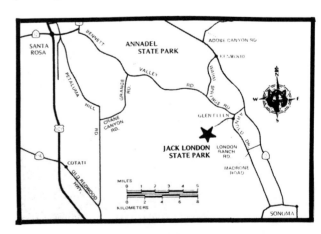

Jack London State Historic Park
2400 London Ranch Road
Glen Ellen, CA 95442
(707) 938-5216

# La Purisima Mission State Historic Park

*Nothing is left there but one long low adobe building with a few arches of the corridor; the doors stand open, the roof falling in; it has been so often used as a stable and sheepfold that even the grasses are killed around it.*

*—Helen Hunt Jackson*

This impression of La Purisima Mission was recorded in 1883 by the author of *Ramona,* Helen Hunt Jackson. The mission buildings continued to deteriorate until restoration work began in the 1930s. In 1934, exactly 100 years after the padres left, the Civilian Conservation Corps began reconstructing the church and a whole complex of buildings. Other restoration projects have continued intermittently ever since and today La Purisima is the most completely restored of California's 21 missions.

Besides the church, you'll see the soldiers' barracks and the priests' and novitiates' quarters. On the mission grounds are reconstructions of the granary, bakery, olive press and soap factory. The ruts of the old El Camino Real are visible where "The King's Highway" passed through the mission compound. In a corral are Mexican sheep and cattle, similar to the breeds of the mission period.

At the mission entrance is a small museum which displays historical information and artifacts recovered from the mission ruins. In a shady grove near the museum is a picnic ground.

The mission is located 3 miles NE of Lompoc on State 246.

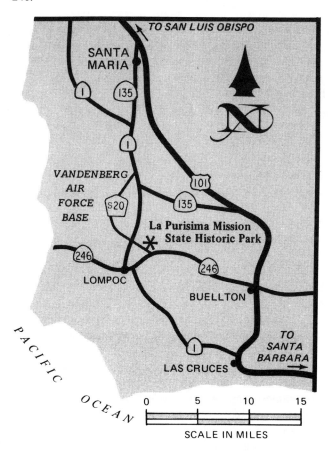

La Purisima Mission State Historic Park
RFD 102 Lompoc, CA 93436
(805) 733-3713

# Mount Diablo State Park

At the eastern fringe of the San Francisco Bay Region, Mount Diablo, elevation 3,849 feet, stands alone on the edge of California's great central valley. The Coast Range at this point consists only of low hills and none are high enough to block the view from the upper slopes of the mountain. Experts say that the panorama visible from the summit of Mount Diablo is unsurpassed in extent by any other mountain in the world with the exception of the 19,000 foot Mt. Kilimanjaro in Africa.

One can look west to the Golden Gate and on out into the Pacific Ocean beyond the Farallon Islands; southwest to the James Lick Observatory on Mt. Hamilton (4,213 ft.) and south to Mt. Loma Prieta (3,791 ft.) in the Santa Cruz Mountains; or north to Mt. Saint Helena (4,344 ft.) and Mount Lassen (10,466 ft.). To the east is the Central Valley with its great winding river delta.

## HISTORY

In 1851 the mountaintop was selected as the starting point for a survey of the public domain. Ignoring the excitement of the gold rush, Leander Ransom and his men erected a flagpole at the summit of Mount Diablo and began to extend base and meridian lines that we use to this day in our official land surveys; the Mount Diablo Base and Meridian lines are referred to in legal descriptions of real estate throughout two-thirds of California.

Toll roads up the mountain were opened in 1874, and there were two stages every day connecting Walnut Creek and Danville with the Mountain House, a sixteen room hotel about three miles from the summit that offered "all conveniences" and was known for its excellent food. The hotel was a favorite spot for weddings, and celebrities from all over Europe and America were among the visitors. In those days, you just hadn't seen the West if you hadn't watched a sunset, sunrise, or full moon from the upper slopes of the mountain.

## NATURAL HISTORY

The geologic story of the mountain revolves around an unusual upthrust of a plug of 160 million-year-old hard red Franciscan rock that has surged upward through six to eight miles of overlying sedimentary rock and soil. The fossilized remains of many sea creatures as well as of mastodons and three-toed horses have been discovered there.

Elevations in the park range from 300 to 3,849 feet, and this rapid change of elevation creates broad variations in temperature, rainfall, and wind exposure that have resulted in a wide variety of plant life in the park. Most of the area is typical Central California vegetation with oak woodland, grassland, and chaparral. Along the lower streams, which have water most of the year, grow isolated stands of knobcone and Coulter pine. The Coulter pine finds its northernmost limit on the lower north slopes of the mountain. The digger pine is found all over the mountain; other trees include the coast live oak, big leaf maple, California laurel and buckeye.

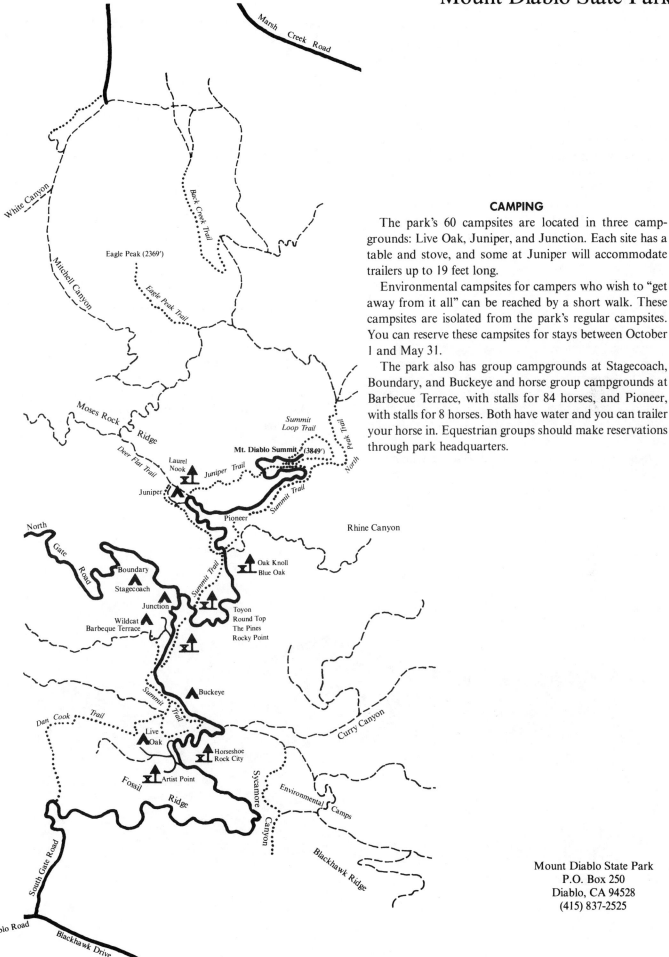

White Canyon

Marsh Creek Road

Back Creek Trail

Eagle Peak (2369')

Mitchell Canyon

Eagle Peak Trail

Moses Rock Ridge

Summit Loop Trail

Deer Flat Trail

**Mt. Diablo Summit (3849')**

Laurel Nook

Juniper Trail

North Peak Trail

Juniper

Pioneer

Summit Trail

Rhine Canyon

North Gate Road

Boundary

Stagecoach

Oak Knoll
Blue Oak

Junction

Summit Trail

Wildcat
Barbeque Terrace

Toyon
Round Top
The Pines
Rocky Point

Buckeye

Summit Trail

Dan Cook Trail

Live Oak

Curry Canyon

Horseshoe
Rock City

Fossil Ridge

Artist Point

Sycamore Canyon

Environmental Camps

South Gate Road

Blackhawk Ridge

Diablo Road

Blackhawk Drive

## CAMPING

The park's 60 campsites are located in three campgrounds: Live Oak, Juniper, and Junction. Each site has a table and stove, and some at Juniper will accommodate trailers up to 19 feet long.

Environmental campsites for campers who wish to "get away from it all" can be reached by a short walk. These campsites are isolated from the park's regular campsites. You can reserve these campsites for stays between October 1 and May 31.

The park also has group campgrounds at Stagecoach, Boundary, and Buckeye and horse group campgrounds at Barbecue Terrace, with stalls for 84 horses, and Pioneer, with stalls for 8 horses. Both have water and you can trailer your horse in. Equestrian groups should make reservations through park headquarters.

Mount Diablo State Park
P.O. Box 250
Diablo, CA 94528
(415) 837-2525

# Petaluma Adobe State Historic Park

The Adobe was the main residence and center of activity for Rancho Petaluma, the fertile sprawling 100-square-mile agricultural empire that helped make General Mariano Guadalupe Vallejo one of the richest, most powerful men in the Mexican province of California.

The land grant that first established the rancho was made in June 1834 by Governor Jose Figueroa on behalf of the promising young Vallejo, who was then commandant of the presidio at San Francisco. It was intended to reward and further encourage Vallejo's leadership in settling the area north of San Francisco Bay.

The rancho stretched eastward from Petaluma Creek over the hills and down to Sonoma Creek, including all the land that lay between these two waterways from the edge of San Francisco Bay to approximately the present site of Glen Ellen. (This was only one of General Vallejo's ranchos. By 1846, he held claim to some 175,000 acres including the site of the present day cities of Vallejo and Benicia, both of which he helped to found.)

Soon after receiving the original grant in 1834, Vallejo started building houses, corrals, and other needed improvements. A commanding site on a knoll overlooking Petaluma Valley was chosen for the rancho's main building. Actual construction of the massive adobe began in April 1836, continued steadily over the years, and was still not complete in 1846 when California's Mexican Era abruptly ended.

Today the Adobe is a National Historic Landmark. Many of the rooms have been furnished with authentic rancho period furniture and equipment, and exhibits in the visitor center make it possible to visualize some of the early-day rancho activities that once took place here.

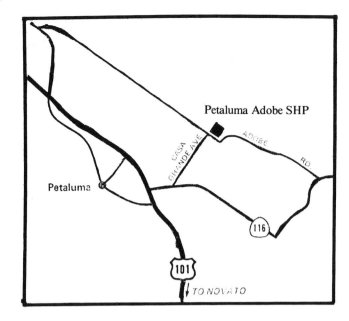

Your visit to the Adobe will be more meaningful and enjoyable if you also visit Vallejo's home and headquarters in the town of Sonoma. Today these buildings as well as others including Sonoma Mission make up Sonoma State Historic Park, and are about a twenty minute drive from Petaluma Adobe.

Petaluma Adobe State Historic Park
3325 Adobe Road
Petaluma, CA 94952
(707) 762-4871

*Petaluma Adobe, 1875*

*Mount St. Helena*

This park honors the author of *Treasure Island,* who spent his honeymoon here in 1880. The locale inspired some of the scenes in this classic novel and also became the setting for another tale, *The Silverado Squatters.*

About 3,000 acres on the upper slopes of Mount St. Helena are preserved in the park. A hiking trail leads to the peak, which provides clear day panoramic views of such mountains as Lassen, Shasta and the Sierra Nevada.

The park, open during daylight hours, is located 11 miles north of Bothe-Napa Valley State Park on Highway 29. Admirers of Robert Louis Stevenson will want to visit the Silverado Museum, which is dedicated to the author.

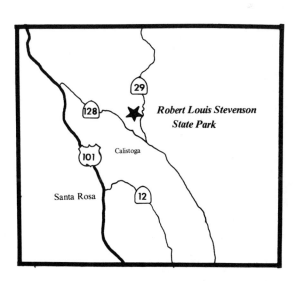

Robert Louis Stevenson State Park
C/O Napa District
3801 St. Helena Hwy., N.
Calistoga, CA 94515
(707) 942-4575

# San Juan Bautista State Historic Park

*Plaza Hotel barroom, 1880s*

San Juan Bautista offers a chance to investigate several successive periods in California history in one compact area. The mission, founded in 1797, is the oldest of the buildings that face the central plaza. The mission church, largest of its kind in California, was completed in 1812 and despite damage from numerous earthquakes it has been in continuous use. Today part of the mission can be toured, and historic artifacts from the mission era are on display.

On another side of the plaza stands the Castro Adobe, once used as an inn. Next door is the Plaza Hotel, built in 1858 by Angelo Zanetta, a professional hotelier. The hotel quickly became famous for its food, drink, and hospitality. The hotel has been restored to its 1870s appearance when the town of San Juan Bautista was an important stop on the stage route between Northern and Southern California.

Another interesting building is the Plaza Stable, designed to handle the extensive stage and wagon traffic that passed through San Juan. At one time there were as many as 11 stages arriving and departing daily. The bulk of the traffic was carried by the Coast Line traveling between San Francisco and Los Angeles. Inside the Stable an assortment of wagons, carriages and contrivances is on display, along with harnesses and other historical items. Behind the Stable is a blacksmith's shop complete with many of the tools used in the wagonwright trade.

Visiting hours are 10 A.M. to 4:30 P.M. (5:00 P.M. Summer)

San Juan Bautista State Historic Park
P.O. Box 1110
San Juan Bautista, CA 95045
(408) 623-4881

In the early nineteenth century, three countries—Russia, Mexico, and America—had designs on the Sonoma Valley. The state historic park in Sonoma preserves several buildings from that era.

The Sonoma Mission, last of the Franciscan missions established in California, is now a museum. The padres' quarters were constructed in 1825, while the church dates from 1840.

In 1833, the Sonoma area became the headquarters of General Mariano Vallejo, sent here to investigate Russian activities at Fort Ross. Vallejo himself laid out the town of Sonoma and secularized the mission. Not far from the plaza is the site of Vallejo's first house, Casa Grande; only the servants quarters still stands.

The General Vallejo Home, a later residence, is about a mile out of town. (Go west 2 blocks from the town square to Third Street, they proceed north to the home.) You may be surprised, after gazing at all that adobe in Sonoma Plaza, to find that Vallejo's home is built in New England style. Vallejo's storehouse is now a museum on the General, who so influenced early California history.

While you're following in the footsteps of Vallejo, you may wish to journey to nearby Petaluma State Historic Park (see description in this guide), where the General's huge adobe hacienda is preserved.

*General Vallejo reviewing his troops at Sonoma*

While on the "History Trail," take a ride to Benicia...

### BENICIA CAPITOL STATE HISTORIC PARK

In the early days after California joined the union, the town of Benicia served as the state capital. The old capitol building, which housed legislative sessions from 1852 to 1854, is preserved as a state historic park.

Although citizens of Benicia offered to introduce legislators to their "twenty or thirty marriageable young ladies," their town couldn't compete with Sacramento. The capitol building, however, continued to be useful for more than a hundred years as a school, jail, courthouse, church, and city hall.

Today, after extensive restoration, the capitol building resembles its 1852 appearance. The legislative chambers with their oil lamps, period furnishings, and winding staircases, evoke the atmosphere of California politics, circa 1852. Many California artifacts from this era are on display.

The historic park is located in downtown Benicia at First and G Streets. There is a small admission fee.

### BENICIA STATE RECREATION AREA

Located along upper San Pablo Bay, this park provides areas for picnicking, waterfront strolling, and tanning. Fishermen cast for striped bass and flounder.

The park is located 1½ miles west of Benicia off Interstate 780. An automatic gate requires an entrance fee in quarters.

Sonoma State Historic Park
20 E. Spain Street
Sonoma, CA 95476
(707) 938-1578

Benicia Capitol State Historic Park
P.O. Box 5
Benicia, CA 94510
(707) 745-3385

# Sugarloaf Ridge State Park

*Sugarloaf Ridge*

Sugarloaf Ridge State Park is located in the midst of the California coastal mountains just 14 miles east of Santa Rosa, in an area of diverse vegetation and topography. The park's 2,500 acres range in elevation from 600 feet at the park entrance on Adobe Canyon Road to 2,729 feet at the top of Bald Mountain.

Two distinct areas of the park can be seen along its 25-plus miles of riding and hiking trails—one, the primarily chaparral-covered ridges leading to Bald Mountain and the other, the linear groves of trees and large open meadows found along the Sonoma Creek drainage. Year-round Sonoma Creek begins in the park and runs for three miles through its southern portion. There is a parking area for day hikers.

An interesting feature of the park is one of the largest bigleaf maples in California; other trees include coast madrone, coast redwood, and several varieties of live and deciduous oak. Among the animals that make their home at Sugarloaf Ridge are blacktailed deer, raccoons, bobcats, gray foxes, rabbits, squirrels, and weasels.

The most popular seasons at Sugarloaf Ridge State Park are fall and spring, when the meadows are alive with wildflowers including the California poppy, cream cups, lupine, penstemon, calochortus, thistles, farewell-to-spring, brodiaea, Indian pinks, buttercups, and varieties of peas.

## CAMPING

Each of the park's 50 developed campsites has a table and stove; they will accommodate trailers and campers up to 24 feet long. Toilets and drinking water are available.

The group camping area, which will accommodate up to 50 people, has a barbecue and also four small corrals and water for horses.

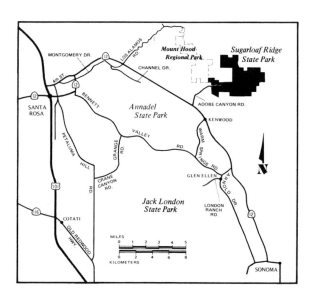

Sugarloaf Ridge State Park
2605 Adobe Canyon Road
Kenwood, CA 95452
(707) 833-5712

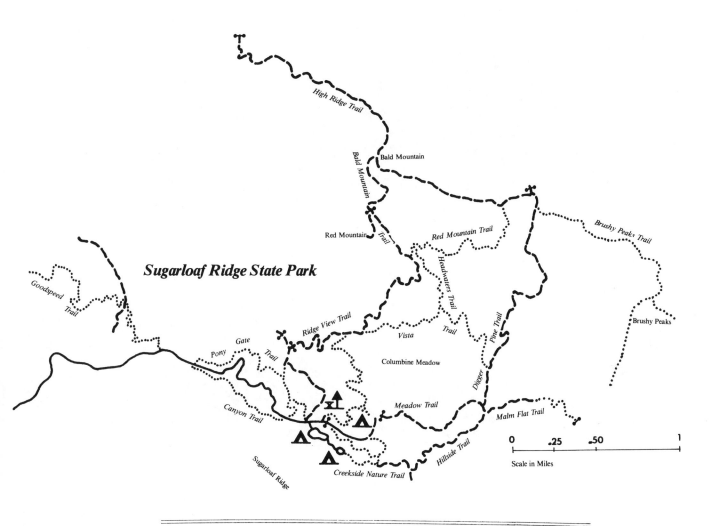

**Sugarloaf Ridge State Park**

High Ridge Trail

Bald Mountain

Bald Mountain

Red Mountain   Red Mountain Trail

Brushy Peaks Trail

Goodspeed Trail

Headwaters Trail

Brushy Peaks

Ridge View Trail

Vista

Pony   Gate   Trail

Columbine Meadow

Pine Trail

Digger

Canyon Trail

Meadow Trail

Malm Flat Trail

Sugarloaf Ridge

Creekside Nature Trail

Hillside Trail

| 0 | .25 | .50 | 1 |

Scale in Miles

THE CALIFORNIA QUAIL.

*Natural Bridges State Beach*

# Central Coast

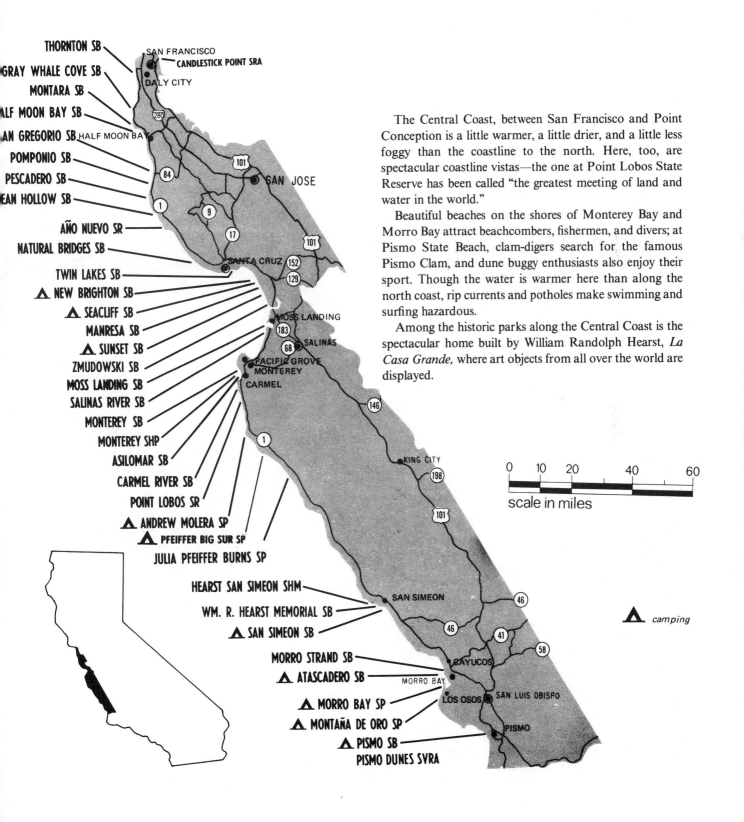

THORNTON SB

GRAY WHALE COVE SB

MONTARA SB

ALF MOON BAY SB

AN GREGORIO SB

POMPONIO SB

PESCADERO SB

EAN HOLLOW SB

AÑO NUEVO SR

NATURAL BRIDGES SB

TWIN LAKES SB

△ NEW BRIGHTON SB

△ SEACLIFF SB

MANRESA SB

△ SUNSET SB

ZMUDOWSKI SB

MOSS LANDING SB

SALINAS RIVER SB

MONTEREY SB

MONTEREY SHP

ASILOMAR SB

CARMEL RIVER SB

POINT LOBOS SR

△ ANDREW MOLERA SP

△ PFEIFFER BIG SUR SP

JULIA PFEIFFER BURNS SP

HEARST SAN SIMEON SHM

WM. R. HEARST MEMORIAL SB

△ SAN SIMEON SB

MORRO STRAND SB

△ ATASCADERO SB

△ MORRO BAY SP

△ MONTAÑA DE ORO SP

△ PISMO SB

PISMO DUNES SVRA

SAN FRANCISCO

CANDLESTICK POINT SRA

DALY CITY

HALF MOON BAY

SAN JOSE

SANTA CRUZ

MOSS LANDING

SALINAS

PACIFIC GROVE

MONTEREY

CARMEL

KING CITY

SAN SIMEON

CAYUCOS

MORRO BAY

LOS OSOS

SAN LUIS OBISPO

PISMO

The Central Coast, between San Francisco and Point Conception is a little warmer, a little drier, and a little less foggy than the coastline to the north. Here, too, are spectacular coastline vistas—the one at Point Lobos State Reserve has been called "the greatest meeting of land and water in the world."

Beautiful beaches on the shores of Monterey Bay and Morro Bay attract beachcombers, fishermen, and divers; at Pismo State Beach, clam-digers search for the famous Pismo Clam, and dune buggy enthusiasts also enjoy their sport. Though the water is warmer here than along the north coast, rip currents and potholes make swimming and surfing hazardous.

Among the historic parks along the Central Coast is the spectacular home built by William Randolph Hearst, *La Casa Grande,* where art objects from all over the world are displayed.

0  10  20  40  60
scale in miles

△  camping

# Andrew Molera State Park

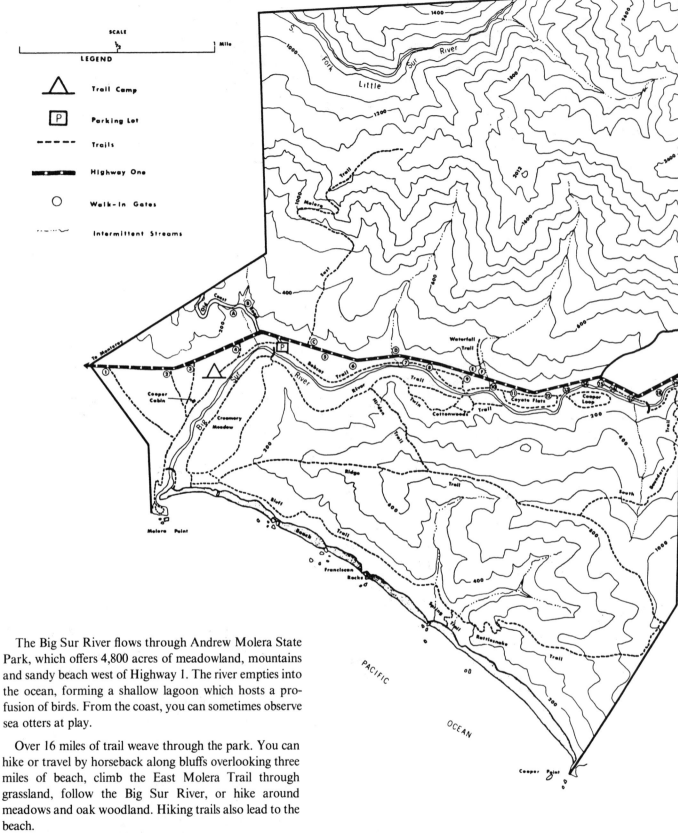

The Big Sur River flows through Andrew Molera State Park, which offers 4,800 acres of meadowland, mountains and sandy beach west of Highway 1. The river empties into the ocean, forming a shallow lagoon which hosts a profusion of birds. From the coast, you can sometimes observe sea otters at play.

Over 16 miles of trail weave through the park. You can hike or travel by horseback along bluffs overlooking three miles of beach, climb the East Molera Trail through grassland, follow the Big Sur River, or hike around meadows and oak woodland. Hiking trails also lead to the beach.

The trail camp is a quarter mile walk from the parking lot. Drinking water, toilets, and fire rings are provided. Each morning a ranger will visit your campsite to collect fees.

Andrew Molera State Park
C/O Pfeiffer Big Sur SP
Big Sur, CA 93920
(408) 667-2315

*Bull elephant seal*

About fifty-five miles south of San Francisco along scenic Coast Highway 1, Año Nuevo State Reserve offers magnificent vistas of shoreline bluffs, coastal lowlands, and the Santa Cruz Mountains.

Punto del Año Nuevo—New Years Point—was named by the chaplain of Spanish explorer Don Sebastain Vizcaino, who sighted it on January 3, 1603. First deeded to Mission Santa Cruz in 1794, Año Nuevo became a rancho under an 1840 land grant; the historic barns, relics of the large dairy farms that once flourished on the coastal bluffs, date from the 1880s. The area has also been the shipping point for a lumber mill, a sand mine, and farmland.

As ship traffic increased along the California coast, the treacherous rocks off Año Nuevo caused their share of wrecks. To warn mariners, the federal government installed a fog whistle on the island in 1872 and added a five-story light tower in 1890. An automatic buoy replaced the station in 1948.

In 1958, the State of California purchased the island and some adjacent mainland to create Año Nuevo State Reserve, which now totals more than 1,191 acres of coastal bluffs, dunes, and beaches. The rocky 13-acre island is now closed to the public to permit the seals and sea lions to breed undisturbed.

### THE ELEPHANT SEALS

A striking feature of Año Nuevo State Reserve is its large colony of northern elephant seals. During most of the year, elephant seals live at sea; they come ashore only to give birth, to breed, and to molt.

The breeding season begins on Año Nuevo Island in December, when the males begin to arrive. From fourteen to sixteen feet long and weighing up to nearly three tons, these huge bulls engage in violent battles to determine dominance; the successful bulls do much of the breeding, with most of the duty falling on the "alpha" bull at the top of the social ladder. Most of the males "hauled out" on the mainland beaches are the unsuccessful males.

In late December the females begin to arrive and form "harems" on the island. Much smaller than the males, they average around ten to twelve feet in length and 1,200-2,000 pounds. They typically give birth to the pups conceived the previous year about six days after they arrive, and nurse their pups—normally only one is born to each female—for 27-29 days. Feeding on its mother's rich (55% fat) milk, the pup will grow from approximately 75 pounds at birth to 300-400 pounds.

During the December-March breeding season you can see the reserve only on one of the scheduled guided tours. These tours, designed to minimize disturbance to the animals and their habitat as well as to give you more insight into the reserve's natural history, will be conducted by park rangers and students from the University of California, Santa Cruz, on a cooperative internship program. Their enthusiasm and love for the reserve will enhance your visit. The tour takes about two and a half hours; you will walk about 5 km (3 miles).

Guided tours are available only by telephone reservation; call (415) 879-0227 or (415) 879-0228 beginning in October.

Año Nuevo State Reserve
C/O San Mateo Coast District
95 Kelley Avenue
Half Moon Bay, CA 94019
(415) 879-0228

# Candlestick Point State Recreation Area

Uncrowded Candlestick Point State Recreation Area is one of the best sites on San Francisco Bay for the car-top boater. Not only is there plenty of patrolled parking, but one can beach their kayak or dinghy on a gentle, protected sand beach. Grassy picnic sites with tables are available for an after-paddle lunch.

The shortest portage to the water is from the turn-around circle at the south end of the parking lot. It is best to avoid low tides when launching or retrieving your boat at Candlestick Point SRA. Consult a tide table or ask a ranger for the best times to launch or retrieve.

Some of the best intermediate, advanced and expert windsurfing conditions on the Bay are to be found on the waters off the fishing piers at the south shore of the Park. The reason for this is a "wind tunnel" effect caused by afternoon winds pouring through the Alemany Gap to the Bay. For this reason, Candlestick Point SRA is recommended only for the experienced windsurfer. Park rangers will direct you to a sheltered lagoon less than ten minutes away if you feel the need for more practice before tackling the "wind tunnel."

Candlestick Point is a park-in-the-making. The new park is unique because it is located on a landfill, initialy created for a U.S. Navy shipyard during World War II. Before the park the landfill consisted of marshlands and mudflats. As the 170-acre recreation area evolves, many different activities and experiences will be offered to visitors. Picnicking and boating will have especially high priority.

At present, Candlestick Point features two fishing piers with fish-cleaning facilities, a large picnic area, biking and hiking trails, and a community garden. All facilities are accessible to the disabled.

Access to the park from San Francisco is quite easy. By auto: Take Highway 101 south to the Candlestick Park exit. Follow the Hunters Point Expressway around the stadium. By bus: Take the No. 56 Rutland MUNI bus to the S.F. Executive Park. Walk across the street to Candlestick.

Candlestick Point State Recreation Area
C/O San Francisco District
P.O. Box 34159
San Francisco, CA 94134
(415) 822-9266

# Hearst San Simeon State Historical Monument

*"La Cuesta Encantada,"* the Enchanted Hill, is the name of the famous castle designed by architect Julia Morgan and built by newspaper publisher William Randolph Hearst. This 146-room monument to the opulence and decadence of the roaring '20s lifestyle, when money was no object, is one of the most popular tourist attractions in California.

George Hearst, a mining baron, first began purchasing land in the area of San Simeon in 1865. He eventually acquired the bulk of five Mexican land grants totaling over 100,000 acres. His son, William Randolph, enlarged the family holdings after World War I to over 240,000 acres.

William Randolph Hearst's original idea was to build a "bungalow" on the site of his favorite childhood campground. His dream quickly evolved from a simply house to a castle from which to run his growing newspaper empire.

Casa del Mar (House of the Sea) was the first of three smaller houses built on the site; Hearst and his wife stayed there when they visited and entertained at the Castle until the magnificent Gothic Suite in the main building was completed in 1927. Both Casa del Mar and the Gothic Suite are part of the monument tours.

Castle tours also offer a glimpse at some of the elaborate collection of Hearst's tapestries, rugs, sculpture, silver and porcelain. The Library contains over 5,000 volumes and houses a large collection of ancient Greek vases. The Assembly Room in the main house has a magnificent doorway of marble bearing the coat of arms of Pope Julius II.

Many of Hearst's fabulous sculptures are located in the gardens, overlooking an inspiring panorama of ocean and coastal mountains. The gardens were designed to link the various building, terraces and pools into the "harmonious whole" envisioned by Hearst and Morgan.

On your way to the Castle from the visitor's center, you may view a zebra or other exotic animal. These are remnants of the 2,000-acre private zoo Hearst began in 1927 to entertain his many guests.

The Castle was in its heyday from the late 1920s to the end of the 1930s. The Great Depression, which saw most of the Hearst newspapers operating in the red, slowed construction on the castle but did not diminish the lavish parties thrown by Hearst and actress Marion Davies. Many famous people passed through the castle, including Charles Lindbergh, Winston Churchill, President Calvin Coolidge, playwright George Bernard Shaw, and a great number of the Hollywood movie colony including Mary Pickford and Douglas Fairbanks, Sr.

After the outbreak of World War II, Hearst closed the castle on the coast and moved to his inland headquarters in Northern California. The Castle was reopened in 1944 and construction resumed. Hearst visited the Castle for the last time in 1948, but it was kept in readiness for his return until his death in 1951. The Hearst family donated the Castle and its fabulous art collections to the State of California in 1958.

The Castle is open to the public daily (except Thanksgiving, Christmas, and New Year's Day). Because the tours are so popular, you are encouraged to make reservations well in advance of your visit. There are four tours available. Each tour lasts about 1 hour and 45 minutes.

## TOURS

The tours begin at 8:20 A.M. daily; the last tour starts at 3:20 P.M. in winter, later in summer. The number of tours is increased during the summer season.

Four tours (each one about 1 hour and 45 minutes long) are offered:

TOUR 1 (capacity 53 persons) includes the gardens, which feature roses and a multitude of outdoor statuary, the two pools, one of the three guest houses, and the lower level of the castle—the Refectory, Assembly Hall, and the movie theater. (150 stair steps) This tour provides the best overview of the castle and is suggested for one's first visit.

TOUR 2 (12 persons) covers the upper levels of the castle—an intimate view of Hearst's personal Gothic Suite and Celestial Suite, the libraries, and a two-level guest room—as well as the kitchen and pools. (300 stair steps)

TOUR 3 (14 persons) covers the castle's guest wing—36 bedrooms, sitting rooms and bathrooms with elaborate furnishings and works of art—and the pools, gardens, and a guest home. (300 stair steps)

TOUR 4 (15 persons) stresses the garden and provides a behind-the-scenes look at a hidden terrace, the wine cellar, two levels of the largest guest house, the two pools, and their dressing rooms. It's given from April through October, depending on the weather. (300 stair steps)

# Hearst San Simeon State Historical Monument

## RESERVATION INFORMATION

Hearst Castle tours are extremely popular and frequently sold out; it's highly recommended that you make your reservations well in advance of your visit. Tickets may be purchased through the **MISTIX** computerized reservation system.

To learn the location of **MISTIX** outlets or to obtain additional reservation information and tour schedules, call 1-800-952-5580 (or TDD 916-324-1891) between 8 A.M. and 5:00 P.M. on business days (recording after hours). Out-of-state residents, dial 916-323-2988.

After you have obtained a reservation application—or photocopied the one in the back of the *California State Parks Guide*—and filled it out, you may make a Hearst Castle tour reservation through the **MISTIX** reservation system by phone, by mail, or by visiting a **MISTIX** outlet in person.

If you are confined to a wheelchair, you must make arrangements for a tour directly with the Castle at least 10 days in advance of your visit. You must provide your own wheelchair and bring someone to push the wheelchair on tour. For information on special tours for person with disabilities, phone 1-800-952-5580, 1-805-927-4622, or write to Hearst San Simeon SHM, P.O. Box 8, San Simeon, CA 94352.

## PHONE-IN RESERVATIONS

Phone Toll Free: 1-800-I-GO-PARK (1-800-446-7275) and charge your reservation to your VISA or MASTER-CARD.

Phone Reservations that do not allow enough time for the tickets to be mailed may be picked up at any **MISTIX** outlet en route to Hearst San Simeon SHM or at the will-call facility at the Visitor Center.

If you plan to pick up your ticket at the will-call facility at the Visitor Center, it is suggested that you arrive at least 20 minutes prior to your scheduled tour to allow enough time to pick up your tickets. The tours leave on schedule and will not wait for people who are in line at the will-call. NO EXCEPTIONS.

## FEES

Tickets for each of the four tours are $8 per adult, $4 for youths age 6 to 12. Children under age 6 are free provided they do not occupy a separate seat on the tour bus.

Tickets purchased at the Hearst San Simeon Visitor Center will be CASH ONLY—no checks or credit cards will be accepted by the State. Senior Citizen Discount Program does not apply.

Times or dates of the tour tickets cannot be changed. You are guaranteed a space on a tour only at the time and date on your ticket. No changes can be made by telephone.

## MAIL-IN APPLICATIONS

Allow at least 10 days before your tour for mailing and processing of individual and group applications. Your request will be returned unfilled if the date(s) and time(s) you specify are not available. Tickets cannot be held at the Castle for your arrival, or mailed to a temporary address such as a hotel. When you get your ticket, check to make sure of the tour, date, and time. If there is an error, immediately call MISTIX at 1-800-I-GO-PARK. To expedite processing of mail requests, write on lower left corner of envelope: HEARST and date requested. Fees for orders outside the United States must be paid in U.S. dollars.

## WILLIAM R. HEARST MEMORIAL STATE BEACH

Protected from heavy surf and the prevailing winds by San Simeon Point directly north, this beach offers excellent swimming. A thousand-foot pier, a bait and tackle shop, and a boat charter service are located on the west end of the main parking lot. Picnicking may be enjoyed in the handsome eucalyptus grove just north of the pier.

San Simeon Bay provides fairly good refuge from northwest and west winds. Fishing boats work the waters near here for albacore in later summer and fall. In 1951 after the death of William Randolph Hearst, his estate donated land south of the general store for a park. In 1957 San Luis Obispo County built the fishing pier. Later the state took over operations of the park.

## SAN SIMEON STATE BEACH

On childhood trips to his family's quarter million-acre ranch, William Randolph Hearst became so enchanted with the site they used as a campground that, when he inherited the vast spread in 1919, he built his castle on the spot. Modern day campers may enjoy the splendors of the San Simeon coast—and perhaps build castles of sand—at San Simeon State Beach.

The beach stretches from San Simeon Creek to Santa Rosa creek, west of Hwy. 1 off San Simeon Road. A short trail to the beach begins at the southwest corner of the campground underneath the Highway 1 San Simeon Creek overpass.

Facilities include 139 campsites, a biker and hiker group site, and an overflow RV camp area south of San Simeon Creek. A trailer sanitation station is adjacent to the ranger headquarters south of the park entrance.

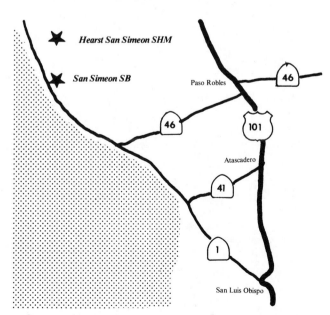

Hearst San Simeon State Historical Monument
P.O. Box 8
San Simeon, CA 93452
(805) 927-4621

# Julia Pfeiffer Burns State Park

Julia Pfeiffer Burns State Park

*A trail through the Big Sur country*

# Julia Pfeiffer Burns State Park

Dramatic McWay Falls, redwood groves and the legendary Big Sur coastline are all offered by Julia Pfeiffer Burns State Park. The park protects two miles of coastline and reaches inland into the nearby ridges of the Santa Lucia Mountains.

## HISTORY

Julia Pfeiffer was a child when her father, Michael Pfeiffer, took up ranching in the Big Sur Country in 1869. In 1915, she married John Burns and for the next few years she and her husband ran a cattle ranch while living at ranch headquarters in McWay Canyon. Julia Pfeiffer Burns was known for her courage, level-headedness and pioneering spirit, as well as for her knowledge and deep love of the Big Sur backcountry.

In the 1920s, Helen Brown and her husband Lathrop Brown, a Congressman from New York and a close personal friend of President Franklin Roosevelt, built the "Waterfall House" on the bluffs near McWay Falls. The Brown's unique house was built before the coast highway was constructed, when the South Coast was a lonely and isolated refuge. The gardens surrounding the house were filled with exotic plants—a Shangri-la in the wilderness.

Helen Brown became friendly with Julia Pfeiffer Burns and was very impressed with this gallant lady. In 1962, 35 years after the death of her friend, Helen Brown gave McWay Canyon and the surrounding ranch land to the state for a park to be named after Julia Pfeiffer Burns, "a true pioneer."

## NATURAL HISTORY

The park is near the southern extremity of the redwood belt, but some fine groves are found here. The trees are restricted to the bottoms of deep canyons and the cool north-facing slopes in order to survive the long, dry summers. Mixed in with the redwoods are madrones, California laurels and tan barks. A trail leads through the fern-covered canyons and climbs into the chaparral country characteristic of Big Sur's coastal slopes.

Another trail passes beneath Highway 1 via a pedestrian underpass and emerges on a steep bluff about a hundred feet above the ocean. McWay Falls cascades over the side of this precipitous bluff into the ocean. In California, it's the only major waterfall to tumble into the ocean.

In December and January, the observation site above McWay Falls is an excellent place to watch migrating gray whales. Sometimes the whales pass very close to shore and may even venture into McWay Cove.

## CAMPING

Though the park has no developed campground, two hike-in environmental campsites in a cypress forest on the coastal bluff are available. The sites are a half-mile's walk from the parking lot. Each site has a fire pit, toilet and food locker. No water.

To use the beautiful campsites, you must contact Pfeiffer Big Sur State Park, 11 miles to the north on Highway 1. You'll be issued a parking permit. The two campsites are subject to reservation.

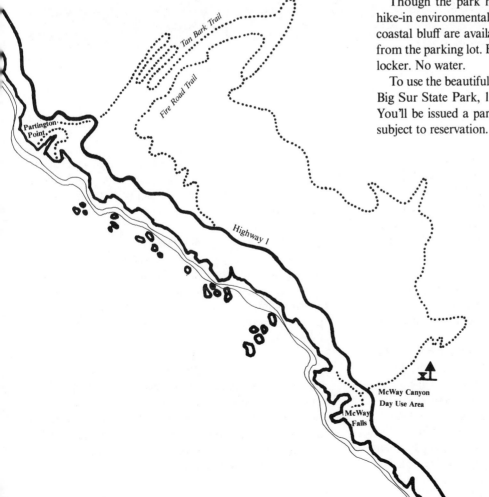

Julia Pfeiffer Burns State Park
C/O Pfeiffer Big Sur SP
Big Sur, CA 93920
(408) 667-2315

# Montana de Oro State Park

Just south of Morro Bay, Montaña de Oro State Park's ten thousand acres include rugged cliffs, secluded sandy beaches, coastal plains, and year-around streams in wooded canyons. The park gets its name—Mountain of Gold—from its profusion of wildflowers in spring; then, you'll find carpets of fiddleneck and California poppy on the slopes that sweep back from the sea, and California buttercups decorating the mountainsides.

The park's most prominent geologic feature is 1,347-foot Valencia Peak. From the summit, on a clear day, you can see nearly a hundred miles of coastline, from Point Sal north to Piedras Blancas.

California live oak and Bishop pine dot the hills; in the canyons are willow, big-leaf maple, box elder, and black cottonwood. The park abounds with wildlife including brush rabbits, black-tailed hares, opossum and raccoons. At dusk, deer come down to browse on the coastal plain.

Of special interest among the park's many birds is the black oyster-catcher, recognizable by its crimson bill; it can be seen along the rocky shore. During the summer, pigeon guillemots with black breeding plumage, white wing-bars, and bright crimson legs and webbed feet nest in the inaccessible holes of the cliffs. Cormorants and western gulls are some of the other residents of the bluffs and offshore rocks.

## HIKING

Coon Creek, Islay Creek and Hazard Creek Trails take you through the wooded areas of the park. The four-mile (roundtrip) Valencia Peak Trail reaches the top of the peak and offers inspiring views of the central coast. The Bluff Trail brings you to overlooks above the coves and sea caves of the park.

## CAMPING

Located just inland from Spooner Cove, the park's 50 primitive campsites beside Islay Creek have tables and woodstoves. Pit toilets are nearby. Trailers and motorhomes up to 24 feet long can be accommodated, but there are no hookups. Water for the campground is trucked in to fill the two large water tanks.

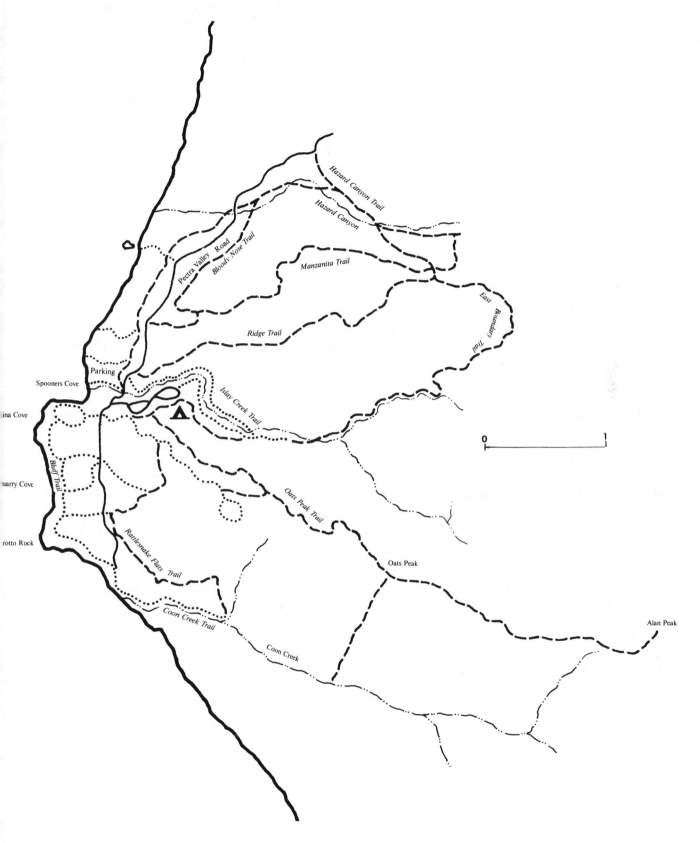

Spooners Cove
ina Cove
uarry Cove
rotto Rock
Parking

Pecira Valley Road
Bloody Nose Trail
Hazard Canyon Trail
Hazard Canyon
Manzanita Trail
Ridge Trail
East Boundary Trail
Islay Creek Trail
Bluff Trail
Oats Peak Trail
Rattlesnake Flats Trail
Coon Creek Trail
Coon Creek
Oats Peak
Alan Peak

0        1

Montana de Oro State Park
C/O Morro Bay State Park
State Park Road
Morro Bay, CA 93442
(805) 772-2560

# Monterey Bay State Beaches

**Natural Bridges—Twin Lakes—New Brighton
Seacliff—Manresa—Sunset—Zmudowski
Moss Landing—Salinas River—Monterey
Asilomar—Carmel River—Marina**

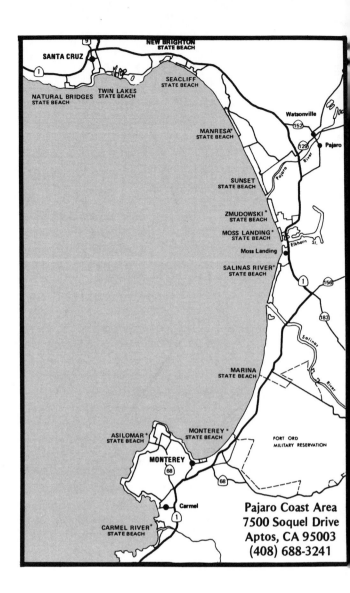

Pajaro Coast Area
7500 Soquel Drive
Aptos, CA 95003
(408) 688-3241

Water activities, fishing, picnicking, and camping are the attractions that draw crowds to these beaches all year long. The climate is favorable—the day's temperature seldom rises above 75 degrees in the summer or drops below 60 degrees in the winter.

Surfers enjoy the bay's relatively warm waters, and the Western Surfing Association holds regular meets here. Surfers may use any of the beaches with due regard for swimmers. There are unpredictable riptides and cross-currents along the coast, and swimming can be hazardous. Lifeguards are on duty only at Twin Lakes, from mid-June

Photographers and artists particularly appreciate the picturesque arches cut by ocean waves in a sandstone outcropping for which Natural Bridges State Beach is named. The interpretive trail here is also popular, and guided nature walks for groups are given on request.

## FISHING

These beaches are popular fishing spots—perch, kingfish, sole, flounder, halibut, bocaccio (tomcod), jacksmelt, lingcod, cabezon, salmon, steelhead, and occasional rockfish are among the species taken from shore or from the old concrete ship at Seacliff. This ship, the *Palo Alto,* was one of two such ships built to serve as a supply ship during World War I, but the war ended before her maiden voyage and it was finally decided that she was too cumbersome to be practical, so the government sold her to a company which had her towed to her present location in 1929 to serve as an amusement center. She was settled on the floor of the bay and a dance floor was built on her main deck with a cafe in the superstructure and a fishing ramp all around. After several years of operation she was closed down and stripped, and heavy storms broke her up, so that the seaward end is now closed.

The Pismo clam is also sought, especially at Manresa and Sunset. Clam diggers should beware of heavy surf, riptides, and the uneven bottom. Deep sea fishing boats are available at the Santa Cruz City Wharf in the summer; boats can be launched or moored at the marina operated by the Santa Cruz Port District at Twin Lakes.

## CAMPING

There are approximately a hundred family campsites each at Sunset and New Brighton, situated on the bluffs above the beach. The sites will accommodate trailers and motorhomes up to 31 feet long; each site has table, stove, and cupboard, and restrooms with hot showers and laundry tubs are nearby. Sunset also has a group campground that will accommodate up to 50 tent campers.

At Seacliff, the 26 trailer sites, with hookups for water, electricity, and sewage, are located right on the sand.

## ASILOMAR

The Asilomar Conference Grounds, operated by the nonprofit Asilomar Operating Corporation, are open all year round to both conferences and individuals. For details of facilities and reservations, write Asilomar Conference Grounds, Asilomar State Beach, 800 Asilomar Boulevard, Pacific Grove, California 93950.

Monterey State Beaches
Monterey District
210 Olivier Street
Monterey, CA 93940
(408) 649-2836

After Mexico obtained its independence from Spain in 1821, the Mexican flag flew over Monterey. The town expanded beyond the old presidio walls, and seafaring men from New England modified the Spanish colonial style to create the "Monterey" style of architecture. The Mexican government built the Custom House and the other public buildings. Comfortable white-washed adobe houses dotted the hills, and stores lined the crooked streets. Visitors were charmed by the picturesque beauty of the pueblo.

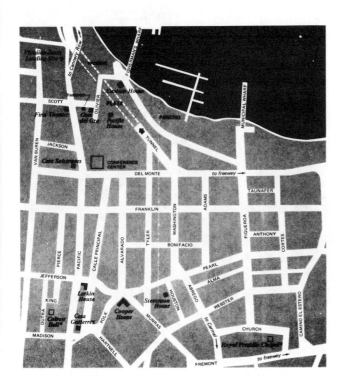

## CASA SOBERANES

336 Pacific Street at Del Monte Ave.

Casa Soberanes is one of the most intriguing examples of the Monterey Colonial style of architecture. The distinctive feature of the home is its half-tiled roof; the other half being covered with shake shingles to relieve the cantilevered balcony from the additional weight of more tiles. It's a well-furnished home, simple but elegant.

## CASA DEL ORO

Corner of Scott and Olivier St.

A general merchandise store operated by Joseph Boston and Co. in the 1850s, later the building was called Casa del Oro because of the unverified story that it had been a gold depository. Restored, it's now operated as a general merchandise store, circa 1850.

# Monterey State Historic Park

## CALIFORNIA'S FIRST THEATRE

Corner of Scott and Pacific Sts.

California owes its first theatre to Jack Swan, an English sailor of Scottish ancestry who settled in Monterey in 1843. He purchased land on Calle Estrada (Pacific Street) where, in 1846, he built a lodging house with a barroom as an added attraction.

Among the first productions were "Nan, the Good-for-Nothing" and a scene from "Romeo and Juliet." Seats were sold at $5 each and the house was packed. The Troupers of the Gold Coast present nineteenth-century plays each week year around. The Jack Swan Tavern serves food and beverages during the day and before evening shows.

## PACIFIC HOUSE

Custom House Plaza

Built in 1847, the Pacific House was first rented to the U.S. Quartermaster for offices and storage of military supplies. Army horses were kept in the large walled corral behind the building, a popular spot for Sunday bull and bear fights.

On the first floor of Pacific House is a museum of California history; on the second floor is an extensive collection of Indian artifacts and a historic costume gallery.

## CUSTOM HOUSE

Custom House Plaza

Here the United States Flag was first raised on July 7, 1846, bringing 600,000 square miles, including California, into the Union. Custom duties collected here from foreign shipping formed the principal revenue source for the government when Monterey was capital of this northern province of Mexico; the building was abandoned as a custom house about 1867.

## STEVENSON HOUSE

530 Houston Street

Juan Girardin, pioneer French resident, and his wife Manuela Perez became the owners of this two story house in 1856. They made some additions and rented spare bedrooms to roomers, among them Robert Louis Stevenson, who occupied a second-floor room during the autumn of 1879. He had come to Monterey to see Fanny Osbourne, who a few months later became his wife.

The house is shown by guided tours only. Tours take approximately 35 minutes.

## COOPER HOUSE

Corner of Polk and Munras

Captain John Rogers Cooper, Larkin's older half-brother, arrived in Monterey in 1823. A dealer in hides, tallow, sea otter pelts, and general merchandise, he travelled to the coast of South America, the islands of the Pacific, and even to China to trade.

The Cooper House, largest complex of Monterey State Historic Park, has recently been restored and is open by guided tour.

## LARKIN HOUSE

Jefferson St. and Calle Principal

Thomas Oliver Larkin arrived in Monterey from Boston in 1832. He started a general merchandise store and other businesses which, combined with his political activities, made him the most influential American resident in Monterey in his time. He served as the first—and only—U.S. Consul to Mexico in Monterey from

Monterey State Historic Park
Monterey District
#20 Custom House Plaza
Monterey, CA 93940
(408) 649-2836

# Morro Bay State Park

*Morro Rock*

Like most of the state park, the popular 18-hole golf course is dotted with pine, eucalyptus, and other trees, many of them planted in the 1930s by the Civilian Conservation Corps. It looks out over a peaceful lagoon with Morro Rock in view a bit to the north. The course includes a driving range, pro shop, and clubhouse.

Along the bay by a small boat harbor, a concessionaire offers launch facilities, mooring space, bicycles, and a snack bar where fishing and other supplies are available.

At the mouth of Los Osos Creek, an extensive marsh opens out into Morro Bay. A haven for countless birds, this is one of the largest marshlands still remaining on the California coast. Spring wildflowers are abundant in the adjacent grass—and brush—covered hills, and the plentiful seed supply attracts birds year-around; more than 250 species of land, sea, and shore birds, both migratory and resident, have been seen in the Morro Bay Area. A rookery of great blue herons is located in eucalyptus trees beside the bay just north of the museum.

The long peninsula that separates Morro Bay from the ocean is made up of sand dunes, some of them up to 85 feet in height. The spit can best be reached by boat; since it is closed to vehicles, it is an excellent spot for birdwatching and nature studies as well as clamming and surf fishing.

*Morro* is the Spanish term for a crown-shaped rock or hill, perhaps the best known of which is El Morro in the harbor of Havana. The rock at the entrance to Morro Bay is a plug dome volcanic outcropping, one of nine similar outcroppings in a line between Morro Bay and San Luis Obispo.

Before it came under the protection of the State Park System, the rock and talus from its steep slopes were being quarried. In 1969 Morro Rock was given Natural Preserve status to protect its considerable scenic, scientific, and historic values; most of the rock is now an ecological reserve operated by the Departments of Parks and Recreation and Fish and Game to protect the nesting area of the peregrine falcons. Though the reserve area is closed to the public, you can take a short trail part way around the rock's base to some excellent fishing sites.

For a good introduction to the wildlife and history of the Morro Bay area, visit the Museum of Natural History located on White Point, a rocky outcropping that rises above the bay. The museum offers interpretive displays, lectures, slide shows and movies. Near the museum you can see Indian mortar holes in the weathered rock and follow a trail that winds up to the top of the White Point for a sweeping view of the bay, sand dunes, and Morro Rock.

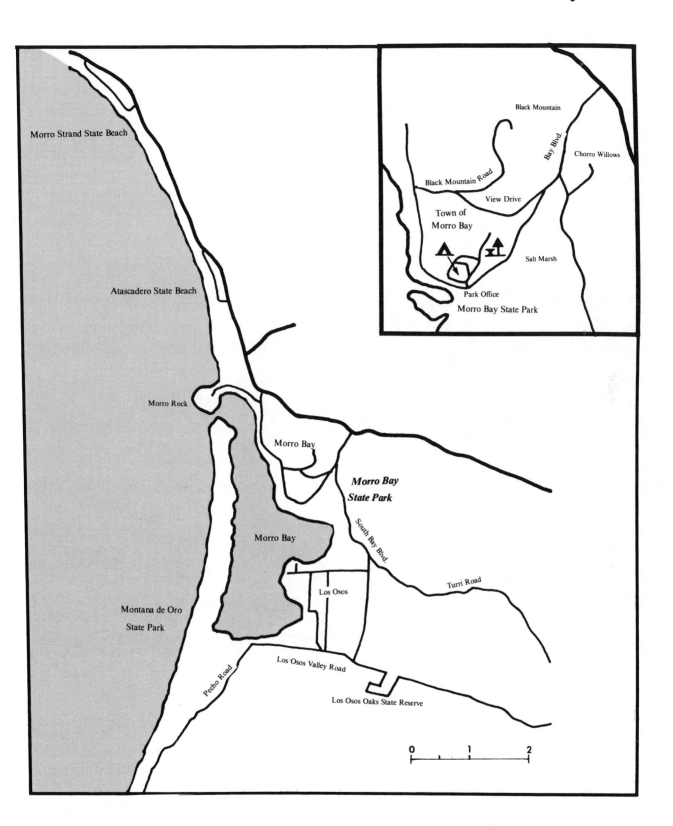

## CAMPING

The park has 135 campsites, each with table, stove and food lockers; restrooms with hot showers are nearby. The sites will accommodate trailers and motorhomes up to 31 feet long and 20 sites have hookups. A trailer sanitation station is available.

Morro Bay State Park
State Park Road
Morro Bay, CA 93442
(805) 772-2560

# Morro Bay Area State Beaches

*Morro Bay*

### ATASCADERO STATE BEACH

Atascadero State Beach, located a mile north of Morro Bay, offers 104 developed campsites. These sites can accommodate trailers and motorhomes up to 24 feet long, but there are no hookups.

Several miles of gentle, sandy ocean front are accessible from this beach, making it a popular place for walking along the shore and for beachcombing as well as for swimming, surf fishing and skin diving. (Clam digging is not allowed.)

### MORRO STRAND STATE BEACH

Two miles north of Atascadero State Beach on Estero Bay is Morro Strand, a beach for day use only. Though no lifeguard is on duty, the surf is seldom rough on this long, sandy beach.

There are no camping or picnicking facilities.

### LOS OSOS OAKS STATE RESERVE

At Los Osos Oaks State Reserve, two miles east of Los Osos on Los Osos Valley Road, two miles of gentle, scenic trail lead through a grove of ancient oaks sculptured by nature into fantastic forms, past panoramic views of Los Osos Valley and the Santa Lucia Mountains.

To help preserve this beautiful place—and avoid the abundant poison oak—please stay on the trail. No facilities have been developed here, and no dogs are permitted.

Pismo State Beach is the northern part of a meeting of land and surf that extends along the central California coastline from the city of Pismo Beach south to the Santa Maria River. The weather here is moderate year-around, with an average temperature of 60 F. summer and winter. Water temperatures are generally cold, often less than 58.

At the southern end of the park, there is an 850-acre off-highway vehicle area for dune buggies, motorcycles and other vehicles that can be operated in soft sand.

### CAMPING

There are two developed campsites on the east side of the sand dunes in the northern part of the park. You may reserve sites in the North Beach Campground (near the city of Pismo Beach) from Memorial Day until Labor Day, and in the Oceano Campground (near the town of Oceano) year-round.

All of Pismo State Beach and State Vehicular Recreation Area except these campgrounds is closed to vehicles from 11 P.M. until one hour before sunrise.

### VEHICLE CODE

The speed limit is 15 mph on the beach or within 50 feet of a campsite. Speed and reckless driving that endanger others are prohibited. Beach driving rules: No erratic driving or weaving in and out of the traffic flow, and no 180- or 360-degree turns.

The provisions of the California Off-Highway Vehicle Code and various local ordinances apply at Pismo State Beach/State Vehicular Recreation Area. It is your responsibility to know beach and dune regulations.

*Pismo Clams, now scarce*

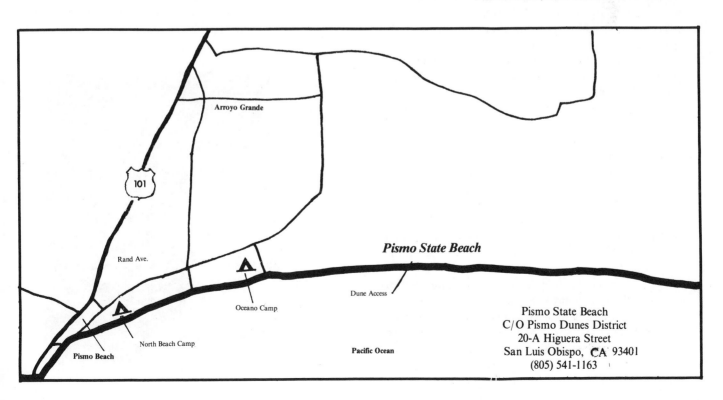

Arroyo Grande

101

Rand Ave.

Oceano Camp

North Beach Camp

Pismo Beach

*Pismo State Beach*

Dune Access

Pacific Ocean

Pismo State Beach
C/O Pismo Dunes District
20-A Higuera Street
San Luis Obispo, CA 93401
(805) 541-1163

# Pfeiffer Big Sur State Park

About thirty miles south of Monterey, State Highway 1 leaves the spectacular views of the ocean's edge for a brief stretch and enters a rugged, wooded canyon. This canyon, cut over long ages by the Big Sur River, contains a coast redwood forest in Pfeiffer Big Sur State Park.

The coast redwood, *Sequoia sempervirens,* grows naturally only in a narrow strip along California's coast from the southern tip of Oregon to San Luis Obispo County; the park's forty inches of rain per year is almost too dry for the trees, and they grow only along stream beds or in canyons and similarly sheltered spots.

In the 810-acre park's river flats and canyons, the redwood makes its home side by side with sycamores, black cottonwoods, big-leaf maples, alders, and willows. Contrasting with this is the dry chaparral country, where the south-facing slopes are covered with coast live oaks, tanoaks, California laurel, and shrubs such as chamise, ceanothus, buckeye, toyon, coffee berry, cascara, manzanita, and yucca. Some redwood lumbering occurred in the area in the early part of the century, but its main lumber product was bark from the tanoak, used for tanning leather at the then-new tannery in Santa Cruz.

In summer, warm days contrast with the cool, foggy evenings; winters are usually mild, though the temperature can drop below freezing and snow on the ground has even been seen briefly. Generally delightful weather makes fall and spring perhaps the best times to visit, despite an occasional rain.

## HISTORY

Though their traces have been found throughout the area its early inhabitants, believed to have been the migratory Esselen Indians, seem to have left the area before the first white settler—a man named Davis—arrived, in the late 1850s or early '60s. Davis built a cabin along the river called by the inhabitants of Monterey, then one of California's major population centers, *Rio Grande del Sur*—Big River of the South—and subsisted by hunting and trapping. Eventually he sold his cabin, the Homestead Cabin still standing near the park's picnic area, to Emanuel Innocenti (for whom Mount Manuel is named) and his family, Indians from Ventura raised and educated by the padres at the Santa Barbara Mission. The family started a small farm, raising melons and vegetables, and planted some fruit trees; Francisca Innocenti and the children cared for the farm while Innocenti worked as vaquero for Captain John Cooper at the Rancho El Sur. None of the Innocenti children reached maturity, though Innocenti lived to be about eighty and his wife almost a hundred years of age. She and six of the children are buried in the park, near the cabin.

In October 1869 Michael Pfeiffer and his family settled at the mouth of Sycamore Canyon, near the beach. His son John homesteaded a 160-acre parcel on the mountain between Sycamore Canyon and the river as soon as he came of age, and in 1884 moved into the Homestead Cabin. At that time, supplies had to be packed in over a rough trail from Monterey, a four-day trip.

*Big Sur River*

A wagon road was built from Monterey, and gradually the area's population grew. Though it still took eleven hours or more to get here from Monterey, sportsmen also found the spot to their liking; one group put in some cabins and a recreation hall in an area now occupied by one of the park's campgrounds, and ran a resort-lodge here for many years.

In 1934 the State Park Commission moved to acquire the nucleus of the present park, 680 acres, from John Pfeiffer, whose holdings by then amounted to some twelve hundred acres. Part of the cost of $164,000 was met by Monterey County and part by the State; Mr. Pfeiffer donated land then valued at $70,000. State Highway 1 was completed in 1937 after 18 years of work at a cost of $10 million, opening a spectacular access to the park. Though it was called a high-speed highway at the time, Highway 1 now is considered a "scenic" route, and park visitors should allow plenty of driving time.

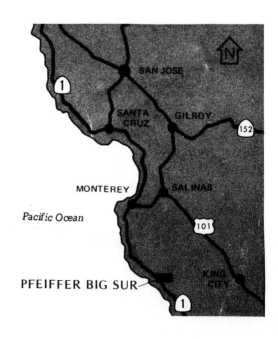

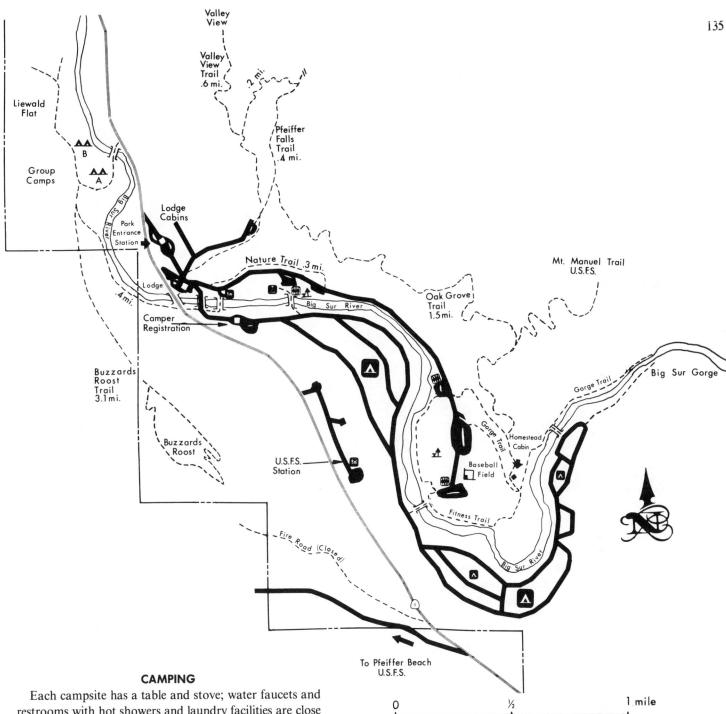

## CAMPING

Each campsite has a table and stove; water faucets and restrooms with hot showers and laundry facilities are close by. Some campsites can accommodate trailers up to 24 feet in length, though there are no hookups, and the park has a trailer sanitation station. Camping is limited to designated campsites with a maximum of eight people and two vehicles (including trailers, all of which should be parked only on paved parking spurs) per campsite. Checkout time is 2 P.M.

There are also concessionaire-operated motel-type accommodations, including a dining room; for information and reservations, contact the Big Sur Lodge, Big Sur, California 93920, phone (408) 667-2171. There are also two grocery stores and a laundromat that are open from the Easter holidays through Labor Day.

In addition to family picnicking and a group picnic area that can handle up to 200 people the park has two group campgrounds, each of which can accommodate 50 campers, open from June 1 to September 15. To make reservations for the group areas, contact the park supervisor.

Pfeiffer Big Sur State Park
Big Sur, CA 93920
(408) 667-2316

# Point Lobos State Reserve

*"The greatest meeting of land and sea in the world,"* is how one writer described Point Lobos. Extravagant praise to be accorded any one portion of the earth's surface, yet those who have come here agree that the beauty of this tree-clad headland is unequaled.

Point Lobos State Reserve, which the National Park Service designated a Registered Natural Landmark in 1968, is an area of 1,250 acres located in Monterey County along the south shore of Carmel Bay. The reserve derives its name from its colonies of California and Steller's sea lions. The sound of their hoarse barking carried inland from the offshore rocks at Punta de los Lobos Marinos, Point of the Seawolves.

Sometimes visitors can glimpse the California sea otter offshore diving for food or floating on its back in the kelp beds. Driven to the brink of extinction by the fur trade many years ago, the otters are now under strict protective laws and today number about 1,000 in California.

In November the gray whale begins to migrate to breeding and calving areas in Lower California, returning to the feeding grounds in the Bering Sea each spring. This large mammal, up to 40 tons and 50 feet long, can be seen as it travels close to shore on its 12,000-mile migration. A whaling station was located here in Whaler's Cove between 1861 and 1884.

Another outstanding feature of the reserve is its grove of Monterey cypress. In earlier geological times the Monterey cypress was widely distributed. Now it is making a last stand in the Monterey region. Clinging to the cliffs above the surf, distorted by wind and weather, sometimes shrouded in drifting fog, the trees tell of the never-ending conflict between sea and land. The still-living trees are rich green with foliage; the dead are stark in silhouette, their bleached and twisted branches red with algae.

Almost miraculously Point Lobos escaped destruction as it passed from one owner to another in years past. Once, in the free and easy days of the Mexican regime, it changed hands in a game of cards. Site of a whaling station, shipping point for a coal mine, proposed as a townsite, grazed over by cattle, and occasionally burned, it finally was acquired by an owner who appreciated its unique qualities. When it passed into the trusteeship of the State of California in 1933, with the help of the Save-the-Redwoods League, it had somehow managed to retain most of its essential, primitive character. And it is still unspoiled. Roads through the park have been kept to a minimum. The finer areas of the reserve can be seen only on foot over unobtrusive trails that lead to its greatest features of beauty and interest.

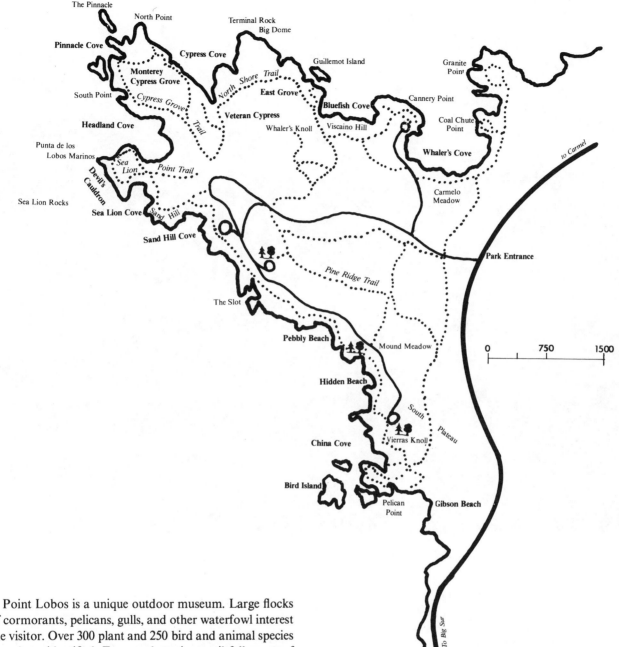

The Pinnacle
North Point
Terminal Rock
Big Dome
Guillemot Island
Granite Point
**Pinnacle Cove**
**Cypress Cove**
**Monterey Cypress Grove**
North Shore Trail
**East Grove**
Cannery Point
South Point
Cypress Grove
**Bluefish Cove**
Coal Chute Point
**Veteran Cypress**
Viscaino Hill
**Headland Cove**
Whaler's Knoll
**Whaler's Cove**
Punta de los Lobos Marinos
Sea Lion Point Trail
Trail
Carmelo Meadow
Devils Cauldron
Sea Lion Rocks
**Sea Lion Cove**
Sand Hill
**Park Entrance**
to Carmel
**Sand Hill Cove**
Pine Ridge Trail
The Slot
0    750    1500
**Pebbly Beach**
Mound Meadow
**Hidden Beach**
South Plateau
**China Cove**
Vierras Knoll
**Bird Island**
Pelican Point
**Gibson Beach**
To Big Sur

Point Lobos is a unique outdoor museum. Large flocks of cormorants, pelicans, gulls, and other waterfowl interest the visitor. Over 300 plant and 250 bird and animal species have been identified. From early spring until fall, acres of wildflowers transform the meadows, the shaded Monterey pine woods, and the seacoast into a variegated pattern of color.

Interesting offshore formations include Sea Lion Rocks, home of the noisy sea lions; Bird Island, sanctuary for thousands of shore and water birds; and the Pinnacles, where the dramatic action of the waves is a grand and never ending spectacle.

In 1960, 750 acres of submerged land were added to the reserve to create the first underwater reserve in our nation; this area was designated as an Ecological Reserve in May 1973. Intertidal and subtidal marine plant and animal species are fully protected so that the normal balance of conditions favorable to the survival of each plant and animal can remain undisturbed.

## GUIDED TOURS

Visitors are offered guided tours twice daily during the summer and on a reduced schedule during the off-season. One can visit six different areas: the cypress grove, the pine wood, Bird Island, the North Shore trail, Whaler's Cove, or the sea lion area.

Point Lobos State Reserve
C/O Monterey District
#20 Custom House Plaza
Monterey, CA 93940
(408) 624-4909

# San Mateo County State Beaches

*Montara Lighthouse and Hostel. Another hostel is located at Pigeon Point.*

### THORNTON—GRAY WHALE COVE
### MONTARA—HALF MOON BAY
### SAN GREGORIO—POMPONIO—PESCADERO
### BEAN HOLLOW STATE BEACHES
### and AÑO NUEVO STATE RESERVE

California's famed scenic Highway 1 connects these beaches that stretch along 50 miles of coastline from Thornton State Beach just south of San Francisco to Año Nuevo State Reserve near the Santa Cruz County line. The nine parks total twelve miles of ocean frontage.

Half Moon Bay is the only beach with a campground. Fifty-one developed sites will accommodate trailers and motorhomes up to 36 feet. A hiker-biker campground is also available.

The other State Beaches are open from 8 A.M. to sunset for day use only. Fishing, picnicking and sunbathing are the major activities. Cold water, rip currents and heavy surf make swimming dangerous.

Though horseback riding on the beaches is not permitted, an equestrian trail runs behind Half Moon Bay State Beach parallel to the ocean.

The famous San Andreas Fault enters the sea just south of Thornton Beach, and earthquake activity in the area has caused landslides which exposed fossilized bone and shell specimens dating from the Pliocene Epoch over a million years ago. Similar remains can be found at Año Nuevo Beach. At Pebble Beach, just north of Bean Hollow, the myriad stone fragments which give the beach its name are washed ashore from an offshore quartz reef.

The tidepools at Bean Hollow and Pescadero show excellent examples of marine life. Also at Pescadero is a marshy 584-acre wildlife refuge, the home of blue heron, kites, deer, raccoons, foxes and skunks. In season, razorback clams can be taken at Thornton.

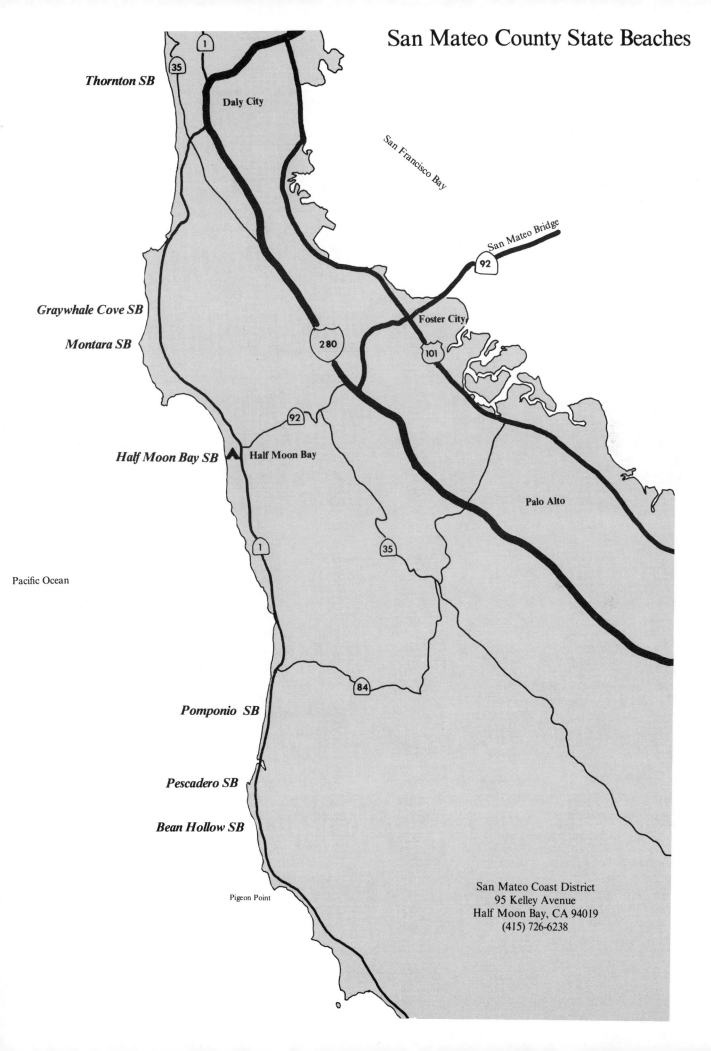

# San Mateo County State Beaches

*Thornton SB*

Daly City

San Francisco Bay

San Mateo Bridge

92

*Graywhale Cove SB*

Foster City

*Montara SB*

280

101

92

*Half Moon Bay SB*   Half Moon Bay

Palo Alto

Pacific Ocean

1

35

84

*Pomponio SB*

*Pescadero SB*

*Bean Hollow SB*

Pigeon Point

San Mateo Coast District
95 Kelley Avenue
Half Moon Bay, CA 94019
(415) 726-6238

# Coast Redwoods

On the map (listed north to south):

JEDEDIAH SMITH REDWOODS SP ▲

CRESCENT CITY

▲ DEL NORTE COAST REDWOODS SP

▲ PRAIRIE CREEK REDWOODS SP

TRINIDAD

EUREKA

FORTUNA

RIO DELL

WEOTT

GRIZZLY CREEK REDWOODS SP ▲

HUMBOLDT REDWOODS SP ▲

GARBERVILLE

▲ RICHARDSON GROVE SP

SMITHE REDWOODS SR

▲ STANDISH-HICKEY SRA

LEGGETT

ADMIRAL WILLIAM STANDLEY SRA

LAYTONVILLE

FORT BRAGG

WILLITS

MONTGOMERY WOODS SR

UKIAH

▲ HENDY WOODS SP

BOONVILLE

PT. ARENA

MAILLIARD REDWOODS SR

CLOVERDALE

GUERNEVILLE

ARMSTRONG REDWOODS SR

SEBASTOPOL

SANTA ROSA

NOVATO

▲ SAMUEL P. TAYLOR SP

SAN RAFAEL

SAN FRANCISCO

HALF MOON BAY

PESCADERO

SAN JOSE

▲ BUTANO SP

▲ PORTOLA SP

FOREST OF NISENE MARKS SP, THE

▲ BIG BASIN REDWOODS SP

▲ HENRY COWELL REDWOODS SP

SANTA CRUZ

WATSONVILLE

▲ camping

0   10   20      40      60

scale in miles

On the western side of the Coast Range, where heavy winter rains alternate with summer fog, is the home of California's famed coast redwood, *Sequoia sempervirens*. The trees stretch in a nearly continuous strip from the Oregon border to below Monterey; some of the finest remaining primeval redwoods can be seen in California's state parks. Many of these groves owe their existence to the Save-the-Redwoods League. Founded in 1918, the League has raised millions of dollars to match State funds for purchase of redwood lands, and spearheaded the drive to establish a State Division of Parks in 1927.

To enjoy the redwoods, plan to take your time—get out of your car to walk some of the many trails that wind through the forests. At the magnificent memorial groves of Jedediah Smith Redwoods and Humboldt Redwoods State Parks, you can see the many variations of redwood forest—all beautiful.

Several of the redwood parks have self-guided nature trails, and a unique Revelation Trail at Prairie Creek Redwoods unfolds the wonders of the redwood forest for blind as well as sighted visitors. At Big Basin Redwoods and Richardson Grove State Parks are exhibits that tell about the growth of the redwood and other plants and animals associated with it, and Humboldt Redwoods State Park offers exhibits on redwoods and history.

*Armstrong Redwoods State Reserve*

## Armstrong Redwoods State Reserve

In the 1870s, Colonel James Armstrong started cutting down the coast redwoods that filled what was then called the Big Bottom country north of Guerneville, a popular resort area along the Russian River. But the Colonel was very much aware of the unique beauty to be found in a virgin redwood forest and so, on the upper reaches of Fife Creek, he set aside one part of the forest to be preserved forever in its natural condition. After his death, his daughter Lizzie Armstrong Jones continued working for the preservation of this area until 1917, when Sonoma County bought the watershed for a park, later deeded to the State.

High ridges trap the rain, which falls abundantly to favor the Reserve's plant growth so that the verdant forest shuts out much of the sunlight and makes passage difficult; the soft forest floor is still and quiet except for the occasional sounds of birds or the gurgling of a brook. It is a redwood jungle—dark, damp, and cool—with few open spaces. Indians shunned the area, referring to it as the "dark hole," and even deer and bobcats seldom wander into the deep, protected canyon.

The quickest way to acquaint yourself with the features of the 680-acre Reserve is to take the self-guided nature trail.

A feature of the trail is the Parson Jones Tree, a coast redwood *(Sequoia sempervirens)* 13.8 feet in diameter, 310 feet tall, and an estimated 1,200 to 1,500 years old, that Armstrong named for his son-in-law, a Congregational minister.

A picnic area containing 100 picnic tables with stoves and barbecue pits is located at the north end of the reserve, at a fork in Fife Creek, and the Reserve also boasts the Redwood Forest Theater, a 1,200-seat natural amphitheater with fine acoustics in a beautiful natural setting, where many visitors attend stage and musical productions, and even weddings.

### CAMPING

There are 24 developed campsites in the campground, each with a table, cupboard, and wood stove. The sites will accommodate most vacation trailers, but there are no utility hookups. Running water and comfort stations with flush toilets are nearby.

## Austin Creek State Recreation Area

"Just isolated, wild, quiet, good country," is how one early resident described the Austin Creek area. And about the only change that has taken place in the last one hundred years is that watersheds of Fife and East Austin Creek are now protected as a state park.

Access to Austin Creek is through Armstrong Redwoods State Reserve on Armstrong Woods Road. This route provides a delightful contrast between Armstrong Redwoods' dark, confining shadows and the bright, open meadows of Austin Creek. After passing through Armstrong Redwoods, the road skirts the eastern side of the recreation area and terminates in the Redwood Lake campground. From there, you can reach the main part of the recreation area only on foot or horseback along twenty miles of trail.

All of Austin Creek's trails are open to horses. Horse trailer parking space is located at the entrance to Armstrong Redwoods.

A year-round stream, East Austin Creek, offers steelhead, salmon, and trout fishing, and Redwood Lake has a resident population of bluegill and black bass.

### CAMPING

The campground at Redwood Lake has 24 units. Each site has a table and a fire ring, and restrooms are nearby. The narrow, winding access road, which climbs a thousand feet to the campground, cannot be negotiated by vehicles pulling trailers, or motorhomes over 20 feet long. It may be closed by bad weather during the winter.

Primitve campsites at Tom King, Mannings Flat, and Gilliam Creek provide overnight areas for equestrians and hikers. Stream water is generally drinkable in spring and early summer, but may need purifying when stream flow decreases. The camps have wood stoves, but you are advised to bring a backpacking stove. Check at the park office before hiking in.

Armstrong Redwoods State Reserve
17000 Armstrong Redwoods Road
Guerneville, CA 95466
(707) 869-2015

# Big Basin Redwoods State Park

Big Basin Redwoods State Park is located on the ocean-facing slopes of the Santa Cruz Mountains about 20 miles north of the city of Santa Cruz. It is the oldest park now in the California State Park System, and preserves a portion of the primeval coast redwood forest of the Santa Cruz area. It was acquired in 1902.

Two access roads leave Highway 9 and wander through the beautiful forests, meadows, and steep canyons of the Santa Cruz Mountains to reach the Waddell Creek watershed where the park is located. The more northerly of these roads is especially narrow and twisting and is not recommended for camper vehicles or cars pulling trailers. Even with these low-speed, scenic access roads, visitors from the San Francisco and Monterey Bay areas can drive to the park in two hours or less.

Because of its convenient location, the park has long been popular as a place where people could find relief from the congestion and hectic activity of urban life; use over several generations has built a tradition of increased respect and admiration for the Big Basin country. At the same time, people have found inspiration and enjoyment through a sharpened awareness of the wonders and immense diversity to be found in the world of nature.

Human beings have probably known about the Big Basin country for thousands of years, although very little is known today about early human—Indian—activity in the region. It is generally agreed, however, that Indians did not often frequent the deep redwood forests, but preferred more open country where food and other commodities were more plentiful. A trail led over the mountains from the Santa Clara Valley to well-established, though perhaps intermittently used, campsites along the coast.

In 1769, the Portola expedition passed along the coast and camped in the Waddell Creek watershed near the ocean shore. They called this area *La Salud* (The Health) because after a brief rest in this place—and despite being drenched by a heavy rainstorm—several ailing members of the expedition began to feel better. The mission padres would later rename this area *Arroyo de los Osos* for the wild grizzlies that roamed the valley. Just a few days earlier, near the Pajaro River, members of this expedition had become the first Europeans to see and wonder at the great Park. It was renamed Big Basin in 1927 and over the years has been enlarged so that today it includes about 15,000 acres, most within the Waddell Creek watershed, and extends to the ocean.

The heart of the park is located on the Opal Creek flatlands at the very bottom of Big Basin. Park headquarters is located here along with a little museum known as the Nature Lodge, which houses a fine collection of historical and natural science exhibits (during the summer season concessionaires operated a snack bar and gift shop here). Not far away Columbian black-tailed deer can usually be seen wandering in the meadow, and a gentle, self-guided nature trail points out some of the most notable features of one of the park's most ancient and impressive redwood groves.

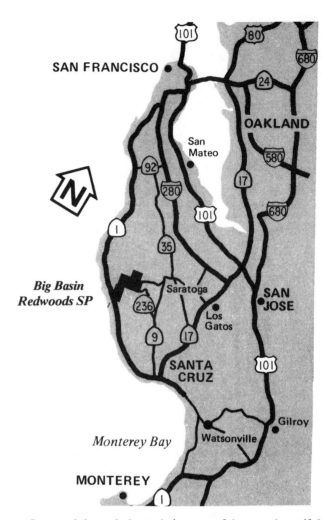

Scattered through the park, in some of the most beautiful areas, are 158 picnic sites, each with table and stove. They are available on a first-come-first-served basis.

Rancho del Oso and Waddell Beach are very pleasant places to spend a day. There is a large day-use parking lot at the beach; overnight camping is not permitted. You can walk up, explore, and enjoy the canyon where Portola's party rested.

In the most exposed parts of the park a mixed forest is found including madrone, California nutmeg, myrtle, and several kinds of oak. Just a short distance from the lush forest of the canyon bottoms, chaparral covers the steep, dry slopes that face west or southwest, and in some places there are groves of knobcone pine—a tree commonly associated with dry, inland climates.

Many kinds of animals live in and around the park, including deer, raccoons, skunks, and squirrels. Animals that are less often seen include opossum, foxes, coyotes, weasels, and an occasional bobcat.

Bird life is also abundant due to the variety of habitats found within the park. Steller's jays and California woodpeckers are often seen and easily identified, and egrets, herons, and other species of water bird can be seen at the marsh and beach at Rancho del Oso near the mouth of Waddell Creek.

# Big Basin Redwoods State Park

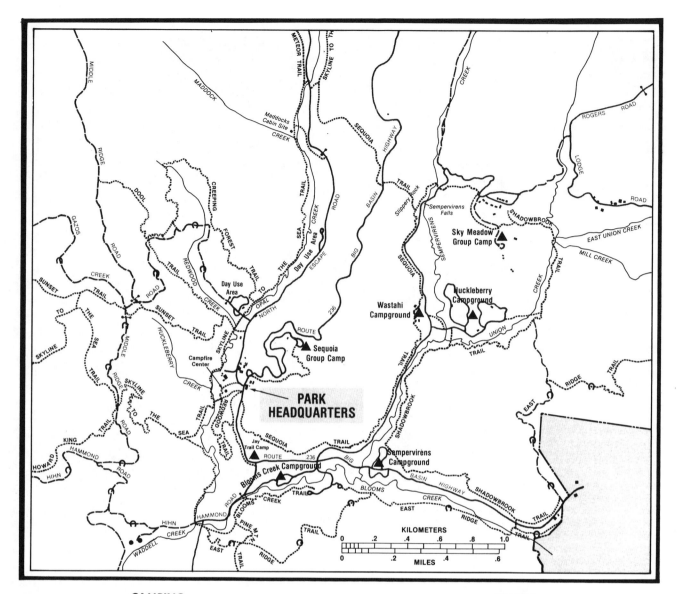

## CAMPING

Each of the 188 family campsites has a table and stove. Combination buildings with restrooms and hot showers are nearby. Wastahi Campground is a walk-in camp; motor vehicles must be left in the nearby parking lot rather than being driven to the individual campsites. In the other campgrounds cars are permitted and there are many sites where there is even room enough for camper vehicles and small trailers. There are no trailer hookups, but a trailer sanitation station is provided in the Huckleberry Campground area.

An extensive interpretive program is carried on at this park. During the summer, and at other times when there is sufficient demand, guided walks and some longer hikes are offered. There are also regular campfires during the summer with informational talks, slide shows, and movies.

## HIKING

Eighty miles (125 km.) of hiking trails lead through the park. Many of these trails follow streambeds through the deep redwood forests of the sheltered basin, but some climb the ridges to scenic vista points from which it is possible to see much of the Big Basin country and to look out over the ocean beyond.

A 23-mile (37-km.) hiking trail connects Big Basin with Castle Rock State Park, and another 12-mile (19-km.) section takes you through Rancho del Oso to Highway 1. Seven trail camps for backpackers are located between Castle Rock and the sea; they are available, on a reservation-only basis, through the Big Basin office. There is a small parking lot inside Rancho del Oso for those who wish to hike in from Highway 1. Hikers are delighted by the surprising number of beautiful waterfalls that occur within the park, and by the wide variety of environments that can be explored.

Big Basin Redwoods State Park
21600 Big Basin Way
Boulder Creek, CA 95006
(408) 338-6132

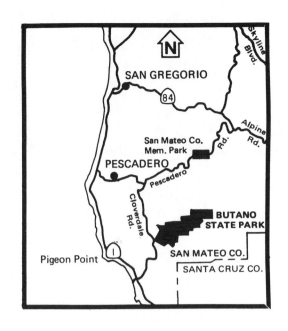

Visitors enjoy camping, hiking, and picnicking in a bit of secluded wilderness at Butano State Park, a 2,200-acre redwood park in the Santa Cruz Mountains of southern San Mateo County. Most of the redwoods are second-growth, but there are some fine mature trees. Butano Creek runs through the park and there is a small, but lush, fern canyon. More than forty miles of trail and fire roads are available for hiking.

Butano is perched on the edge of the fog belt, so fog can be expected nights and mornings in summer. By noon, the temperature is usually just about perfect for picnicking.

### CAMPING

The park has 40 campsites, each with a table and stove; restrooms are nearby. Nineteen of the sites cannot be reached by car; campers must carry their equipment a short distance.

Use of the Butano Trail Camp must be arranged in advance; contact the park for information and reservations.

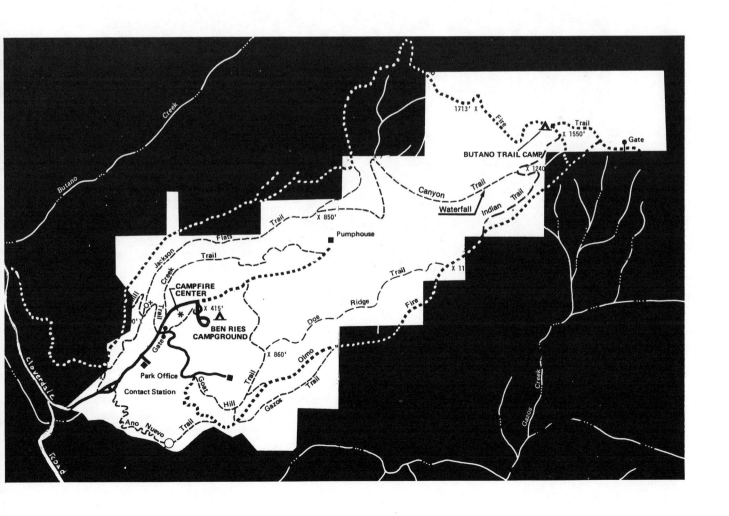

# Del Norte Coast Redwoods State Park

At Del Norte, dense redwood forest growing almost to the ocean's edge gives you an idea of what Jedediah Smith and his party were up against when they passed through this country in the late 1820s. Much of the park is virgin forest, but in the 1920s Hobbs, Wall & Co. conducted logging operations where the campground is now located, so the lush forest there is second-growth redwood, mixed with red alder. In the fall, the leaves of the alders and maples make a colorful display. In addition to the remains of the logging operation, there are traces—old ties and a decaying trestle—of the Crescent City and Smith River Railroad that once ran through the park.

## CAMPING

The park is open from April 1 to October 31. There are 145 family campsites, each with a food locker, stove, and table; restrooms with showers are nearby. Some of the sites will accommodate trailers up to 27 feet long and motorhomes up to 31 feet; others are walk-in sites that provide privacy for tent campers. Sites for hikers and bicyclists are available on a first-come-first-served basis.

## HIKING

MILL CREEK TRAIL—2.6 mi. (4.2 km.), EASY. This trail along Mill Creek (the same stream that flows through Jedediah Smith, though the trails do not connect) gives you a chance to wade and watch the activities of birds and small animals. The stream is generally too shallow to afford good fishing. The trail begins along the campground entrance road.

ALDER BASIN TRAIL—1 mi. (1.6 km.), MODERATE. Beginning across the bridge from the Mill Creek trailhead, this trail takes you through a streamside habitat of alders, maples, and willows. The scene is colorful in the fall.

TRESTLE LOOP TRAIL—1 mi. (1.6 km.), MODERATE. This is a good chance for bird-watching in a second-growth redwood forest.

NATURE LOOP TRAIL—0.8 mi. (1.3 km.), EASY. Beginning across from the campground entrance station, this trail gives you a quick view of a redwood forest, highlighted by the red peeling bark of a madrone tree.

HOBBS-WALL TRAIL—3.8 mi. (6.1 km.), MODERATELY STRENUOUS. This trail, named for the old lumber company that logged off the campground area, leads through the second-growth redwoods past abandoned logging cables and machine parts. It can be started from the campground, just past the west winter closure gate, from Saddler Skyline Trail, from the Nature Loop, or from the park entrance near Highway 101.

SADDLER SKYLINE TRAIL—1.5 mi. (2.4 km.), MODERATE. You can start this trail from the Nature Loop or from the campground, between Sites 7 and 8; it will take you through a Douglas-fir and young redwood forest, with plenty of opportunities for birdwatching and lots of huckleberries in the fall.

These trails can be reached from Highway 101.
MEMORIAL GROVE TRAIL—0.9 mi. (1.4 km.), EASY. This trail leads from a turnout on Highway 101 through the second-growth redwood forest to the Hobbs-Wall Trail.

DAMNATION CREEK TRAIL—2.5 mi. (4 km.), STRENUOUS. Used by the Yurok Indians to gather shellfish and seaweed, this steep trail leads you from Highway 101 through a dense forest with redwoods growing almost to the water's edge to a hidden sea cove with a small beach. The Highway 101 trailhead is at the Henry Solon Graves Memorial Grove in a turnout about four miles (six kilometers) south of the campground entrance.

LAST CHANCE TRAIL—6 mi. (9.6 km.), MODERATELY STRENUOUS. On this trail you walk along the original route of the highway through redwood, spruce, and red alder forests to the coastal bluff and spectacular ocean vistas. Begin at the south end of the trail on Highway 101, about a third of a mile (half a kilometer) south of the Damnation Creek trailhead.

FOOTSTEPS ROCKS TRAIL—0.8 mi. (1.3 km.), MODERATE. This trail leads from the highway to a small rocky beach, and takes about an hour round trip. The trailhead is north of the Lagoon creek picnic area and vista point, 6 miles (9.7 km.) south of the campground entrance.

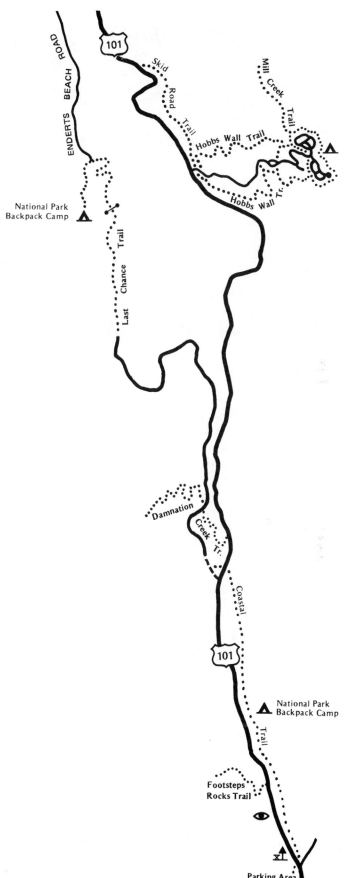

Del Norte Coast Redwoods State Park
C/O Klamath District
3431 Fort Ave.
Eureka, CA 95501
(707) 464-9533

# The Forest of Nisene Marks

*California Youth Conservation Corps helps repair storm damage*

The Forest of Nisene Marks is on land which was clear-cut during a forty-year logging frenzy (1883-1923). When the loggers left Aptos Canyon, the forest began to heal itself and now the scars grow fainter with each passing year. The Forest of Nicene Marks State Park is a monument to forest regeneration and the future.

The forest's land is a maze of ridges and canyons formed by the twisting and contorting of the earth due to faults which run diagonally across the park. The land is dominated by the watersheds of Aptos and Hinckley Creeks. The watersheds were so forbidding that 19th century surveyors used the ridge tops as boundaries rather than attempt to enter the country. Those ridge tops today mark the boundaries of the park.

In narrow Aptos Canyon, the Loma Prieta Lumber Company built the largest lumber mill in Santa Cruz County and created a small company town named Loma Prieta (Loma Prieta means "dark mountain" and is taken from the highest peak in the Santa Cruz Mountains). Using oxen, steam donkeys, trestles, high lines, skid roads, inclines, and tenacity, it took loggers forty years to push up every canyon in the watershed. When they were finished, they had removed a staggering total of 140 million board feet of lumber. Only a handful of the first-growth redwoods survived; two along the Aptos Creek Road were spared because they had large flaws and several groves on distant ridges were saved by their isolation.

The lumber company's 9,600 acres were purchased in the 1950s by the Marks, a family of Danish ancestry active in Salinas Valley farming. In 1963, Herman, Agnes, and Andrew Marks, with assistance from the Nature Conservancy, donated the property to the State of California in memory of their mother, Nisene Marks. The donation was made with the stipulation that the property be left undeveloped so that the natural process of restoration might continue.

The natural inaccessibility of the canyons was brought into dramatic focus during the winter storms of 1982 and 1983; creeks raged through the canyons scouring creek bottoms and tossing logs about like tinker toys. Many of the hiking trails which had been placed atop hundred-year-old railroad grades were washed away; trestles which had witnessed a century of storms vanished without a trace. Some of the trails on the Bridge Creek and West Ridge sides of the park have been restored by volunteer workers and the California Youth Conservation Corps, but it will be many years before the trails again reach deep into Aptos Canyon.

• The park is open from dawn to dusk each day.

• Mountain bicycles should use the fire roads north of the steel bridge. Bicyclists should be courteous to hikers using the park. Downstream of the bridge, joggers, hikers, horseback riders, and bicycles will all be using the same trail system.

• Steelhead fishing is permitted during open Winter season downstream of the steel bridge. A valid California fishing license is required.

## CAMPING

To stay overnight at the Westridge Trail Camp you must make advance reservations. Only backpacking stoves are allowed. Drinking water and a restroom is at the camp. Parking for vehicles left overnight is either the Westridge Trailhead or Georges Picnic Area, depending upon the time of year.

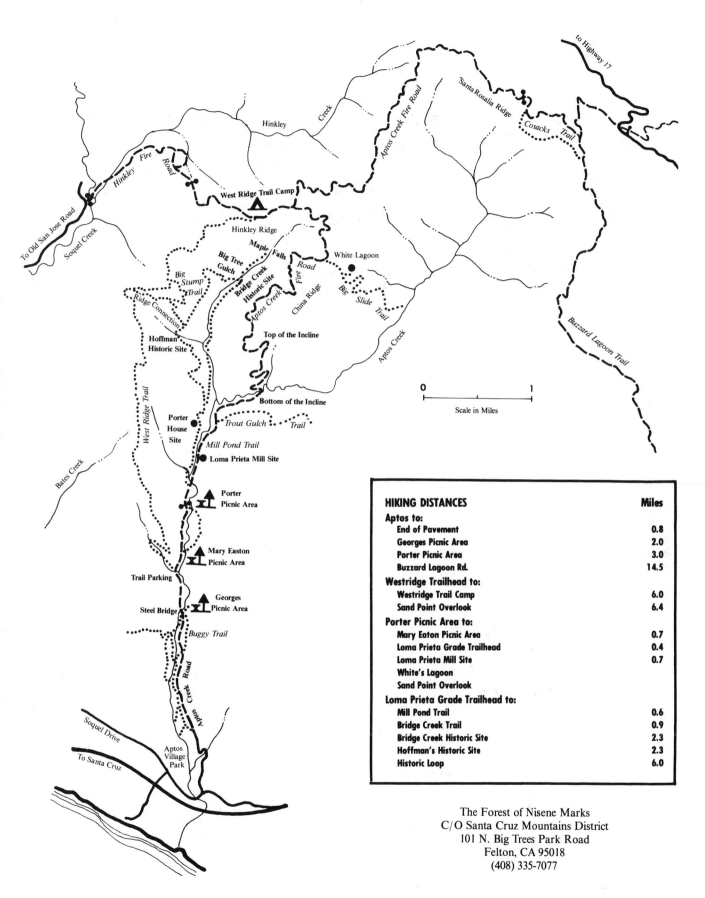

**HIKING DISTANCES** — **Miles**

| | Miles |
|---|---|
| **Aptos to:** | |
| End of Pavement | 0.8 |
| Georges Picnic Area | 2.0 |
| Porter Picnic Area | 3.0 |
| Buzzard Lagoon Rd. | 14.5 |
| **Westridge Trailhead to:** | |
| Westridge Trail Camp | 6.0 |
| Sand Point Overlook | 6.4 |
| **Porter Picnic Area to:** | |
| Mary Eaton Picnic Area | 0.7 |
| Loma Prieta Grade Trailhead | 0.4 |
| Loma Prieta Mill Site | 0.7 |
| White's Lagoon | |
| Sand Point Overlook | |
| **Loma Prieta Grade Trailhead to:** | |
| Mill Pond Trail | 0.6 |
| Bridge Creek Trail | 0.9 |
| Bridge Creek Historic Site | 2.3 |
| Hoffman's Historic Site | 2.3 |
| Historic Loop | 6.0 |

The Forest of Nisene Marks
C/O Santa Cruz Mountains District
101 N. Big Trees Park Road
Felton, CA 95018
(408) 335-7077

# Grizzly Creek Redwoods State Park

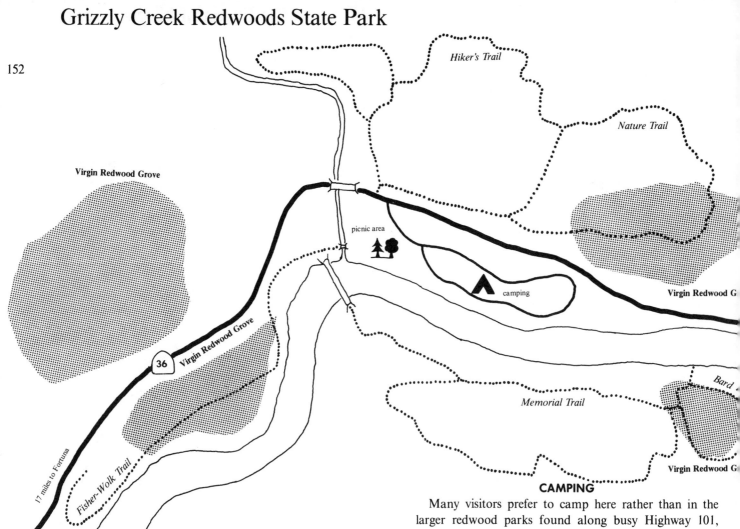

Hiker's Trail

Nature Trail

Virgin Redwood Grove

picnic area

camping

Virgin Redwood G

Bard

Memorial Trail

36 Virgin Redwood Grove

Virgin Redwood G

17 miles to Fortuna

Fisher-Wolk Trail

Grizzly Creek Redwoods State Park lies in the Van Duzen River Valley 30 miles from the ocean. It is the smallest—only 234 acres—and the farthest inland of California's twenty-two popular coast redwood parks.

In the 1860s, after the Indians were resettled north in the Hoopa Indian Reservation, farms and ranches were established around the mouth and upper reaches of the Van Duzen River. Lush grass and abundant water made the present park site an excellent feed and rest stop for the many herds that were driven down the river to coastal markets and shipping ports.

Stagecoach drivers reined their teams to a stop where the park's only campground now lies. This verdant spot on the north bank of the river offered shade and drinking water for the weary passenger traveling between Bridgeville and Strong's Station.

Today the Indians, the cattle drives, and the stage lines are gone, and so are the bears that gave their name to Grizzly Creek, a small stream near park headquarters. But the forest has changed very little, and the visitor is fortunate to see it much as it must have appeared to the Wiyots when they searched for game under the towering redwood trees and fished for salmon in the river.

## CAMPING

Many visitors prefer to camp here rather than in the larger redwood parks found along busy Highway 101, twenty miles west. Grizzly Creek's 30 campsites are all close to piped drinking water, and each has a table, stove, and cupboard.

For those who plan to stay in the park for just a day, there is a 30-unit picnic area adjacent to park headquarters. Trails from the picnic area and the campground lead to the river where one can wade or fish for trout.

Across State highway 36 from the campground and picnic areas are two short trails that wind through virgin stands of coast redwoods and secondary tree growth. One, the Nature Trail, is marked with signs explaining the plant life. Across the river is the 1¼-mile Memorial Trail, which is open in the summer from June 15 to September 15, when the bridge across the Van Duzen River is in place. The forest is dense and the vistas are limited, but there is an open view of the park and the Van Duzen Valley at Devils Elbow, a river overlook close to the highway on the park's west side.

Along the river's edge where the ground is soft, one is likely to find the tracks of black-tailed deer, night-roaming skunk, raccoon or bobcat. When the river recedes after winter rains, bobcats and other scavengers search the banks for spawned-out salmon. Many anglers come to the park in the fall and winter to try their luck during the salmon and steelhead runs.

Grizzly Creek Redwoods State Park
Star Route, Box 75
Carlotta, CA 95528
(707) 777-3683

# Hendy Woods State Park

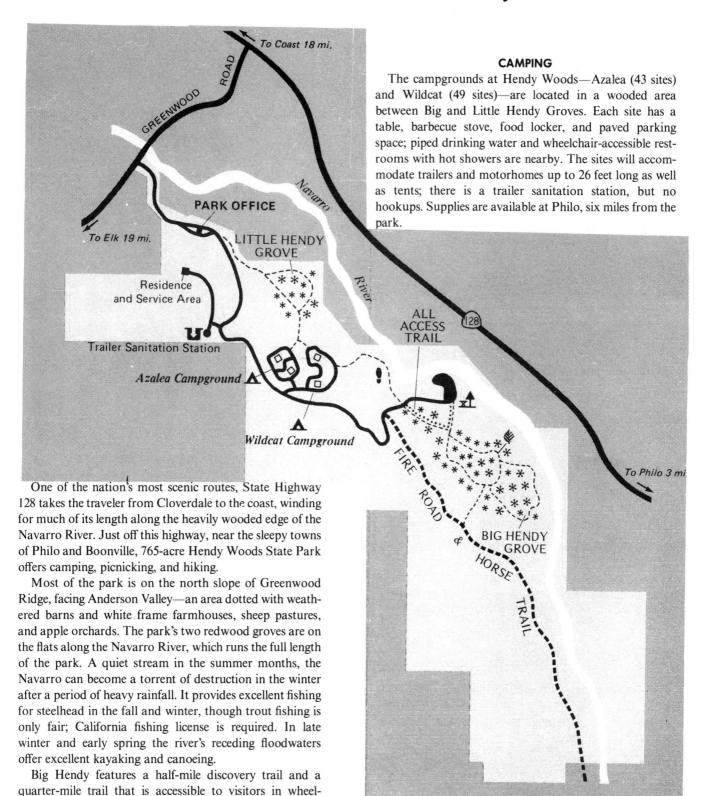

## CAMPING

The campgrounds at Hendy Woods—Azalea (43 sites) and Wildcat (49 sites)—are located in a wooded area between Big and Little Hendy Groves. Each site has a table, barbecue stove, food locker, and paved parking space; piped drinking water and wheelchair-accessible restrooms with hot showers are nearby. The sites will accommodate trailers and motorhomes up to 26 feet long as well as tents; there is a trailer sanitation station, but no hookups. Supplies are available at Philo, six miles from the park.

One of the nation's most scenic routes, State Highway 128 takes the traveler from Cloverdale to the coast, winding for much of its length along the heavily wooded edge of the Navarro River. Just off this highway, near the sleepy towns of Philo and Boonville, 765-acre Hendy Woods State Park offers camping, picnicking, and hiking.

Most of the park is on the north slope of Greenwood Ridge, facing Anderson Valley—an area dotted with weathered barns and white frame farmhouses, sheep pastures, and apple orchards. The park's two redwood groves are on the flats along the Navarro River, which runs the full length of the park. A quiet stream in the summer months, the Navarro can become a torrent of destruction in the winter after a period of heavy rainfall. It provides excellent fishing for steelhead in the fall and winter, though trout fishing is only fair; California fishing license is required. In late winter and early spring the river's receding floodwaters offer excellent kayaking and canoeing.

Big Hendy features a half-mile discovery trail and a quarter-mile trail that is accessible to visitors in wheelchairs. The two loops take you through a forest of towering redwoods, moss-covered stumps, and fallen trees. In the more open areas are a variety of plants associated with the redwood forest community—Woodwardia, sword, bracken, and deer ferns as well as huckleberry, redwood sorrel, and an occasional trillium.

Other trails include one that winds through Little Hendy Grove, another that leads from the campgrounds to the ranger station, and a trail that climbs through the more remote sections of the park.

Hendy Woods State Park
C/O Mendocino Dist. Hdqtrs.
P.O. Box 440
Mendocino, CA 95460
(707) 937-5804

# Henry Cowell Redwoods State Park

The forest at Henry Cowell Redwoods State Park looks much the same today as it did 200 years ago when Zayante Indians found shelter, water, and game here. Franciscan monks changed the Indians' way of life when they founded a mission at Santa Cruz in 1791. The Zayantes left the mountains, but the beauty and solitude of the forest that they once knew are still here to enjoy.

A notable feature of the 1,737-acre park is its coast redwood trees *Sequoia sempervirens.* Few other trees approach them in size, height, or botanical interest. Although the park has a tree 285 feet in height, taller coast redwoods grow farther north where heights of more than 350 feet have been measured.

The park's better examples of coast redwoods, in size and height, grow in Redwood Grove, the most visited site in the park. A self-guided nature path, the Redwood Grove Trail, loops through the grove. From the trail you can see a cross section of the park's plant life and view coast redwoods from excellent vantage points. The trail begins and ends at an exhibit shelter where an interpretation of the park, its history, and paintings of the park's wildflowers are on display.

A day-use area for individual and group picnicking is near the grove. The picnic grounds, which have tables, stoves, and parking spaces, overlook the San Lorenzo River from its east bank. The river is a popular spot for swimmers and fishermen, and when the winter runs of steelhead and silver salmon begin, many anglers visit the park to test their skill and tackle on these lively game fish. The fish congregate at the mouth of the river in Santa Cruz until winter rains raise the water level. Then they migrate upstream to spawn. Best fishing is usually from November to February.

The protection of coast redwood trees and other living things at Henry Cowell Redwoods State Park began in the 1860s with two men—Joseph Warren Welch and Henry Cowell Sr. Both men bought property of the Rancho Canada del Rincon, an original Mexican land grant of 1843, and shared similar views on protecting the virgin forest.

Part of Welch's land holdings included the Big Trees Grove—now called The Redwood Grove. Welch sold the grove and 80 acres to Santa Cruz County in 1930 for a local park. This land was combined with more than 1,500 acres gift-deeded to the State by Cowells' son, Samuel, in 1954.

## CAMPING

Eagle Creek, a small tributary of the San Lorenzo River, meanders along the northeast boundary of the park. Its source is a spring located east of Graham Hill Road. Paralleling the creek is a trail that passes close to the park's first overnight area, the 113-unit Eagle Creek Campground.

The campground may be reached from park headquarters by driving to the nearby town of Felton and turning right on Graham Hill Road. There are campsite spaces for trailers less than 36 feet long. Piped drinking water is provided close to all campsites and there are hot showers and flush toilets.

The campsites are located in a stand of ponderosa pine, the most unusual feature of the park. These trees are common to drier inland areas and at higher elevations, but at Henry Cowell they represent one of the two groves in the Santa Cruz Mountains. The foggy and wet weather found in the mountains favors the growth of Douglas fir, madrone, tanbark oak, and coast redwood.

Day Use Entrance

River

Trail

Graham Hill Road

Lockwood Lane

Redwood Grove

9

| Trail Chart | Miles |
|---|---|
| ...ampground to San Lorenzo River | |
| ...ia Powder Mill & Buckeye Trails | 1.4 |
| Pine Ridge & Rincon Trails | 1.9 |
| Pine & Ridge Trails to | |
| mouth of Eagle Creek | 1.5 |
| ...ia Eagle Creek Trail | 1.4 |
| | |
| ...ampground to Redwood Grove | |
| ...ia Eagle Creek & River Trails | 1.3 |
| ...ia Ridge and River Trails | 1.8 |
| | |
| ...icnic Area to Eagle Creek | |
| ...a River Trail | 0.7 |
| ...an Lorenzo River to Ridge Trail | 1.0 |
| ...ampground to Graham Hill Rd. | |
| ...a Powder Mill Trail | 1.5 |
| ...ampground to Water Tank | |
| ...a Pine Trail | 0.4 |
| ...ater Tank to Eagle Creek | |
| ...a Pine Trail | 0.9 |

FIRE RD.

N. Powder Mill Trail

Campground Entrance

Pipe

PIPE

Eagle Creek

LINE

Ox Road Trail

P

Observation Deck
Water Tank
(view of Santa Cruz)

Trail

Graham

Powder

Mill

SERVICE

Ridge

Powder

Mill

Garden of Eden

ROAD

Rincon

San Lorenzo

Trail

Trail

S.P. R.R.

Cathedral Redwoods

Buckeye

Very Steep Trail

ROAD

Big Rock Hole

River

Rincon

Trail

P

9

## HIKING

A semi-wilderness area lies south and west of the campground. This area may be reached by one of three hiking and riding trails that pass through the campground. A short and easy hike by way of the North Powder Mill Trail or Pine Trail will take you to the water tank where a panoramic view of the park and Santa Cruz is possible on clear days. A concrete observation platform with a wooden railing allows a better view of the area.

Fifteen miles of trail have opened all areas of the park to the hiker and horseback rider. The Rincon Trail, which intersects with the Ridge Trail midway through the park, originates from a parking lot alongside State Highway 9 at the park's south end. It passes by the Cathedral Redwoods, a ring of trees growing from a single base.

Henry Cowell Redwoods State Park
101 N. Big Trees Park Road
Felton, CA 95018
(408) 335-4598

# Humboldt Redwoods State Park

Great forests of redwood have existed on the planet for someting like 160 million years. Due to climatic and geologic change they have been retreating and disappearing, and yet, since the time of the dinosaur—long before the coming of mankind—redwoods have managed to survive and in some places even to prosper. Today in the Eel River Basin of Northern California, within the fifty-thousand-acre Humboldt Redwoods State Park, magnificent forests of primeval coast redwood, *Sequoia sempervirens,* are being carefully and thoughtfully protected. Here, amid 2,000-year-old trees in a 20-million-year-old forest, one can sense the long, slow, venerable yet joyous procession of life on Earth.

In the spring, countless wildflowers bring color and variety to the forest floor. Dogwoods and occasional rhododendrons or azaleas are perhaps the most spectacular, but a surprising variety of smaller blossoms are found throughout the forest. The clover-like oxalis, or redwood sorrel, opens its lavender-pink blossoms and is joined by sugar scoops, fairy lanterns, glade anemone, calypso—the delicate redwood orchid—and many others.

Following the south fork of the Eel River, the spectacular 33-mile-long Avenue of the Giants Parkway, now bypassed by U.S. 101, has turnouts and parking areas from which short loop trails reach out into the forest. Following the river, the road passes through occasional open, sun-filled meadows with views of distant mountain slopes, then goes back into colonnades of trees where the air is cool and fragrant and long beams of sunlight slant down through the green foliage.

On the Dyerville Flats just across the river from the Rockefeller Forest, Founder's Grove is dedicated to the early leaders of the Save-the-Redwoods League. A gentle, and very scenic, self-guiding nature trail describes some interesting aspects of redwood and other plant life in what may well be the world's most beautiful and impressive forest area.

Another outstanding area is across the river in the more extensive Rockefeller Forest. Hiking trails and a park road make it easy for visitors to see some of the highlights of this forest, including the awe-inspiring Tall Tree and the Giant and Flatiron trees.

Picnic areas have been developed in some of the park's most delightful locations. Williams Grove, with 90 tables and some 56 camp stoves, is the largest picnic area. Other picnic areas are located in the F.K. Lane Memorial Grove, the Garden Clubs of America Grove, and the California Federation of Women's Clubs Grove, where the beautiful Hearthstone Fireplace is also located.

## HISTORY

The Sinkyone Indians who lived in this region for thousands of years had relatively little impact on the old redwood groves, but during the 1850s and '60s the first white settlers began to cut some redwood trees to develop pasture land for this stock. Later, as the virtues of redwood lumber became known, and as roads and railways were developed into the redwood country, lumbering became an important industry, and during the 1880s and '90s land that had been sold by the government for as little as $1.25 an acre began to be highly prized as timberland.

But many people felt that the best of the ancient groves were too unusual, too beautiful, too valuable to be cut down simply for lumber. Formed in 1918, the Save-the-Redwoods League has succeeded in preserving within the State Park System more than a hundred thousand acres of redwood forest land, roughly half of it in Humboldt Redwoods State Park.

However, the floods of 1955 and 1964 made it painfully clear that majestic old groves on the alluvial flats cannot be saved without controlling complete watersheds. Hundreds of giant trees that had been considered safe were lost as Bull Creek left its well-established channel and became a 300-foot-wide, gravel-filled destroyer. With considerable help from the Save-the-Redwoods League, the Department of Parks and Recreation has now acquired almost all of the Bull Creek watershed, badly damaged by fire after logging, and begun the long and difficult task of restoration.

## CAMPING

Because of the high fire hazard, camping is permitted only in established sites. Hikers and bicyclists can use the primitive Marin Garden Club Grove area (see map).

At Burlington, near the park headquarters, there are 58 family campsites, each with a table, stove, and food locker. Piped drinking water is available here, as it is in all of the developed areas of the park, and combination buildings with restrooms, hot showers, and laundry tubs are located within easy access of all campsites. During the summer season, evening campfire programs are held here and at Hidden Springs Campground with group entertainment and informal interpretive talks.

The 155 family campsites at Hidden Springs have the same facilities as those in the Burlington area. The 32 sites at Albee Creek are all complete with table, stove, and food locker; restrooms are nearby.

Family campsites will accommodate trailers up to 24 feet long and motorhomes up to 30 feet long; although hookups are not provided, there is a trailer sanitation station at Williams Grove.

Backpackers can enjoy six trail camps in Humboldt Redwoods State Park. Johnson Camp, once a tie camp (where railroad ties were made) has four rustic cabins that are still standing and can be used for an overnight stay. Hanson Ridge Camp offers an outstanding view of the Bull Creek drainage and surrounding area. A hike to Indian Orchard Camp will reward the explorer with a stay in an apple orchard planted by a settler.

Whiskey Flat was once the setting for at least one moonshine still. Today, it offers a cool respite under a remote grove of redwoods. Bull Creek Camp is right along the upper stretch of Bull Creek and is a good area for spotting wildlife. Grasshopper Camp is just below Grasshopper Peak, the highest point in the park (3,379 feet) and the site of a fire lookout tower.

# Humboldt Redwoods State Park

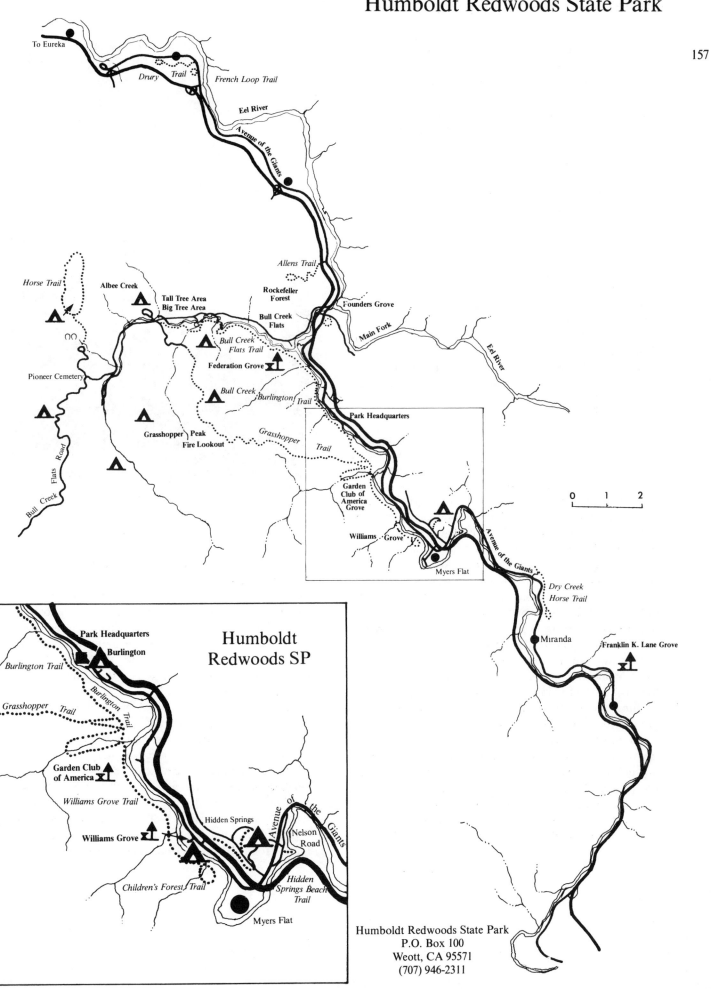

## Humboldt Redwoods SP

Humboldt Redwoods State Park
P.O. Box 100
Weott, CA 95571
(707) 946-2311

# Jedediah Smith Redwoods State Park

Jedediah Smith Redwoods State Park lies at the confluence of the Smith River and Mill Creek on U.S. 199, less than twelve miles north of Crescent City. It is the northernmost of the redwood parks which dot the California coast from Monterey County to the Oregon border. The park offers camping, picnicking, fishing, hiking trails, and solitude. It also offers a wide variety of forest types, including many of the more impressive forest trees that share this northwestern California landscape with *sequoia sempervirens*—the coast redwood.

It is a most attractive setting—white, fast-running water with many deep pools; primeval forests with a lush undergrowth of rhododendron, western redwood sorrel, azalea, banks of ferns on giant fallen trees, huckleberry, salmonberry, salal, and oxalis; and a streamside habitat which is the home of a wide variety of birds.

In contrast to the cool, damp, fogbound summers along the coast just a few miles to the west, summer days in this park are usually warm and sunny. On the other hand, winters are rainy—a hundred inches of rain during the season is not uncommon—and the Smith River has been known to rise twenty feet in twenty-four hours during a storm.

*Stout Grove*

### MEMORIAL GROVES

In 1929 the Frank D. Stout Memorial Grove was presented to the state, and the Webber tract was purchased in 1931. The 75-acre Musick Tract came in 1932 to make Hiouchi Redwoods State Park, named for the Indian tribes native to the area. The Mill Creek redwoods area of 6,708 acres was purchased in 1944 through donations to the Save-the-Redwoods League, and the park name changed to Mill Creek Redwoods State Park. With another expansion, the park was again renamed, this time for Jedediah Smith, the first white man to see this area.

There are now eighteen memorial groves in the park. Stout Memorial Grove contains the park's largest known tree, which is 20 feet in diameter and 340 feet high. Half of the funds for the 5,000-acre National Tribute Grove, which includes the Daughters of the American Revolution unit of about 500 acres, were contributed through the Save-the-Redwoods League by thousands of citizens and national organizations such as the Garden Club of America. This grove's magnificent virgin redwoods, combined with hemlock, fir, cedar, tan oak, and madrone, stand in majestic silent tribute to those who served the cause of freedom in the armed forces of the United States during World War II.

### JEDEDIAH STRONG SMITH

Smith, referred to as the Bible-Toter, was the first white man to cross directly overland from the Mississippi to the Pacific. It is claimed that he was the first to discover the South Pass in the Rocky Mountain divide, through which most of the subsequent overland emigration to Oregon and California was to flow, and the first to traverse the West Coast by land from San Diego past the Columbia River, almost to the Canadian border.

The Smith River is also named for this intrepid explorer, who crossed it in the summer of 1828 while leading the first party of white men through what is now Del Norte County. Smith led many parties of fur trappers to the West before he was killed by Comanche Indians in 1831, but few white men came to the area until 1849, when the Gold Rush began. The sudden influx of miners produced friction with the Tolowa Indians who lived along the Smith River, and trouble continued until 1869 when the Indians were remove to the Hoopa Reservation on the Klamath River.

# Jedediah Smith Redwoods State Park

## NATURAL HISTORY

Much of the park is very rugged, and is best seen from the foot trails which lace the area. The park contains an unusually wide variety of trees and shrubs, with both coastal and interior species represented. Ponderosa pine and incense cedar occur here in small numbers, with many other inland and upland species.

Bear are seen occasionally, as are deer, gray squirrel, Douglas squirrel, redwood chipmunk, and other small mammals. Raccoons are numerous, as many campers find to their sorrow when food is left on camp tables at night. A rare treat is the sight of river otter playing in the riffles of the river, and patient observers may be rewarded by the sight of beaver working in some of the deep pools.

## CAMPING

Jedediah Smith is a busy park both summer and winter. When summer vacationers leave, the fishermen move in to take advantage of the fine salmon and steelhead fishing—catches of thirty-pound salmon and twenty-pound steelhead are not uncommon. Fly-fishing for trout is usually good from late August until the rains begin, while the best fishing for winter salmon and steelhead is from October to February.

The park has 107 family campsites, each with table, stove, and cupboard, plus nearby restrooms with hot showers and laundry facilities. While there are no trailer hookups, the park has a trailer sanitation station; the campsites will accommodate trailers up to 30 feet long. In addition to fishing, swimming, sunbathing, and hiking, summer campers will enjoy the park's interpretive program.

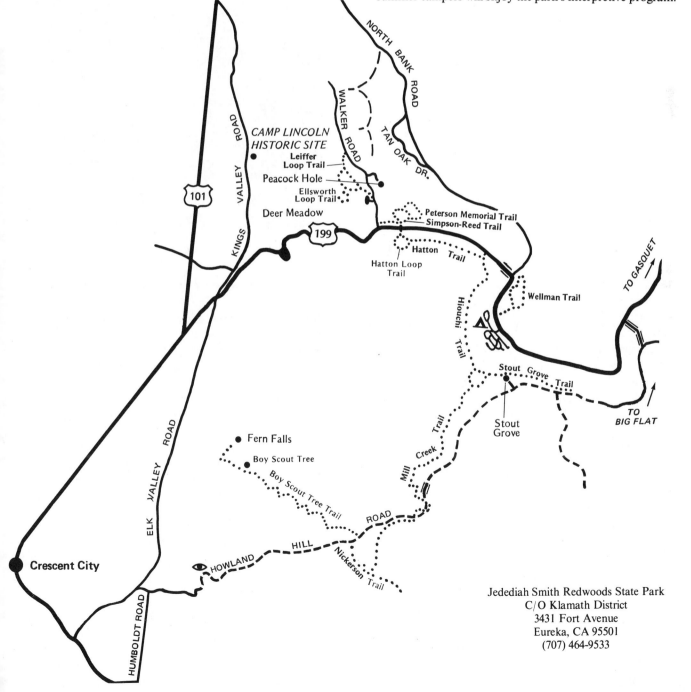

Jedediah Smith Redwoods State Park
C/O Klamath District
3431 Fort Avenue
Eureka, CA 95501
(707) 464-9533

# Mailliard Redwoods SR/Montgomery Woods SR

Mailliard Redwoods State Reserve is a quiet, out-of-the way locale, ideal for a picnic or walk in the redwoods. The Reserve was named for conservationist John Ward Mailliard, Jr., member of a ranching family whose members have large holdings nearby.

Virgin redwoods grow along a creek which winds along with Fish Rock Road. Second-growth redwoods are on the upper slopes. Douglas fir, lowland fir and tan oak are also found in the Reserve. The creek which runs through the park is the headwaters of the Garcia River. Salmon and steelhead spawn in this river. Fishing is prohibited.

The isolated Reserve is hot and dry during the summer months. October boasts an Indian summer. Winter months are wet, with an average rainfall of 34 inches.

The only development at Mailliard is a picnic table. Five vehicles can park in the small lot.

The Reserve is located 3½ miles south of Highway 128 on Fish Rock Road.

*Montgomery Woods*

### MONTGOMERY WOODS STATE RESERVE

With the help of the Save-the-Redwoods League, the Reserve has grown from the nine acres donated by Robert Orr in 1945 to its present size of 1,142 acres. Donations for the memorial groves through the League enabled the state to purchase the Reserve from private owners before the trees were logged.

A trail follows the course of Montgomery Creek, connecting five of the Reserve's memorial groves, to give you a good view of its small but impressive virgin stand of coast redwood, *Sequoia sempervirens.* This stand is a "climax forest" where a limited number of acid-soil-tolerant plants live in a stable environment. Among them are ferns, oxalis (redwood sorrel), huckleberry, poison-oak, wild iris, trillium, and miner's lettuce.

The trail is approximately two miles (three kilometers) long and takes about an hour to walk.

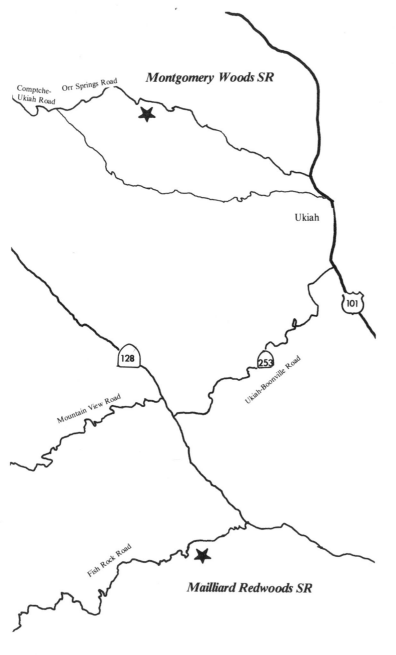

Mailliard Redwoods State Reserve
C/O Mendocino Dist. Hdqtrs.
P.O. Box 440
Mendocino, CA 95460
(707) 937-5804

In the rugged terrain of a deep canyon between Skyline and Butano Ridges, Portola State Park offers solitude and relaxation just over the hill from the Bay Area.

The park is a natural basin forested with coast redwoods. Ferns and dense patches of California huckleberry cover the forest floor. Douglas fir and coast live oak thrive on the park's upper ridges and south-facing slopes.

The park's ten miles of hiking trails extend an invitation to observe the parks diverse natural scenes. Some trails lead upward through the redwoods into the chaparral; others follow streams and a forest floor of azaleas, fern and oxalis.

Peters Creek and Pescadero Creek flow in earth faults; frequent oil slicks in the streams give evidence of ancient deposits. Clam shells and other marine fossil deposits indicate that the ocean once covered the area.

The park is open all year. There's not much change in the average summer or winter temperatures—in summer, highs are usually in the mid-70s with cool, foggy nights. The winter brings the rainy season, with daytime temperatures around 50 degrees.

### HISTORY

In 1769, noted Spanish explorer Don Gaspar de Portola led an expedition through present-day San Mateo County in search of Monterey Bay, discovered in 1602 by Sebastian Vizcaino. Instead, they found a new anchorage, the huge bay later named San Francisco.

Lumbermen were the original settlers of the Santa Cruz Mountains, in the 1860s; stumps still showing the notches cut for loggers' springboards are evidence of their activities. Many larger trees remained untouched because they were unsuitable for cutting by lumber standards of that time.

Chris Iverson, believed to have been a Pony Express rider, acquired 80 acres on Pescadero Creek in 1868. He sold this property to a lumber company and bought a 40-acre parcel where he built a cabin that still stands. The Islam Shrine used the property from 1924 to 1945, when the state purchased the approximately 1,700 acres.

### CAMPING

The park has 52 developed family campsites, each with table and stove; restrooms with hot showers are nearby. Some campsites will accommodate trailers up to 21 feet long or motorhomes up to 27 feet, but there are no hookups.

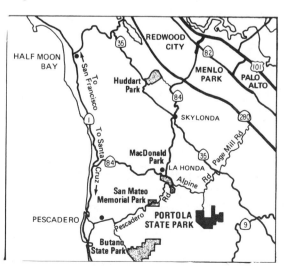

Portola State Park
Star Route 2
La Honda, CA 94029
(415) 948-9098

# Prairie Creek Redwoods State Park

*Roosevelt Elk*

The "prairie" is a large meadowland bordering U.S. 101. Here, opposite Elk Prairie Campground, the redwoods give way to open grasslands where Roosevelt elk roam. The elk may also be glimpsed in the meadows above Gold Bluffs Beach.

Magnificent stands of virgin redwood and lush fern canyons highlight the park. Dense summer fogs and about one hundred inches of yearly rainfall support a forest understory as lush as that of a tropical rainforest. Fern Canyon is probably the most spectacular of the many "fern canyons" found in the coast redwood belt. Lady, sword, bracken, and licorice ferns cover the walls of the canyon. A trail follows the white pebbly floor of the canyon along Home Creek. Other trails lead to groves of the world's tallest trees.

**CAMPING**

There are two developed family campgrounds in the park: Elk Prairie Campground with 75 sites, and Gold Bluffs Beach Campground with 25 sites. Each site has a cupboard, table, and stove; piped water and restrooms with flush toilets and hot showers are nearby. Elk Prairie will accommodate trailers up to 24 feet long or motorhomes up to 27 feet, though there are no hookups.

To drive to Gold Bluffs Beach, you must take Davison Road, which intersects Highway 101 3.6 miles (5.8 km.) south of park headquarters. This unpaved road is maintained by the county, which prohibits vehicles over twenty feet long or seven feet wide, or weighing over 3 tons. The road is often closed during the rainy season.

Separate camps for hikers and bicyclists are adjacent to both campgrounds, and there is also a backpackers' camp near Butler Creek, a 7.5-mile (12.1 km.) hike along West Ridge and Butler Creek Trails from Highway 101.

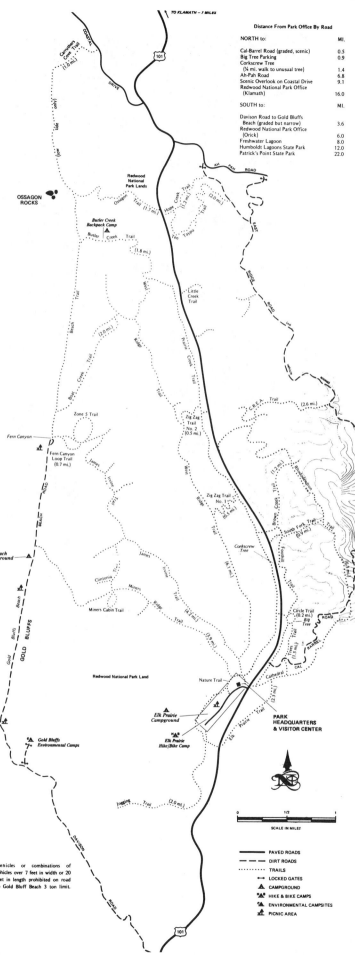

## HIKING

The Rhododendron, Clintonia, and California Real Estate Association Trails pass by stands of old-growth redwood. Streamside habitats are explored by Ten Taypo, Hope Creek, and Brown's Creek trails. The James Irvine Trail, which was once a supply route to the Gold Bluffs mining camp, leads from park headquarters through a forest of redwood, Sitka spruce, and Douglas fir to Fern Canyon.

You may see elk browsing as you hike the Elk Prairie or Cathedral Trees Trails. Ossagon Trail leads through a redwood and alder forest to the open, grassy area above Gold Bluffs. Miner's Ridge Trail connects park headquarters the beach campground.

The Big Tree Circle Trail lets you view one of Prairie Creek's largest redwoods, and as you take the Five-Minute Nature Loop around the visitor center you will see a hollowed-out "Chimney Tree," partly boarded up, where a family lived during the 1930s.

## THE REVELATION TRAIL

Feel the rough bark of a redwood and compare it to the smoother covering of a tanoak. Smell the aromatic leaves of the California bay and listen to the splash of a stream. The Revelation Trail, with wood-and-rope guide rails is designed to take the blind or disabled visitor into the midst of the forest. The trail is one-third of a mile long and has seventeen stops. Tape players are available in the visitor center bookstore.

## Azalea State Reserve

The creamy blossoms of the Western Azalea come into full flower around Memorial Day. The peak of bloom varies a few weeks each year, depending upon weather.

Hiking trails lead under the blossoms hanging overhead. East Trail offers an overlook of the reserve. Rangers from nearby Prairie Creek State Park sometimes lead nature hikes through the reserve.

The park has restrooms and a picnic area.

The Reserve is located a few miles north of the town of Arcata and can be reached via North Bank Road either from U.S. 101 or U.S. 199.

Prairie Creek Redwoods State Park
Orick, CA 95555
(707) 488-2171

# Richardson Grove State Park

Soon after you enter Humboldt County from the south on Highway 101, you drive into a cool, dark, verdant forest of towering coastal redwood trees. This is Richardson Grove, named in honor of the state's 25th governor, Friend W. Richardson.

The park's tranquil setting is one of shadows and semi-darkness. Even when the sun is at its zenith only a fraction of the light filters through the closely growing trees and their protective branches. Sounds are shut out by the profusion of plant life, and the wind is tempered by the tall trees. The forest stillness is not easily forgotten.

Highway 101 traverses the park from north to south, following the South Fork of the Eel River and passing close to the area's tallest trees. Over the past twelve hundred years, the river has deposited more than eleven feet of new soil, and it is here on the river flats in soil of this kind that coast redwoods, *Sequoia sempervirens,* grow best.

Richardson Grove is a year-round park with more than half a million visitors annually. It is most popular during the summer when the weather is mild and warm. An interpretive program is offered to acquaint visitors with the park's history and its animal and plant life. A schedule of events is posted at park headquarters and on bulletin boards throughout the park. An interpretive display telling the story of the coast redwods and their environment is on Highway 101 directly across from Richardson Grove Lodge.

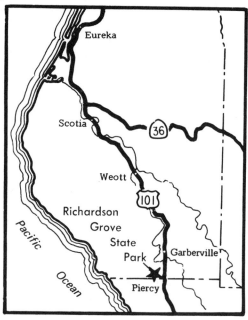

it should be noted that due to high water during the rainy season the footbridge at the north end of Toumey Trail is kept in place only from June to September.

There is a picnic area with 15 tables and stoves between the highway and the river. A trail leads to the river and a beach where sunning and swimming are popular activities. There is no lifeguard on duty.

## HIKING

The park area can be explored by a widely varied system of trails ranging from short, gentle, self-guided nature walks to more ambitious trails that climb the nearby ridges and reach scenic vantage points. The shorter trails generally remain within the cool, shaded redwood groves. There are some nearby sunny areas where a wide variety of plant and animal life can be observed. The Lookout and Toumey Trails are among the longer and more scenic walks, though

## CAMPING

There are 169 campsites in the park's three campgrounds, each with a cupboard, tale, and stove. Piped drinking water and combination buildings with hot showers are nearby.

Winter runs of silver and king salmon and steelhead trout draw many fishermen to the park. The fishing is good during the rainy season. In the summer, when the water is low, fishing is a popular activity for children.

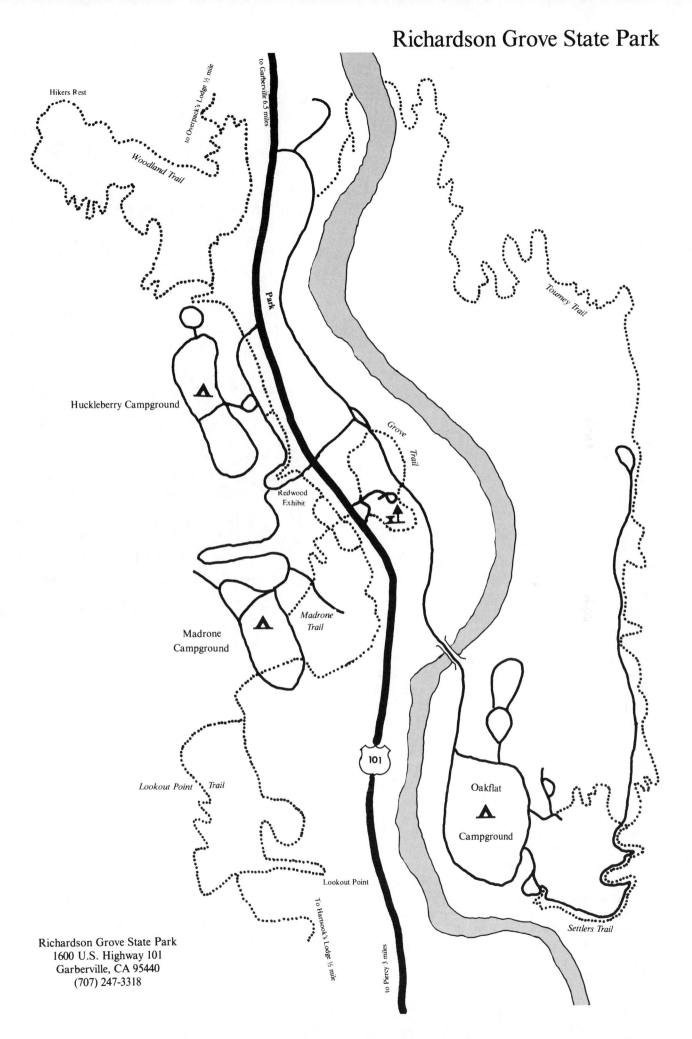

# Richardson Grove State Park

165

Hikers Rest

Woodland Trail

to Overpack's Lodge ½ mile

to Garberville 6.5 miles

Park

Toumey Trail

Huckleberry Campground

Grove Trail

Redwood Exhibit

Madrone Trail

Madrone Campground

101

Lookout Point Trail

Oakflat Campground

Lookout Point

Settlers Trail

To Hartsook's Lodge ½ mile

to Piercy 3 miles

Richardson Grove State Park
1600 U.S. Highway 101
Garberville, CA 95440
(707) 247-3318

# Samuel B. Taylor State Park

Samuel P. Taylor State Park is located just north of San Francisco in the steep, rolling hills of central Marin County.

The park, with its 2,600 acres of beautifully wooded countryside, is within easy driving range of some of northern California's most dramatic outdoor scenery. It is just seven miles east of the spectacular Point Reyes National Seashore, and is also close to Mount Tamalpais State Park and Muir Woods National Monument.

The park's landscape includes some sharp contrasts. Along the canyon bottoms and up the north-facing slopes there are cool, shaded, fern-filled groves of coast redwoods where a wonderful variety of flowers is found during the spring and summer. Among the lush green ground covers that thrive in this environment is the striking elk clover, with immense green leaves that drape low over the stream banks and, in early summer, huge clusters of cream-colored blossoms.

Just a short distance away, on the canyon's dry north side, is a more open grassland area where oak, tanoak, madrone, and other hardwoods are the dominant trees.

Black-tailed deer are the most common large animal in the park, and of course there are countless squirrels and other small animals in residence. Raccoons, striped and spotted skunks, and the gray fox are less often seen, while badgers and bobcats are seen only occasionally.

In the winter, silver salmon and steelhead trout migrate up Paper Mill Creek to spawn, and during the regular season (May to November) fishing is allowed along the creek and in the nearby lakes. The lakes are outside the park on Marin Municipal Water District land, and both a state fishing license and a special permit from the Water District are required for fishing in them.

### HISTORY

In 1849, upon the news of the California gold discovery, Samuel Penfield Taylor and a group of adventurous young friends purchased and fitted out an old schooner and set sail for California from Boston Harbor. Ten months and several repair stops later, the little schooner finally arrived in San Francisco.

After a flurry of business transactions in San Francisco, Taylor joined his friends in the gold country. In August 1852, he shipped 6,173 pennyweight of gold dust to his San Francisco bankers Curtis, Perry and Ward. The dust netted him $5,691.99 and gave him his start in California.

Back in San Francisco, Taylor entered the lumber business and shortly afterward purchased 100 acres of timberland along what is now Paper Mill Creek within the area of the present State Park. Timber was plentiful, but Taylor installed a paper-making process that utilized only scrap paper and rags gathered from San Francisco and other coastal towns. The mill produced newsprint for the dailies in San Francisco, fine paper for use as election ballots and other official documents, and square-bottomed paper bags, which were quite a novelty at the time.

*Taylor's paper mill produced newsprint for San Francisco's papers.*

Thirty thousand kegs of blasting powder were manufactured by a powder mill that Taylor built and operated at another site in the canyon. The mill was an extremely profitable venture at first but Taylor's dream of becoming a major black-powder supplier ended with a violent explosion in November 1874. The mill never reopened.

A little town with about 100 families sprang up around Taylor's paper mill. This was one of the first areas in the United States to offer outdoor camping as a recreational pursuit. Access to the area remained difficult until 1874, when a narrow-gauge railroad was built through the canyon to serve the Point Reyes-Tomales Bay area. In the same year, Taylor built a resort hotel beside the new railroad, and nearby he opened Camp Taylor. During the late '70s and early '80s Taylorville was one of California's most popular and well-known weekend recreation areas.

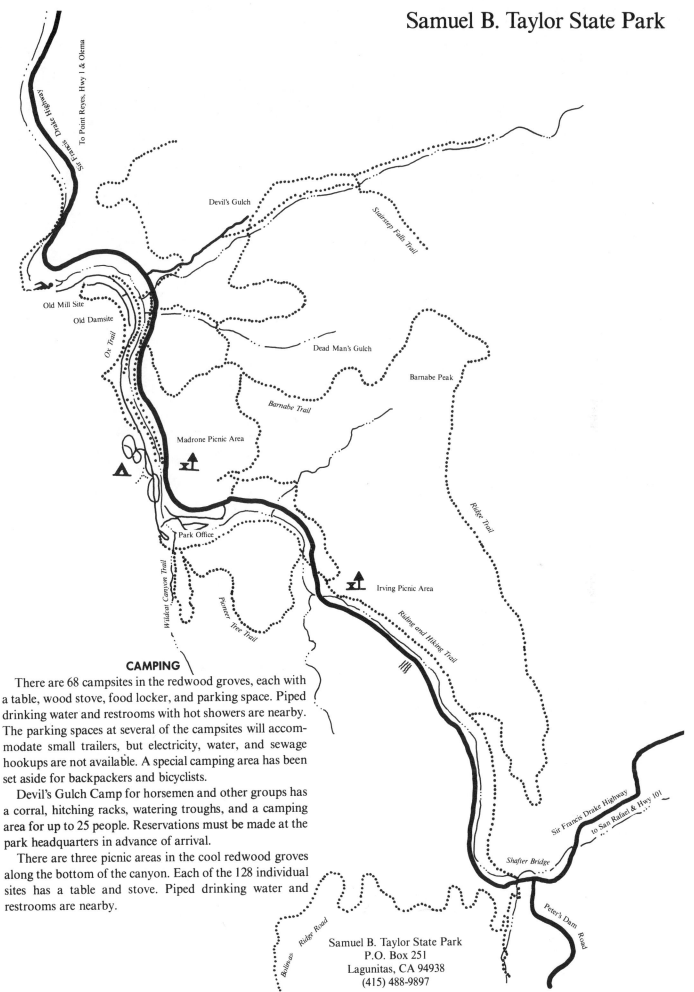

To Point Reyes, Hwy 1 & Olema

Sir Francis Drake Highway

Devil's Gulch

Stairstep Falls Trail

Old Mill Site

Old Damsite

Ox Trail

Dead Man's Gulch

Barnabe Peak

Barnabe Trail

Madrone Picnic Area

Ridge Trail

Park Office

Irving Picnic Area

Wildcat Canyon Trail

Pioneer Tree Trail

Riding and Hiking Trail

## CAMPING

There are 68 campsites in the redwood groves, each with a table, wood stove, food locker, and parking space. Piped drinking water and restrooms with hot showers are nearby. The parking spaces at several of the campsites will accommodate small trailers, but electricity, water, and sewage hookups are not available. A special camping area has been set aside for backpackers and bicyclists.

Devil's Gulch Camp for horsemen and other groups has a corral, hitching racks, watering troughs, and a camping area for up to 25 people. Reservations must be made at the park headquarters in advance of arrival.

There are three picnic areas in the cool redwood groves along the bottom of the canyon. Each of the 128 individual sites has a table and stove. Piped drinking water and restrooms are nearby.

Sir Francis Drake Highway

to San Rafael & Hwy 101

Shafter Bridge

Peter's Dam Road

Bolinas Ridge Road

Samuel B. Taylor State Park
P.O. Box 251
Lagunitas, CA 94938
(415) 488-9897

# Smithe Redwoods SR/Admiral William Standley SR

*Admiral William H. Standley SRA*

## Smithe Redwoods State Reserve

Smithe Redwoods State Reserve, located about four miles north of Leggett on Highway 101, contains a fine stand of old-growth redwoods and a 60-foot waterfall. Trails lead to the waterfall and to the Eel River.

The park, named for Frank and Bess Smithe, who contributed the land, is one of the first large redwood groves one encounters in northern Mendocino County along the Redwood Highway. The 600-acre Reserve offers picnicking and swimming. Its proximity to the river make it a popular rest stop for Highway 101 travelers.

## Admiral William H. Standley State Recreation Area

Admiral William H. Standley State Recreation Area is a small, lovely grove of redwoods traversed by the South Fork of the Eel River. The grove was named for a naval officer born in the county.

The 45 acre park is located about 14 miles west of Laytonville on Branscomb Road. There are no developed facilities at the grove, but it is open to picnicking and hiking.

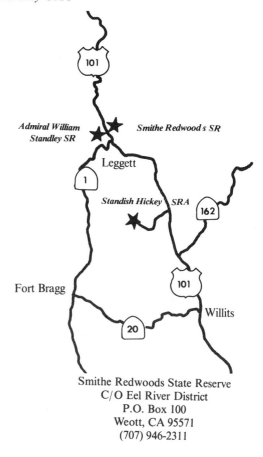

Smithe Redwoods State Reserve
C/O Eel River District
P.O. Box 100
Weott, CA 95571
(707) 946-2311

# Standish Hickey State Recreation Area

Standish-Hickey State Recreation Area is named after Edward Hickey, who gave the first 40 acres of the recreation site to the state, and A.M. Standish, a direct descendant of Captain Miles Standish who came to Plymouth, Massachusetts on the Mayflower in 1620, who also donated acreage. The park offers camping, picnicking, hiking, swimming, and fishing on the south fork of the Eel River which winds through the area for almost two miles.

One park feature is the Captain Miles Standish tree. This redwood is the only remaining tree of its size here and is typical of the kind of forest that existed before logging took place. Scarred by fire and saw cuts, the tree is 225 feet tall, 13 feet in diameter, and about 40 feet in circumference. Estimated age is 1,200 years.

There are several redwood groves in the recreation area, all second growth. Ferns include sword, woodwardia, lady, western bracken, gold-back maindenhair and licorice. Common wildflowers are Indian pink, redwood sorrel, shooting star, lupine and buttercup.

Steelhead and salmon spawn in the Eel River and its tributaries in the fall and winter. This is when fishing is at its best.

Because of heavy rainfall, the Eel River floods regularly so the river bottom and the swimming holes change each year. Swimming is good wherever the terrain is flat enough to allow access to the river. The river is 15 to 20 feet deep at the holes.

### HIKING

The area lies within the canyon of the South Fork of the Eel River and the trails are steep; hikers should be in good condition.

Trails include the half-mile trail to the swimming hole, the 2.1-mile Big Tree Loop Trail, the 4.7-mile Mill Creek Loop Trail which is an extension of the Big Tree Trail, and the 3-mile Lookout Point Trail.

### CAMPING

Standish-Hickey contains three campgrounds—Rock Creek, Hickey, and Redwood—each with 35, 64, and 63 campsites respectively. Each campsite has a stove, cupboard, and table; restrooms with hot showers are nearby. Reservations are advisable.

Redwood Campground is closed in winter because the bridge is removed to prevent it from being washed out by the Eel River. Trailers and motorhomes are not allowed in this campground because of the steep, winding access roads, but Rock Creek and Hickey Campground will accommodate these larger vehicles. No hookups. One campground is kept open all year.

Standish-Hickey State Recreation Area
P.O. Box 208
Leggett, CA 95455
(707) 925-6482

# Inland Mountains

Evergreen forests, sparkling streams and lakes, and magnificent vistas make the state parks in California's inland mountains among the most popular. The foothills, like the coast Range, are covered with oak, madrone, chaparral, and grassland; at higher elevations are found pine, spruce, fir, cedar, and, at Calaveras Big Trees State Park, the gigantic Sierra redwood, *Sequoia-dendron giganteum.*

Some parks at higher elevations are open in winter for snow play, snowshoeing, or cross-country skiing. At Calaveras Big Trees and the parks on Lake Tahoe, regular winter hikes are offered, and winter camping is available at McArthur-Burney Falls Memorial and Sugar Pine Point SPs and Tahoe SRA.

Several parks in this region have exhibits telling the story of the Gold Rush.

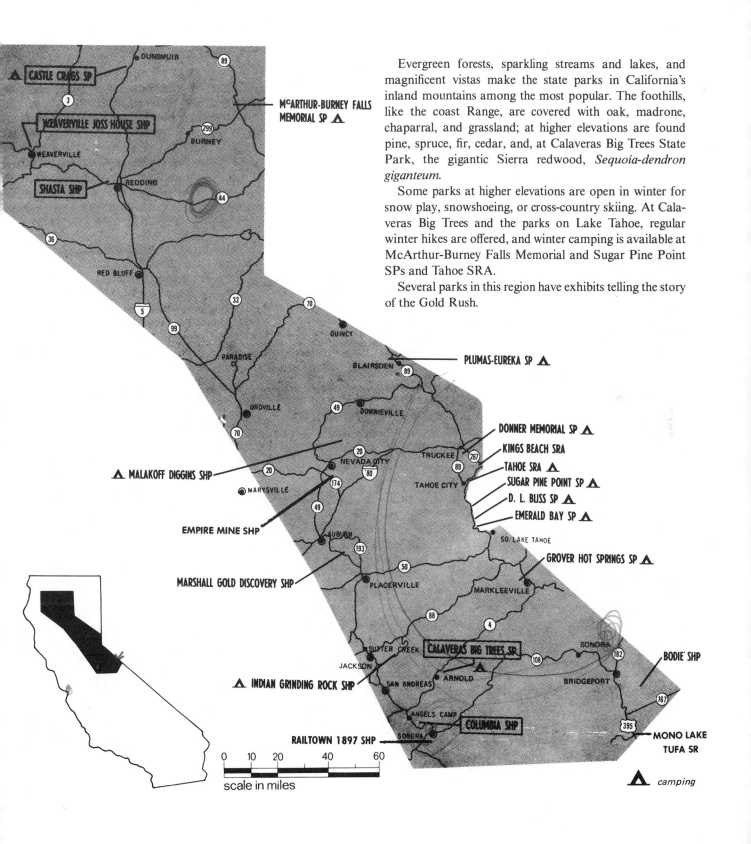

CASTLE CRAGS SP
DUNSMUIR
McARTHUR-BURNEY FALLS MEMORIAL SP
WEAVERVILLE JOSS HOUSE SHP
BURNEY
WEAVERVILLE
SHASTA SHP
REDDING
RED BLUFF
QUINCY
PARADISE
PLUMAS-EUREKA SP
BLAIRSDEN
OROVILLE
DOWNIEVILLE
DONNER MEMORIAL SP
MALAKOFF DIGGINS SHP
NEVADA CITY
TRUCKEE
KINGS BEACH SRA
TAHOE SRA
TAHOE CITY
SUGAR PINE POINT SP
D. L. BLISS SP
MARYSVILLE
EMERALD BAY SP
EMPIRE MINE SHP
AUBURN
SO. LAKE TAHOE
GROVER HOT SPRINGS SP
MARSHALL GOLD DISCOVERY SHP
PLACERVILLE
MARKLEEVILLE
SUTTER CREEK
CALAVERAS BIG TREES SP
SONORA
BODIE SHP
JACKSON
INDIAN GRINDING ROCK SHP
SAN ANDREAS
ARNOLD
BRIDGEPORT
ANGELS CAMP
COLUMBIA SHP
RAILTOWN 1897 SHP
SONORA
MONO LAKE TUFA SR

0  10  20  40  60
scale in miles

▲ *camping*

# Bodie State Historic Park

This is Bodie—or rather the remains of Bodie. Only about five percent of the buildings it contained in its 1880 heyday still remain: it stands just as time, fire, and the elements have left it—a genuine California gold-mining ghost town. Designated a State Historic Park in 1962, it is now maintained in a state of "arrested decay."

Bodie was named after Waterman S. Body, who discovered gold here in 1859. The change in spelling has often been attributed to an illiterate sign painter, but was a deliberate change by the citizenry to insure proper pronunciation of the town's name.

Bodie rose to prominence with the decline of mining along the western slope of the Sierra Nevada. Prospectors crossing the eastern slope to "see the elephant"—search for gold—in 1858 discovered what was to be the Comstock Lode at Virginia City, and started the wild rush to the high desert country.

A museum is open in summer and sometimes on weekends in spring and fall. Guided tours are given of the Standard Mill (a gold stamp mill) which is otherwise closed to the public. On a hillside nearby there is an old cemetery, which is reached by a trail from the town. Rangers are at Bodie all year, but the road is not plowed; much of winter the park is accessible only by snowmobiles or skis.

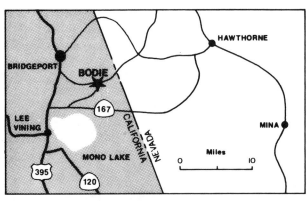

Bodie State Historic Park is best visited during the summer. At other times the weather is unpredictable, and off-season visitors are cautioned to check at Bridgeport, Mono County seat, for road and weather conditions before making the trip. The park is on Bodie Road 13 miles east of its junction with State Highway 395 seven miles south of Bridgeport.

When you take your walk through old Bodie, please stay on the streets and sidewalks—most of the buildings are unsafe. Do not enter hazardous areas posted to prohibit public entry. Also, *do not smoke;* fire is an everpresent danger here.

*"Goodbye God, I'm going to Bodie,"* prospectors used to say.

Bodie State Historic Park
P.O. Box 515
Bridgeport, CA 93517
Sierra Dist.: (916) 525-7232

# Calaveras Big Trees State Park

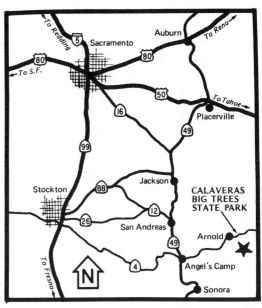

The giant sequoia groves in Calaveras Big Trees State Park offer a rare opportunity to visit a truly ancient forest—one in which giant sequoias, the largest living things on Earth, still play their age-old role. Experts at survival both as individuals and as a species, these gigantic redwood trees come down to us from out of the Mesozoic Era—the age of dinosaurs. They are, in effect, holdovers from a time of giants.

The park is located at middle elevation (four to five thousand feet) on the western slope of the Sierra Nevada, and is thus right in the heart of one of the world's most impressive forest areas. Along with two groves of giant sequoias, it also includes some six thousand acres of pine forest (Ponderosa and sugar pine, white fir, incense cedar, etc.) on both sides of the Stanislaus River and Beaver Creek watersheds.

## THE NORTH GROVE

The one hundred or so large giant sequoias that were discovered in the North Grove during the height of the California gold rush were the first to come to the attention of Western civilization, and were for a time thought to be the only ones of their kind anywhere in the world. After 1852, as word of the Big Tree discovery went out to a somewhat disbelieving world, journalists, botanists, and tourists began to search out the grove in ever-increasing numbers. Leading American and European newspapers and magazines carried stories about the newfound giants—often exaggerating the already astonishing facts—and described (as colorfully as possible) the circumstances of their "discovery." The local Indians, of course, had known about the sequoias, and considered them sacred, for thousands of years.

A summer resort, the Mammoth Grove Hotel, was built close beside the North Grove and began to record the visits of miners, merchants, scientists, and celebrities from every corner of the Earth. Botanical specimens from the North Grove were used to classify and officially name the Big Trees, while trees were carved out of the North Grove for display in the most important exhibit halls of both North America and Europe.

All of these activities tended to keep the spotlight of world attention on Calaveras Big Trees even after most of the Sierra Nevada's other sequoia groves were discovered. As a destination for tourists even the spectacular scenery and diversity of Yosemite could not compete with the charm, easy accessibility, and fame of the Calaveras North Grove until the 1870s, when the words of John Muir and others (plus a new wagon road) finally began to shift the balance toward Yosemite and the Mariposa Grove. Even then, and until the turn of the century, according to most guide books of the time, the North Grove of Calaveras big Trees including John Sperry's Mammoth Grove Hotel (he also built the Murphy's Hotel) continued to be a very stylish and popular place to visit—second only among Sierra Nevada attractions to the imcomparable grandeur of Yosemite.

# Calaveras Big Trees State Park

### THE SOUTH GROVE

While millions of people have visited the North Grove, the far larger South Grove has remained remote and primeval. The road ends a mile from the South Grove, and visitors must walk the trail up Big Trees Creek to reach its westernmost fringe. From there a self-guiding loop trail explores a representative portion of the grove but beyond this, the sequoia-filled wilderness of the South Grove with all its many interrelated plants and animals remains absolutely untouched by the hand of modern man—a pristine sample of an ancient and once widespread forest community that has now almost completely disappeared from the face of the Earth.

### OFF-SEASON USE OF THE PARK

Calaveras Big Trees State Park is enjoyable in all seasons. Springtime brings a rush of renewed vitality throughout the forest, and there are lovely displays of white dogwood and azalea blossoms as well as the colorful flowers of countless other plants and shrubs. In late autumn many people come to the park to enjoy the fall color, particularly the brilliant red or magenta tones of the dogwood. The park remains open throughout the winter, and an increasing number of people enjoy the park most of all at this time of year for cross-country skiing and snowshoe hikes.

### HIKING

Along with trails through North Grove and South Grove, a number of other interesting trails lead through other parts of the park. Perhaps the most ambitious of these trails is the one that runs between the North Grove and the Stanislaus River. Since this four-mile long trail descends some 1,500 feet, many park visitors would be well advised to have an automobile waiting for them at the river parking area.

Another interesting walk begins at the Lava Bluffs Trail parking area and explores the relatively warm, dry terrain on the south-facing slope above the Stanislaus River. The scenic canyon of the North Fork of the Stanislaus can be enjoyed from overlooks along this trail, which also visits some bold outcroppings of lava that rise above the surrounding forest.

A number of fire roads, particularly in the South Grove area, make it easy to get away from the main activity areas and explore other parts of the park on foot.

### CAMPING

Developed campgrounds with piped drinking water and hot showers are located in the North Grove and Oak Hollow areas. Winter temperatures are generally rather mild at this elevation and portions of the North Grove Campground remain open all year, except when unusually heavy snow or cold weather force a closure.

Facilities for summer group camping are available and should be reserved well in advance of arrival. There are also group picnicking areas and a rustic hall with a large stone fireplace. Environmental walk-in campsites are also located in the park. Contact the park for more information.

"See and Touch" natural and human history exhibits are on display in the Visitor Center. Ask the park staff about ranger-guided walks.

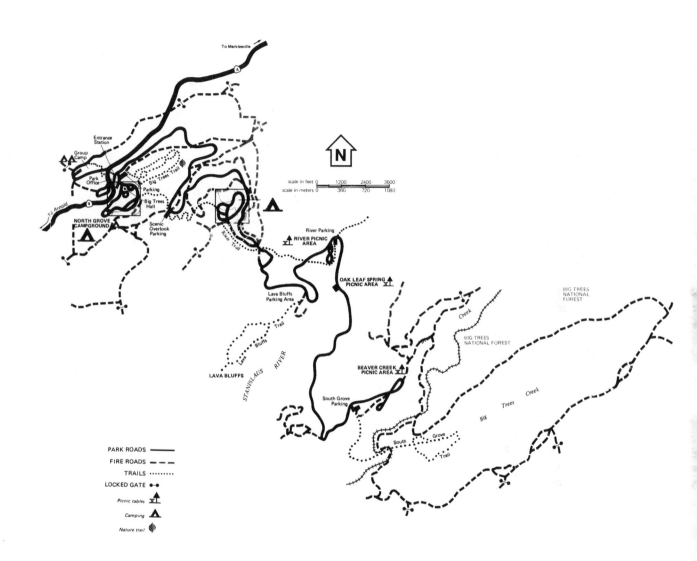

Calaveras Big Trees State Park
P.O. Box 120
Arnold, CA 95223
(209) 795-2334

# Castle Crags State Park

Dominated by soaring spires of ancient granite, Castle Crags State Park is located in the forested mountains north of the Sacramento Valley about twenty-five miles north of Lake Shasta on Interstate 5. The most popular activites here are swimming and fishing in the park's two miles along the cool, quick-running Sacramento River, and hiking in the park or the surrounding backcountry.

From the park, you can see several dramatic geologic features. To the north, dominating everything else for a hundred miles around, is 14,162-foot Mount Shasta, an incredibly beautiful, snow-covered, inactive volcano. Closer to hand are the glacier-polished crags for which the park is named. Unrelated to the geologically recent volcanic activity of Mount Shasta, the Crags are made up of granitic material that was formed some 225 million years ago, far beneath the surface of the earth, and forced upward through a blanket of serpentine and glacial debris.

A still different formation can be seen to the southwest, where the Grey Rocks form the crest of Flume Creek Ridge. Geologically unlike either the Crags or Mount Shasta, the Grey Rocks consist of a great weathered slab of metamorphic rock—principally greenstone—that has been thrust sideways, over and on top of serpentine and glacial material.

Elevations range from 2,000 feet along the river to more than 6,000 feet at the top of the Crags. Most of the area is beautifully forested with a wide variety of evergreen cone-bearing trees including ponderosa and sugar pines, Douglas fir, white fir, Port Orford and incense cedars, and western yew. Intermixed with the evergreen forest, especially at the lower elevations, are a number of deciduous trees—alders, vine and big-leaf maples, black and canyon oaks—most of which contribute to the wonderful display of color that can be seen here in the autumn.

For many years travelers, including the horse-drawn stages of the California-Oregon Stage Company, struggled up and over Kettlebelly Hill on the Pioneer California-Oregon Toll Road that passed through the area west of the present freeway. In 1886-87 the Southern Pacific Railroad came through the canyon, opening the country to mining and lumbering operations. Even today, though the rails have long since been removed, you can see the carefully levelled beds of narrow-gauge steam railways and other signs of early-day logging in the park.

With the coming of the railroad, a number of little hotels sprang up that boasted about their friendly atmosphere, fresh air, good food, and—most important of all—the restorative value of the area's mineral springs, like the one that bubbles out of a rock fountain near the park's picnic area. For many years its water was bottled and sold as Castle Rock Mineral Water.

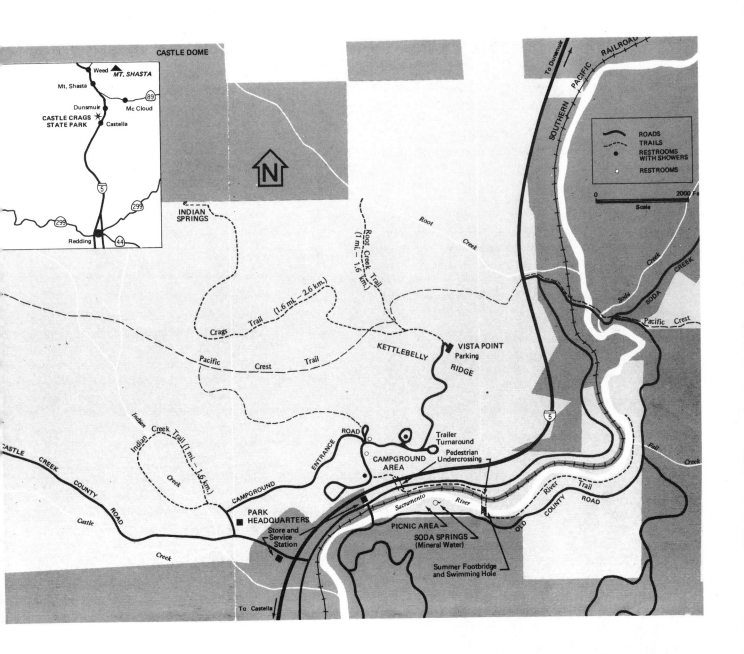

## CAMPING AND PICNICKING

With its long, warm summers and easy access, the park is a popular place to camp or picnic from about the first of April to the end of October. Even though winter brings snow and cold temperatures, the park remains open all year around.

There are 64 family campsites, each with table, stove, and storage locker; restrooms with hot showers and wash-tubs are nearby. Many of the sites are large enough to accommodate trailers up to 21 feet long or motorhomes up to 27 feet long, though there are no hookups.

Across the river from the park's main entrance, in a cool forest grove along the river, are 21 picnic sites with tables and stoves. A tunnel under the freeway and a bridge make it easy to reach the river and picnic area for fishing and swimming.

When you visit, keep food in the trunk of your car or where its odor will not attract bears.

Castle Crags State Park
Drawer A
Castella, CA 96017
(916) 235-2684

# Columbia State Historic Park

Columbia is the best-preserved gold mining town in America and the best-known of all the state's historic parks. Today it's a living museum. As you stroll down the Main Street boardwalk, you'll pass the elegant City Hotel, a blacksmith's shop, a newspaper office, and a saloon. Some of the shopkeepers are dressed in Gold Rush era clothing.

Unlike many of these settlements, which long ago succumbed to fire, vandalism, and the elements, Columbia was never completely deserted. Its brick buildings withstood the ravages of time. Through the years it has retained much of the same appearance as when miners thronged its streets. So, recognizing an opportunity to preserve a typical Gold Rush town as an example of what was the most colorful era in California history, the State Legislature in 1945 created Columbia State Historic Park.

Of particular interest is a museum located in the Knapp Building, a brick structure once used as a general store. Exhibits tell the story of Columbia's early days. The Wells Fargo Express Building, a fancy two-story brick building built in 1858, contains displays explaining business and commerce activity during Columbia's boom years. In summer stagecoach rides depart from the Wells Fargo building.

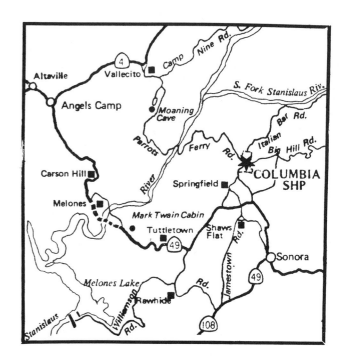

Within a mile of Columbia are campgrounds, trailer courts, and motels. The park itself contains no camping facilities, but there are many picnic table and restaurants.

The University of the Pacific presents nineteenth-century plays in the restored Fallon Theater during July and August. Square dancing clubs meet in Angelo's Hall several nights a week, and other entertainment is also scheduled there. Park exhibits and businesses are open daily except Christmas and Thanksgiving.

Columbia was only one of hundreds of settlements that sprang up during the exciting years when the cry of "Gold!" brought Argonauts from all over the world to seek their fortunes in California. Located in the heart of the Mother Lode—a mile-wide network of gold-bearing quartz that extends 120 miles along the western edge of the Sierra Nevada, from Mariposa northward to Georgetown—Columbia yielded, at 19th Century prices, $87 million in gold.

Columbia State Historic Park
P.O. Box 151
Columbia, CA 95310
(209) 532-0150

*Overlooking Emerald Bay*

D.L. Bliss and Emerald Bay State Parks include over six miles of magnificent Lake Tahoe shoreline. At the crest of Eagle Falls, a brilliant panorama of Emerald Bay, Fannette Island, Lake Tahoe, and the distant Nevada shore can be enjoyed.

D.L. Bliss State Park is named for a pioneering lumberman, railroad owner, and banker of the region. His family donated 744 acres to the park system in 1929. The nucleus of Emerald Bay, including Vikingsholm, was given to the state by Placerville lumberman Harvey West in 1953.

The grandeur of the parks and their setting is a product of successive upheavals of the mountain-building process which raised the Sierra Nevada. Lake Tahoe, which to the Indians meant "Lake in the Sky," lies east of the main Sierra crest at an elevation of over 6,000 feet. After the mountains rose to the east and west of this area, glaciers and lava seeping from volcanic vents completed its basin. The lake is over 22 miles long, 12 miles wide, and over 1,600 feet deep in some places. From promontories such as Rubicon Point one can see several hundred feet into its depths.

The Lake Tahoe area has a wide variety of trees and plant life. In addition to the gnarled and stunted sugar pines growing on the thin granitic soil in the center of D.L. Bliss, the parks also contain ponderosa and Jeffrey pines, white and red firs, Sierra juniper and black cottonwood. Along the streams grow a lush combination of alders, quaking aspen, mountain dogwood, and a host of wildflowers such as columbine, leopard lily, lupine, bleeding heart, mint, and nightshade.

## VIKINGSHOLM

In 1928 Mrs. Lora Knight of Santa Barbara purchased this isolated site at the head of Emerald Bay. She instructed Lennart Palme, a Swedish-born architect, to design a home without disturbing a single tree. After a trip to Scandanavia, they decided to reproduce a Norse fortress of about A.D. 800 in full detail. Vikingsholm, considered the finest example of Scandanavian architecture in the Western Hemisphere, was completed in September 1929, and Mrs. Knight spent her summers in this 38-room castle until her death in 1945. In addition to the main house, she had guest houses and the teahouse on Fannette Island built.

The methods and materials used in the construction of Vikingsholm, including the granite boulders of the foundations and walls, are those used in ancient Scandanavia. Turrets, towers, intricate carvings, even hand-hewn timbers were used to recreate the fortress, and the sod roof with its living grass is like those used in Scandanavia to feed livestock during the winter.

Vikingsholm is open from July 1 to Labor Day. The building is reached by trail from the parking lot at the Emerald Bay Overlook. It's about a mile down the trail, but according to some visitors, at least two miles back up! From Vikingsholm, another trail leads to Eagle Creek Falls.

# D.L. Bliss/Emerald Bay State Park

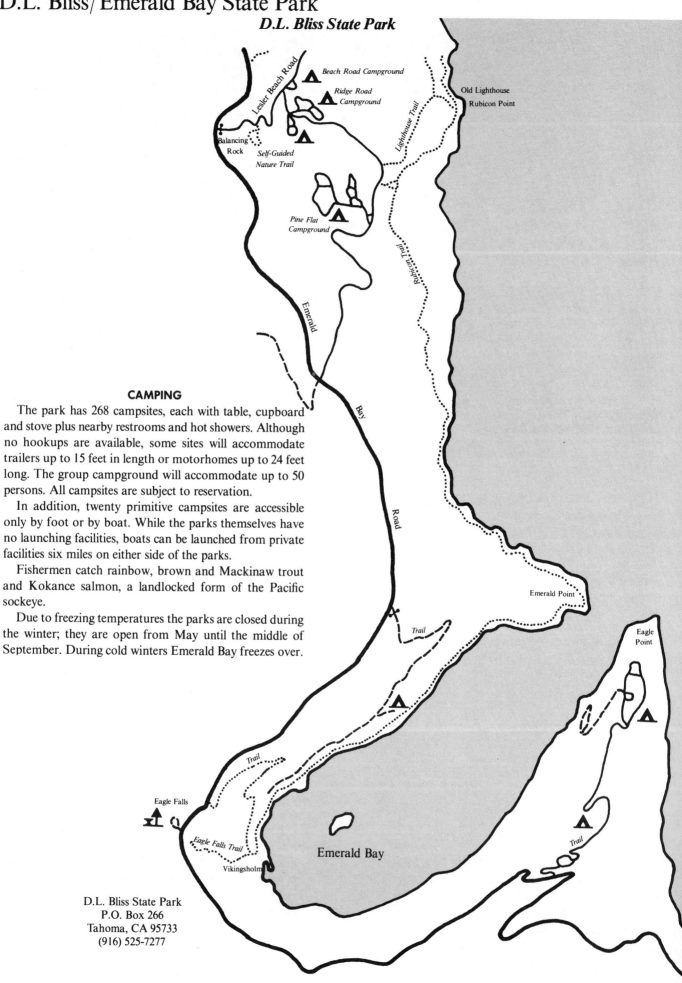

## D.L. Bliss State Park

Lesler Beach Road

Beach Road Campground

Ridge Road Campground

Old Lighthouse
Rubicon Point

Lighthouse Trail

Balancing Rock

Self-Guided Nature Trail

Rubicon Trail

Pine Flat Campground

Emerald

Bay

Road

Emerald Point

Eagle Point

Trail

Trail

Eagle Falls

Eagle Falls Trail

Vikingsholm

Emerald Bay

Trail

## CAMPING

The park has 268 campsites, each with table, cupboard and stove plus nearby restrooms and hot showers. Although no hookups are available, some sites will accommodate trailers up to 15 feet in length or motorhomes up to 24 feet long. The group campground will accommodate up to 50 persons. All campsites are subject to reservation.

In addition, twenty primitive campsites are accessible only by foot or by boat. While the parks themselves have no launching facilities, boats can be launched from private facilities six miles on either side of the parks.

Fishermen catch rainbow, brown and Mackinaw trout and Kokance salmon, a landlocked form of the Pacific sockeye.

Due to freezing temperatures the parks are closed during the winter; they are open from May until the middle of September. During cold winters Emerald Bay freezes over.

D.L. Bliss State Park
P.O. Box 266
Tahoma, CA 95733
(916) 525-7277

180

*Donner Lake*

Located in the beautiful Sierra Nevada, Donner Memorial State Park offers the summer vacationer opportunities for camping, picnicking, boating, fishing, waterskiing, and hiking.

Exhibits in the park's Emigrant Trail Museum give the natural history of the Sierra Nevada, tell the dramatic story of how the Central Pacific Railroad was built over its forbidding ramparts, and recount the tragic tale of the Donner Party trapped here in the savage winter of 1846-47.

The park is forested primarily with lodgepole and Jeffrey pine and white fir. It is home to deer, squirrels, chipmunks, porcupines, raccoons, beaver, and a wide variety of birds.

In and around the park you can see some of the Sierra Nevada'a geologic history—the granite that rose within the crust of the earth in enormous bubbles, then cooled and hardened, to be exposed by erosion; the older sedimentary rocks, transformed by temperature and pressure; and of course the Sierra's steep eastern face, the barrier that faced the Donner Party and other California immigrants, created when gigantic upheavals tilted a section of the earth's crust as if it were a door with its hinge on the western edge. The glaciers that dominated the area a few thousand years ago have left their traces, too—the huge boulders and other debris that remained when the ice melted, scattered as if by a giant hand.

While the park has no boat launching ramp, a public ramp is available in the northwest corner of Donner Lake. The lake is open to both power and sail boats.

The park has over three miles of frontage on Donner Lake and Creek, but fishing is not usually spectacular, though there are trout and kokanee in the lake and the creek is planted with catchable trout; a fishing license is required. Many fishermen prefer to use the park as a base to visit nearby lakes—for suggestions, ask a ranger.

The park has about 2½ miles (4 km.) of hiking trails, and more enthusiastic hikers can also explore the neighboring Tahoe National Forest.

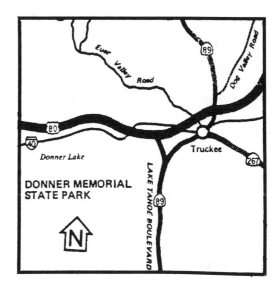

Donner Memorial State Park
P.O. Box 9210
Truckee, CA 95737
(916) 587-3841

# Empire Mine State Historic Park

This state park preserves the Empire Mine, the oldest and richest hardrock gold mine in California. The 367 miles of underground workings which made up the Empire-Star Mine complex yielded 5.8 million ounces of gold in its 106 year history and reached an incline depth of 11,007 feet. Visitors may observe the Empire Mine shaft from a viewing platform and learn the story of hardrock gold mining.

Within two years of James W. Marshall's discovery of gold in 1848, great hordes of '49ers had panned out most of California's gold-bearing streambeds. Few of them had any idea of the enormous amounts of gold that were locked beneath the surface of the Sierra in sheet-like veins of quartz. But in the fall of 1850, a lumberman named George Roberts discovered flecks of gold in a surface outcropping of quartz located where today's parking lot is now.

Hundreds of miners soon flocked here to take out placer claims, but soon found that they lacked the skills necessary to tunnel deep into the earth. Chipping and blasting rock was dangerous work; cave-ins were frequent, and tunnels were continually flooded by mountain springs. By 1851, the land was perforated with hundreds of "coyote holes," mines resembling 40-foot-deep wells into which miners were lowered in buckets. George Roberts, like many others, became discouraged and sold his claim for a few hundred dollars to a group that consolidated these claims and named the new property the Empire Mine.

Ownership of the mine changed rapidly during the 1850s and '60s, and the processing plants were repeatedly rebuilt and modernized. The Empire prospered after capitalist William Bourn gained a controlling interest in 1870.

In 1877, when Bourn's son, William Jr., reached the age of 21 and took over management of the mine, all indications pointed to the mine's imminent closure; many believed that profitable operations could not be conducted below the four-hundred foot level. But young Bourn pushed several shafts much deeper. For several years operating expenses were barely paid, but by 1884 the profits began to roll in.

During tour seasons, park visitors will enjoy viewing the Empire Cottage, an Elizabethan Manor style home used by the Bourn family on their visits to Grass Valley. The Cottage was built by noted San Francisco architect Willis Polk in 1898. Also included in the park are several offices, shops, and the large mining machinery display area. The Park and visitor center are open daily from 9 to 5 with tours and audio visual programs offered on a seasonal basis.

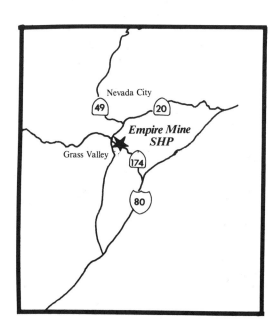

Empire Mine
State Historic Park
10791 E. Empire Street
Grass Valley, CA 95945
(916) 273-8522

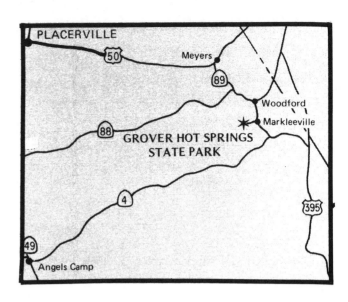

The 519-acre park lies in Hot Springs Valley at an elevation of nearly 6,000 feet, with mountains rising abruptly on three sides. Hawkins Peak, at 10,023 feet, is three miles northwest of the valley, and Markleeville Park, 9,417 feet, lies four miles to the southwest.

You can see the bare granite peaks better from Burnside Trail, which begins at Quaking Aspen Campground and ascends rapidly from the west end of the valley. A branch at Charity Valley Creek goes southwest to Charity Valley and a country road; Burnside Trail continues northwest, passing a small waterfall before switchbacking up a steep mountainside. The trail rises more than 2,000 feet in less than four miles before it reaches Burnside Lake, which is also accessible by road from State Highway 88.

Ever since the mid-1850s, when journalists began putting into words their impressions of Grover Hot Springs, the descriptions have been generous. The area is one of alpine beauty with a large variety of plant and animal life. A self-guided loop trail describing the area's natural history begins at the Hot Springs Creek bridge.

During the summer months, the nighttime temperature at the park drops to around 50 degrees, and the daytime reading reaches around 80. Frost is not uncommon in early June and may come again in late August or early September, when the colder weather brings a rich display of orange and gold in stands of quaking aspen. In winter, visitors enjoy Nordic skiing and snowshoeing as well as soaking in the hot pools.

## THE HOT SPRINGS

The park's hot springs are a phenomenon associated with the faulting that developed when the Sierra Nevada began to rise, millions of years ago. Surface water courses its way through the cracks in the earth's crust until it reaches hot rock thousands of feet below; then it bubbles to years before the advent of modern medicine, people sought the curative powers they believed existed in the water from Grover Hot Springs. The springs, they said, cured a long list of chronic illnesses.

The water's total mineral content of 74.4 grams per gallon breaks down as follows: sodium chloride 19.91, sodium sulphate 12.02, sodium carbonate 34.10, calcium carbonate 6.38, magnesium carbonate 1.16, iron and alumina 0.32, and silica 0.82, plus a trace of organic matter. Unlike the water from most hot springs, it contains little sulphur.

One of the park's two concrete pools is fed by the runoff from six mineral springs. Although the water leaves the ground at 148 degrees Fahrenheit, the pools' inflow is regulated so the temperature remains between 102 and 105 degrees in the hot pool. Excess water and overflow from the pools are diverted into nearby Hot Springs Creek, a year-round stream that flows through the middle of the park's large meadow. Pool hours depend on the season; call the park for them when you plan to visit.

Visitors can fish the creek during the summer months. Catchable-size trout are planted periodically as long as it maintains an adequate waterflow. Four miles east of the park is the Carson River and farther upstream is Silver Creek, both noted for their excellent trout fishing.

## CAMPING

The two campgrounds—Quaking Aspen and Toiyabe—have 76 sites equipped with stoves, cupboards, and tables. Each campsite is close to piped water and restrooms with showers.

The campgrounds are closed from early October to May, but you can camp in the picnic area adjacent to the park entrance during the winter. Each of the 30 units has a stove and a table; piped water and restrooms are accessible.

Grover Hot Springs State Park
P.O. Box 188
Markleeville, CA 96120
(916) 694-2248

# Indian Grinding Rock (Chaw'se) State Historic Park

The main grinding rock is a limestone outcropping measuring 173 feet by 82 feet. It is covered with 363 petroglyphs, or rock carvings, and 1,185 *chaw'ses,* or mortar cups.

The 1,185 mortar cups, the largest number found at one site in California, were an important tool in Northern Miwok Indians' hunting and gathering economy. They were used to pulverize acorns and other seeds to make palatable foods.

In the fall, when the acorns were ripe, the Miwok gathered and spread them out to dry in the shade. When they were thoroughly dry, the acorns were stored in large granaries *(cha'ka).* These huge basket-type affairs, sometimes as much as eight feet high, were made of four or more poles arranged over a stump. The poles were interwoven with slender brush stems tied with willow and wild grapevine to form a network which was lined with pine needles and wormwood to discourage insects and rodents. After the granary was filled, the exterior was thatched with short boughs of white fir or incense cedar with the needles pointing downward to shed snow and rain; the top was covered with pine needles, wormwood, and sections of incense cedar bark.

Acorns were removed from the granary as needed. They were cracked and shelled; then the dry meats were pounded with a stone pestle in the holes in the mortar cups *(chaw'se)* until they became a fine meal of flour. Seeds, bulbs, greens, and edible fungi were also pulverized.

Though acorns are rich in food value, they contain a poisonous, bitter-tasting tannin. To remove the tannin, the flour was leached with hot and cold water. Then the mush, made of acorn meal and water, was cooked in a large basket; heat was supplied by hot stones that were put into the basket with wooden tongs and moved about with a

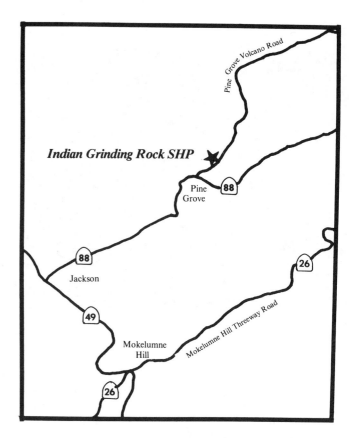

*Ground acorns provided sustenance for many tribes of California Indians.*

paddle to prevent them from burning the basket. The acorn meal, whether finely ground for gruel or thin soup, more coarsely ground for mush, or still more coarsely ground for patties (cakes) that were baked on hot rocks, was a staple in the Indians' diet.

At Chaw'se you will also see a round house, or *hun'ge,* of the type that the Indians used for meetings and religious activities; a bark conical dwelling, or *u'macha',* and an Indian football field, or *poscoi a we'a.*

The Museum Cultural Center, which offers group tours, an informative slide show, and displays of artifacts from several Indian tribes, is open five days a week, Wednesday through Friday, from 8:30 A.M. to 4:30 P.M. and Saturday, Sunday and holidays from 9:30 A.M. to 5:30 P.M.

School, youth and organized groups can arrange for special interpretive tours by contacting the Resident Ranger.

### CAMPING

The park has 21 campsites with tables and stoves; piped water and restrooms are available, but there are no showers. There is also a small picnic area.

An isolated environmental campground called U'macha'tam'a features five Miwok bark dwellings for sleeping and is suited for both large (up to 30 campers) and small groups. Reservations are made through the park.

Indian Grinding Rock State Historic Park
14881 Pine Grove-Volcano Road
Pine Grove, CA 95665
(209) 296-7488

# Malakoff Diggins State Historic Park

The great Malakoff mine pit, seven thousand feet long and three thousand feet wide, is nearly six hundred feet deep in places. Slides and erosion have filled it in somewhat and the waters of the lake that has formed in its bottom contrast with the colorful cliffs.

Between 2,200 and 4,200 feet in elevation, Malakoff Diggins State Historic Park's terrain varies from open meadows to tree- and chaparral-covered slopes and deep canyons. During the winter there's usually some snow on the ground; temperatures range from the low 20s to the 40s. Summers are pleasantly cool in comparison with the Central Valley—highs during the day are in the middle 80s, dropping to the 50s in the evening.

The 2,700-acre park's wildlife includes deer, rabbits, raccoons, porcupines, skunks, and squirrels; bobcats, coyotes, and bears visit on occasion. Birdwatchers will see quail, doves, pigeons, hawks, and numerous songbirds.

For fishermen, the lower sections of Humbug Creek and the South Yuba River offer rainbow and brown trout, and there are black bass, bluegill, and catfish in Blair Reservoir. The reservoir is also used for swimming (be careful, as no lifeguard is available) and there is a small picnic area on its banks. Or, after lunching in the Clampicnic area in the center of town, picnickers can enjoy a leisurely stroll to see the park's displays.

Early every June, on the Sunday before Father's Day, the park hosts a Homecoming. The celebration, which started out as a reunion of former North Bloomfield residents, has grown each year and now features a picnic, parade, musical performances and various special events.

During the second weekend in June, the park hosts a Homecoming. The celebration, which started out as a reunion of former North Bloomfield residents, has grown each year and now features a picnic, parade, musical performances and various special events.

Displays in the park's museum tell the story of hydraulic miners and their way of life. The museum is open on weekends during the fall and spring; in the early afternoon on an intermittent basis during the winter. In the Ostrom Livery Stable, you will see some of the many types of wagons in use when the mine was operating.

Saint Columncille's Catholic Church was originally built in 1860 near French Corral. Donated to the park by Babe Pinaglia, it was restored by the park staff with the aid of Forestry crews. Many North Bloomfield residents believe that Saint Columncille is the patron saint of bartenders.

### CAMPING

The park contains 30 primitive family campsites; drinking water and restrooms (no showers) are available, and each site has a table, cupboard, and stove. Though there are no hookups, trailers up to 24 feet in length or motorhomes up to 30 feet long can be accommodated in some of the sites.

Recreational vehicles should take the primary roads to North Bloomfield to reach the park. North Bloomfield-Graniteville Road from Nevada City is not recommended for R.V. and trailer use. R.V. units should use Tyler-Foote Crossing Road, 12 miles north of Nevada City off State Highway 49.

In addition, the park has two rustic cabins for family use, but bring your own bedding, utensils, etc. These cabins can be reserved through the park office.

Campfire programs are held during the summer months; a film that vividly shows how hydraulic mining was done is shown each weekend, in the museum. Tours of the park's historic sites are given each summer weekend, and by appointment during the rest of the year.

Malakoff Diggins State Historic Park
23579 North Bloomfield-Graniteville Rd.
Nevada City, CA 95959
(916) 265-2740

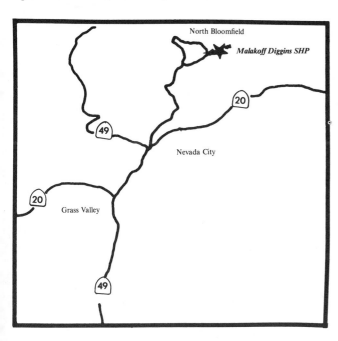

# Marshall Gold Discovery State Historic Park

*The whole country from San Francisco to Los Angeles, and from the seashore to the base of the Sierra Nevadas, resounds with the sordid cry of gold, Gold, GOLD, while the field is left half planted, the house half built, and everything neglected but the manufacture of shovels and pickaxes.*

—*San Francisco Californian*
*May 29, 1848*

When James Marshall discovered gold in January 1848 in the tailrace of the little lumber mill he was building for John Sutter, he set off one of the most remarkable chapters in modern history. Within a year people from every corner of the world were throwing off their occupations and swarming into California in an attempt to make their fortunes in the Mother Lode.

James W. Marshall did not greatly benefit from his momentous discovery. He ended his days in bitter disillusionment living in a rustic cabin that is now part of the park.

The park includes about three-fourths of the town of Coloma, birthplace of the Gold Rush. A few old buildings line Highway 49, but most are tucked away on steep narrow backstreets. Among these is the Chinese store, a stone building dating from 1860.

Also in the park is a replica of Sutter's Mill where the first fateful traces of gold were actually found. The replica is a working model, with demonstrations given on the weekends.

Ore cars, stamp mills, and *arrastres* (ore crushers) help you visualize the hard work of hard rock mining. Exhibits at the Gold Discovery Museum tell of Sutter, Marshall and the gold rush. Museum staff members can direct you to the trails, picnic sites, and other attractions of the park.

Marshall Gold Discovery State Historic Park
P.O. Box 265
Coloma, CA 95613
(916) 622-3470

# McArthur-Burney Falls Memorial State Park

McArthur-Burney Falls Memorial State Park is located in the beautiful evergreen forests of the Pit River country in northern California, halfway between Mount Shasta and Lassen Peak in an area little changed from the time of the Hudson's Bay Company fur hunters. One of the oldest in the State Park System, the 875-acre park dates from 1920 when Frank McArthur gave 160 acres to the state as a memorial to his parents, John and Catherine McArthur.

A spectacular waterfall, one of the wonders of the world, is the park's main attraction. The forest is mostly Ponderosa pine, but there are also incense cedars, Douglas firs, white firs, black oaks, willows, and black cottonwoods as well as shrubs such as vine maple, buck brush, redbud, and dogwood. Five-fingered ferns grow in the moist places near Burney Falls, and during the spring and early summer wildflowers include tiger lilies, starflowers, monkeyflowers, columbines, lupines, shooting stars, and mule's ears.

Camping and picnicking are popular here, and the park has frontage along Burney Creek and Lake Britton, a nine-mile-long man-made lake where swimming, fishing, boating, and waterskiing are popular.

### BURNEY FALLS

Just inside the southern boundary of the park, Burney Creek wells up from the ground and hurries along to divide into two flows of water and stream over a 129-foot cliff into an emerald pool. On sunlit mornings a little rainbow can be seen in the ever-present mist at the foot of the falls. But Burney Falls owes its unique beauty to the countless small streams of white water that issue from the fern- and moss-covered rock all across the cliff behind the two main cascades.

Although Burney Creek goes dry between the park and the town of Burney, some ten miles to the south, from June to September, Burney Falls flows undiminished year 'round, and the temperature of the water remains a constant 48 degrees summer and winter. This suggests that the creek flows from extensive underground reservoirs. Geologists believe these reservoirs are fed by runoff water trickling down through gravel-filled fissures and fault lines in the volcanic cap rock until it reaches the impermeable materials underlying old watersheds that were buried by volcanic eruptions. Then, in places like the "spring" above Burney Falls, the water comes rushing back up out of the ground, cool and refreshing even in the hottest, driest season.

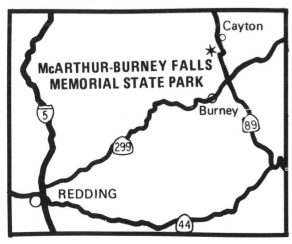

### BOATING

The concessionnaire rents canoes and small power and rowboats for fishing, and the park also has a launching ramp.

### FISHING

Bass, pike, and brown and rainbow trout are the most frequently caught in Lake Britton, Burney Creek, Hat Creek, and the many other lakes and streams nearby. A fishing license is required.

### CAMPING

Scattered through the forest not far from Burney Creek are 118 family campsites, each with table, stove, and food locker; piped drinking water and restrooms with hot showers and laundry tubs are nearby. Some of the sites can accommodate motorhomes and trailers up to 32 feet long, though there are no hookups. A concessionaire-operated store in the park, open from mid-April to the end of September, sells groceries and other supplies including fuel for the campstoves. The park is open year-round though there is no running water in the campground during the winter. In summer, rangers lead campfire programs and interpretive hikes.

McArthur-Burney Falls Memorial State Park
Rt. 1, Box 1260
Burney, CA 96013
(916) 335-2777

# Mono Lake Tufa State Reserve

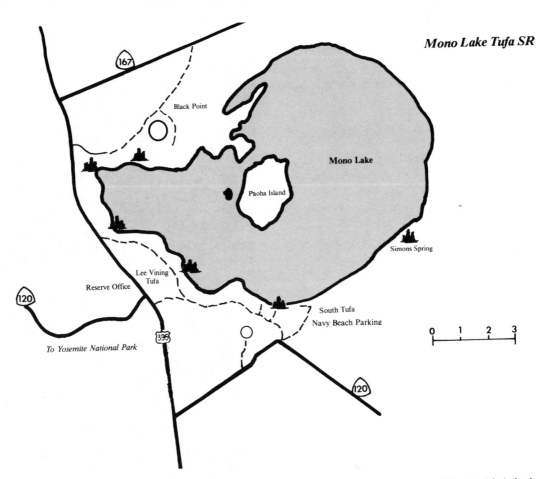

Cradled by volcanoes, glacier-sculpted canyons and snowy peaks, Mono Lake is one of the most dramatic landscapes of the American West. Visitors marvel at the lake's grand setting and the tufa formations on the lake's island and shore.

The main feature of the Reserve are the tufa formations; these are towers of calcium carbonate formed when alkaline lake water combines with fresh water from streams located beneath the lake. Calcium carbonate is the principal mineral in limestone, so tufa's resemblance to cave formations is not surprising. Scientists believe tufa formation may be promoted by algae living in the lake. The algae grows around the precipitating tufa and directs its texture, color and growth.

Mistakenly called "California's Dead Sea," Mono Lake is actually a life-sustaining lake that is immensely important to birds. One-fourth of the world's population of the California gull nests on Negit Island. As many as 800,000 eared grebes, a duck-like diving bird, have been tallied on its waters. Supplying food for the birds is the brine shrimp, which, like other organisms in Mono's waters, has adapted over the last million years to an extremely saline habitat. Since aquatic habitat is scarce in the arid American West, birds depend on Mono for the rest and sustenance they need to cross hundreds of miles of desert.

Mono's waters are slippery to the touch and extremely salty. Because the lake has no outlet, salt and minerals are concentrated as the water evaporates. Mono Lake is three times as salty and eight times more alkaline than the ocean.

The lake's salty water offers a wonderfully buoyant swim. Oldtimers claim the waters cure a multitude of ailments. Keep the water out of your eyes!

Navy Beach on the south shore is the best swimming spot. Be careful when you enter the water—parts of the shore are very muddy.

During the summer months, rangers lead nature walks through the tufa. Check the schedule posted at the park office.

Mono Lake Tufa State Reserve
P.O. Box 99
Lee Vining, CA 93541
(619) 647-6331

High on the east slopes of the Sierra Nevada 80 miles north of Lake Tahoe, Plumas-Eureka State Park sits amid spectacular mountain scenery in the headwaters country of the Yuba and Feather Rivers. Within the park, the historic mining town of Johnsville and the partially restored Plumas-Eureka stamp mill vividly recall the time when hard-rock gold mining was the primary activity in this region and an important part of the California economy. Today, during the summer months, the most popular activities are camping, hiking, fishing, and general sightseeing. During the winter the park's high mountain location (elevation 4,000 to 8,000 feet) means lots of cold and snow. Nevertheless, the park's headquarters and the fine mining history museum remain open throughout the year.

Glacier-carved granite peaks rise above the timberline to dominate the horizon, and beautiful forests cover the lower slopes of the area. Red and white fir, Douglas fir, incense cedar, Ponderosa, Jeffery, and sugar pines make up much of the surrounding forest, with alder, black cottonwood, aspen, and willow along the stream courses. Brushy areas, especially at the higher elevations, are filled with manzanita, chinquapin, ceanothus, and buckthorn.

### HISTORY

Today there are still many reminders of this area's colorful history in and around the park. Not the least of these are the seventy miles of long-silent, sealed-off mine shafts and tunnels. Another is the partially restored Plumas-Eureka Mill where eight millon dollars' worth of gold is said to have been processed. The building that houses the park headquarters and museum originally served as a bunkhouse for one of the mines.

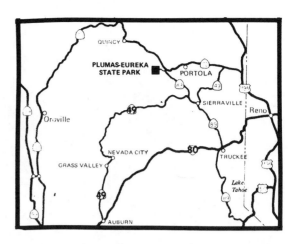

The old tramway, no longer standing, is said to have served as the world's first ski lift. In fact, it may well be that the early-day miners who wintered here were the first Americans to organize, advertise, and wager on highly competitive, high-speed, downhill ski races using what were then called Norwegian-type "snow shoes" or "long boards."

Eureka Lake and Madora Lake are both within the park, and there are other lakes in the nearby region, many of them in the U.S. Forest Service-administered Lakes Basin area just south of the park. Trails, many of which are actually old mining-era roads, reach out from the park to these lakes and to other outstanding features of the surrounding country.

### HIKING

Hiking is especially rewarding because of the spectacular scenery, the many fine trails, and the excellent fishing for trout and other high mountain, cold water fish that thrive in the area's many nearby lakes and year-round streams.

### CAMPING

There are 67 campsites in the forested canyon alongside Jamison Creek each with table, stove and food locker. Piped drinking water and combination buildings with restrooms, hot showers, and laundry tubs are located conveniently nearby.

Due to extremely cold weather and heavy snows associated with this high mountain area, the campground is closed after about October 1. During the winter, though, the park is a delightful place for family snow-play and skiing. In the Eureka Bowl area a ski-lift is operated on Wednesdays, Saturdays, and Sundays by the non-profit Plumas County Ski Club. The ski-lift facilities are also used for a skiing instruction program administered by the club in cooperation with various local schools.

Plumas-Eureka State Park
310 Johnsville Road
Blairsden, CA 96103
(916) 836-2380

*Plumas-Eureka stamp mill*

# Railtown 1897 State Historic Park

The Iron Horse is almost vanished from America's railroads, but visitors can get a glimpse of a steam locomotive and what it took to keep them rolling at Railtown 1897 State Historic Park. Tools and equipment are displayed in a roundhouse and shops that look much as they did when they were built, shortly after the turn of the century.

Thomas Bullock had owned a small Arizona railroad until the Santa Fe came through and took away his business. He saw the potential of the Sierra foothills and began planning a new railroad venture that would make it possible to get the area's products to market.

The Sierra Railway Company was founded early in 1897, and by the end of the year track was laid from Oakdale to Jamestown. Later, the line was extended to Sonora, Angels Camp, and Tuolumne. Meanwhile, Bullock was buying up timber acreage and planning a sawmill; the railroad's mainstay throughout its history has been hauling lumber.

The company came on hard times during the Great Depression, and was reorganized as the Sierra Railroad Company in 1935. Business improved during and after World War II; today, its freight business is operated by Silverfoot Inc.

Though the line had discontinued regular passenger operations in 1939, there was still demand for steam-train excursions, and private groups chartered the Sierra's equipment for many such trips during the late 1950s and early '60s.

Because of this demand, the railroad opened "Rail Town 1897," offering a variety of sightseeing trips, at Jamestown in 1971. Increasing costs and decreasing ridership halted this operation in 1979.

However, local railroad enthusiasts and others were unwilling to see Railtown die, and their efforts convinced the Legislature to purchase the property, equipment, and trackage rights on the Sierra Railroad's line for a park.

Until recently, a concessionaire offered weekend steam excursions and guided tours of the old roundhouse.

The State is currently looking for a new operator for the railroad and scenic tours may again be offered. Write or phone the park for more information.

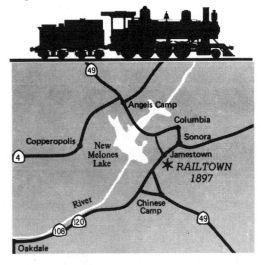

Railtown 1897
C/O Columbia SHP
P.O. Box 151
Columbia, CA 95310
(209) 532-0150

Shasta was Northern California's center of wagon transportation during the time of the northern gold rush in the 1850s. Shasta merchants did a thriving wholesale and retail business. As many as a hundred wagons a day rolled into Shasta, where the goods were transferred to pack mules and taken into the backcountry—sometimes all the way to Oregon.

Shasta faded away when the hydraulic mining petered out about 1884. One writer later observed:

> Shasta, through which a stream of golden treasure once flowed, now lies in ruins. Six miles west of Redding, its crumbling brick structures flank the highway in serried rows. Roofs have long since caved in, and paneless windows stare vacuously into the grass-grown street.

The old courthouse building, seat of Shasta County between 1861 and 1888 had deteriorated until only its brick walls and the iron bars of the jail cells remained. The state has restored it and added many artifacts of the boom years to a small museum. Down the road is a Masonic Lodge, which has been in use since 1853 and is the oldest in the state.

The park is open daily from 10 A.M. to 5 P.M. Interpretive specialists are on duty. A few picnic tables are available.

The park occupies both sides of a short stretch of State 299, six miles out of Redding.

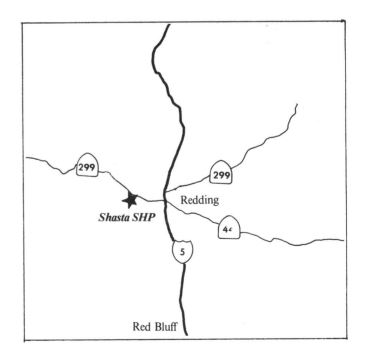

Shasta State Historic Park
P.O. Box 2430
Shasta, Ca 96087
(916) 243-8194

# Sugar Pine Point State Park

*Sugar Pine Point's location in the deep snow belt makes it
a popular winter destination.*

Sugar Pine Point, a beautifully situated promontory on the western side of Lake Tahoe, includes nearly two miles of lake frontage. Delightful little sandy beaches occur along the natural area north of General Creek, where the untouched primeval forest of the Lake Tahoe Basin marches down to the water's edge. In the developed area south of General Creek are a number of historic buildings including a pioneer-built, hand hewn log cabin and an elegant summer home, the Pine Lodge.

The forest at Sugar Pine Point is dominated by sugar and Jeffrey pine, red and white firs, Lodgepole pine, quaking aspen and black cottonwood. Some exceptionally large Sierra junipers grow near the lake shore. John Muir called them the largest he had ever seen.

Sugar Pine Point is one of the few areas of gentle, easily accessible lakeshore that has not been significantly modified. The land just north of General Creek has been set aside as a natural preserve. A nature trail explores part of the area and ranger-naturalists conduct walks during the warmer months.

## HISTORY

One of the first permanent Tahoe residents was an old frontiersman from Kentucky by the name of "General" William Phipps (1813—1891). Known as an Indian fighter, hunter and fisherman, Phipps staked out a 160-acre homestead claim on Sugar Pine Point in the spring of 1860, and soon afterward built himself a rough-hewn log cabin. He supported himself by fishing and hunting and apparently took great pleasure in the solitary life of a backwoodsman. About 1870 he built a second cabin near the lake and it is this cabin that can be seen today near the beach just south of General Creek.

The Pine Lodge, a sumptuous High Sierra home built at the turn of the century, is a fascinating example of the "opulent" tradition in Lake Tahoe architecture. Today the home is a museum.

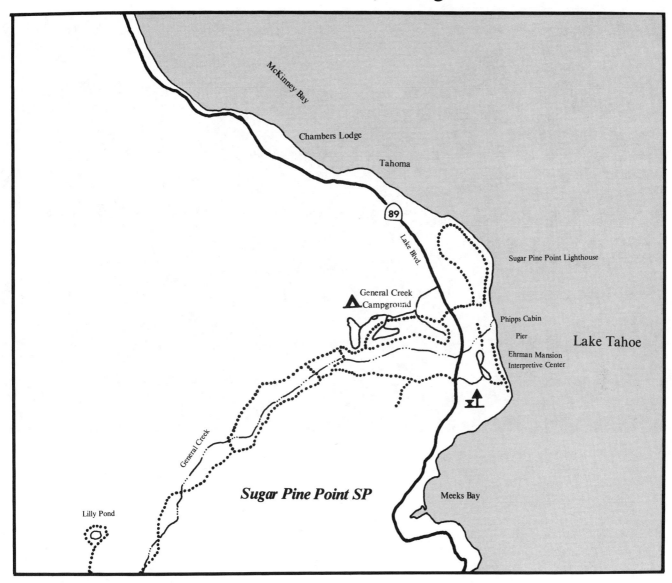

### SWIMMING AND BOATING

The park's half-mile sandy beach and central pier are popular places for swimming, sunbathing, picnicking, and fishing. A number of nearby marinas provide boat launching, mooring, and rentals for fishing and waterskiing.

### FISHING

Deep-line fishermen try their luck along Lake Tahoe's 300-foot deep underwater ledges by fishing for Mackinaw trout and Kokance salmon. Top-lining or trolling near the surface and shore fishing are also popular. Fishermen enjoy the challenge presented by General Creek and many of the lakes and streams in the nearby Desolation Wilderness.

### HIKING

The park features about ten miles of trail, including a trail for the handicapped along the lakeshore. Sugar Pine Point is a popular jumping off place for the High Sierra backcountry west of Lake Tahoe, including the northerly part of the Desolation Wilderness. The park also has different cross-country ski trails.

### CAMPING

The park offers 175 campsites complete with hot water and laundry facilities. The campsites can accommodate trailers up to 25 feet in length, motorhomes up to 30 feet long. No hookups.

Groups of up to 400 people can be accommodated in the group camping area; reservations should be made well in advance of arrival.

The park remains open throughout the winter months. Restrooms are heated and roads and parking spaces are kept clear of snow, but considerable forethought and good camping equipment are important during the winter because conditions at this elevation include frequent snow storms and deep snow packs, as well as temperatures that are apt to dip to near zero.

Sugar Pine Point State Park
P.O. Box 266
Tahoma, CA 95733
(916) 525-7982

# Tahoe State Recreation Area

*We plodded on—and at last the Lake burst upon us—a noble sheet of blue water lifted six thousand three hundred feet above the level of the sea, and walled in by a rim of snowclad mountain peaks that towered aloft full three thousand feet higher still! It was a vast oval, and one would have to use up eighty or ninety good miles in traveling around it. As it lay there with the shadows of the mountains brilliantly photographed upon its still surface I thought it must surely be the fairest picture the whole earth affords.*

—*Mark Twain*
*"Roughing It"*

Located in the midst of Tahoe City, Tahoe State Recreation Area is a little lakeshore park offering picnicking and water sports. Boaters can launch or moor their craft here.

The park has 39 improved campsites and a picnic area with a dozen sites.

Seven miles from Tahoe SRA is Kings Beach State Recreation Area, which is operated by the North Tahoe Public Utility District. The park features picnicking, boating, and a nice beach on Lake Tahoe.

Tahoe State Recreation Area
P.O. Box 583
Tahoe City, CA 95730
(916) 583-3074

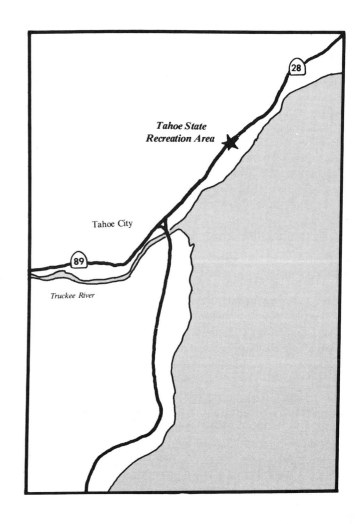

# Weaverville Joss House State Historic Park

The characters over the door of the Weaverville Joss House, oldest continuously used Chinese temple in California, mean "The Temple of the Forest Beneath the Clouds." They served as a vivid reminder of the Chinese contribution to this area.

In 1852, 2,500 Chinese were gold prospecting along the Trinity River. They tended to work less profitable claims than other miners, but they worked hard and prospered despite the high tax—$4 each per month—on foreign miners; they sent much of the money they earned back to their families in China. Their prosperity triggered jealous resentment in the other miners, leading to episodes of violence.

Life in the mining camps was rugged, and most of the Chinese in Trinity County during this period were men, although some brought their families when finances and laws permitted. Not all Chinese worked as miners—many opened stores and restaurants.

About 1852, the Chinese erected a place of Taoist worship at Chimney Point in Weaverville. The original building and most of its furnishings, some of which had come from China, were destroyed by fire in 1873 but local Chinese rebuilt it the following year.

The temple has been in continuous use as a place of worship since its construction. Descendants of the men who built the temple still worship here, along with other Chinese from all over California. Worshippers visit the temple alone, with their families, or with a small group of close friends to pray and to place some incense, candles, and other offerings such as food and paper money, before the images of the gods of Health, Decision, or Mercy. Worshipers are forbidden to pray for such things as wealth (though they might ask for help in making the right business decision) or revenge on an enemy, and the temple attendant would punish with a fine those who made such a request.

In addition to the temple, visitors can view Chinese art objects, pictures, mining tools, and wrought iron weapons used in the 1854 tong war.

Weaverville Joss House State Historic Park is open at 10 A.M. daily. In summer, tours are given every half hour with the last tour starting at 4:30 P.M.; in winter, tours are given every hour and the last tour starts at 4 P.M.

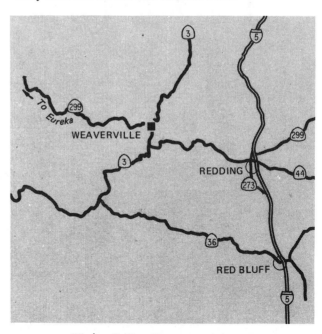

Weaverville Joss House State Historic Park
Drawer W
Weaverville, CA 96093
(916) 623-5284

PELICAN SB

CRESCENT CITY

199

DRY LAGOON SP

▲ PATRICK'S POINT SP

TRINIDAD SB — TRINIDAD

LITTLE RIVER SB

AZALEA SR

ARCATA

299

FORT HUMBOLDT SHP

EUREKA

FERNDALE — FORTUNA

36

▲ SINKYONE WILDERNESS SP

101

WESTPORT-UNION LANDING SB

WESTPORT

▲ MacKERRICHER SP

FT. BRAGG

JUG HANDLE SP

WILLITS

▲ RUSSIAN GULCH SP

20

MENDOCINO

▲ VAN DAMME SP

UKIAH

▲ MANCHESTER SB

128

PT. ARENA

KRUSE RHODODENDRON SR

HEALDSBURG

▲ SALT POINT SP

FORT ROSS SHP

116    101    128

JENNER

SEBASTOPOL    SANTA ROSA

▲ SONOMA COAST SB

BODEGA BAY

NAPA    FAIRFIELD

TOMALES BAY SP

PETALUMA    116    37    29    12

INVERNESS

BENICIA

SAN RAFAEL    CHINA CAMP SP

MILL VALLEY

▲ MOUNT TAMALPAIS SP

STINSON SB

ANGEL ISLAND SP

# North Coast

Stretching from the Oregon border to San Francisco, the North Coast has a cool, foggy climate with heavy winter rains. Here summer mornings may be foggy, but there are usually some brilliantly clear days in the spring and fall when you can see spectacular vistas of the rocky coastline.

There are few good swimming beaches in North Coast parks, and cold water and unpredictable ocean currents make swimming hazardous. Hikers, fishermen, and divers, however, enjoy the rugged shore.

At Van Damme and Russian Gulch State Parks, you can see pygmy forests where sixty-year-old trees have attained a height of only a few feet because of the impoverished soil, podzol, a type which is found in only a half-dozen places in the world. Near these areas, you may see a grove of huge second-growth redwoods.

Other attractions of the North Coast include watching the gray whales that pass within sighting distance of many points along the shore during their annual round trip from their breeding grounds in Baja California to spend the summer feeding in the Bering Sea.

Exhibits at several parks tell about the area's history.

0    10    20    40    60

scale in miles

▲ camping

# Angel Island State Park

Angel Island is a mountainous, grass- and forest-covered island in San Francisco Bay that offers spectacular overviews of Marin County, San Francisco and the Golden Gate. Naturalists enjoy the 740-acre island because a wide variety of land and marine animals, birds, and plant life can be observed. The island also has a varied and fascinating military history stretching back to the American Civil War.

Trails and fire roads circle the island, pass through historical areas, climb to the summit of 781-foot high Mount Caroline Livermore, and provide access to several small, sandy beaches. Bicycles can be used on the island fire roads and can be brought to the island on the ferry boats.

## BEACHES

The beaches at Quarry Point and Ayala Cove are both sandy and protected from the afternoon breezes that so often blow in from the ocean through the Golden Gate. Quarry Point Beach is especially pleasant for sunbathing or playing in the water. There are no lifeguards, however, and swimming can be hazardous because of the very strong currents that run past the island with each change of the tide. The water at Perle's Beach is considerably rougher, and the beach itself more exposed to the wind and weather. The area does have a spectacular view, however, and the beach is a delightful place to walk.

## FACILITIES

Facilities for family picnicking in the Ayala Cove area include tables, charcoal stoves, piped drinking water, and restrooms. A concessionaire operates a snack bar. Group facilities include tables, barbecue pits, piped drinking water, and restrooms. A volleyball court and softball diamond are also available at East Garrison. The number of people who can use the area is limited and a reservation for use is required.

Picnicking is permitted throughout the island but fires are restricted to designated areas at Ayala Cove and East Garrison. Charcoal can be purchased on the island.

There is a fishing pier at Ayala Cove and one can fish from a number of other places on the island. Rock fish, striped bass or salmon may be caught.

Organized groups are welcome to use the playing field and other facilities at East Garrison. Reservations for group use of these facilities can be made up to 90 days in advance by contacting Marin District Headquarters, (415) 456-1286.

Private boats can use the boat slips or mooring buoys at Ayala Cove or East Garrison. Mooring buoys can be used overnight, but the boat slips—and the island itself—are for day use only.

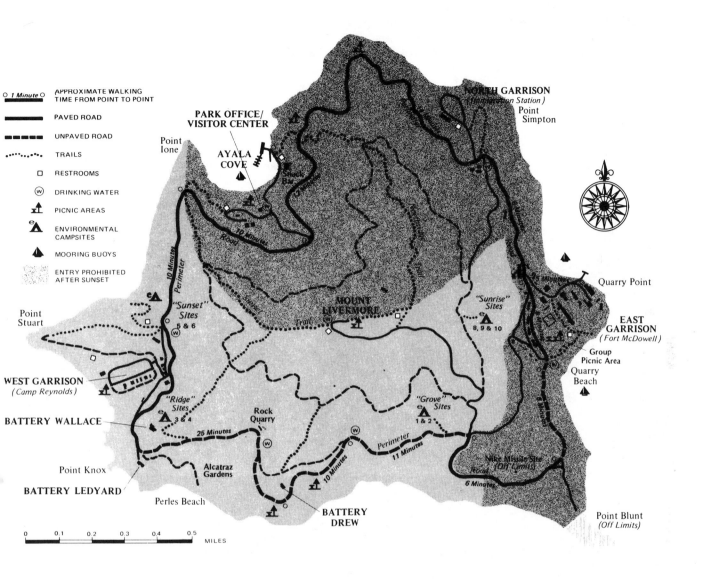

APPROXIMATE WALKING
TIME FROM POINT TO POINT

PAVED ROAD

UNPAVED ROAD

TRAILS

RESTROOMS

(W) DRINKING WATER

PICNIC AREAS

ENVIRONMENTAL CAMPSITES

MOORING BUOYS

ENTRY PROHIBITED AFTER SUNSET

## CAMPING

The park has nine environmental campsites in four areas. Shelter Grove (1) and Cypress Grove (2) in the Grove Area are protected from the wind. Bay Ridge (3) and Ridgecrest (4), in the Ridge Area, are more exposed and windy, but offer a view of San Francisco and the Golden Gate Bridge. Tiburon Sunset (5) and Tam Sunset (6) are on the west side of the island closest to the ferry dock. Leafy Sunrise (8), Peeking Sunrise (9), and Noon Sunrise (10) in the Sunrise Area are clustered on the east side of the island and make a good group camp area for up to 24 people. All sites have tables, barbecues, water and toilet. The sites are open all year around. You can reserve Angel Island's environmental campsites only through the Department of Parks and Recreation reservations office in Sacramento—1-800-952-5580.

## GETTING THERE

Ferries run to the island from San Francisco and Tiburon daily during the summer, June 1 through Labor Day. The Tiburon Ferry runs Saturday and Sunday year around and daily from June 1st through Labor Day. The Red/White Fleet runs Saturday and Sunday from May through October with additional daily service June 1st through Labor Day.

For information on ferry schedules and fares, call the Angel Island State Park Ferry, Tiburon, at (415) 435-2131, or the Red and White Fleet, San Francisco, (415) 546-2815.

Angel Island State Park
P.O. Box 318
Tiburon, CA 94920
(415) 435-1915

# China Camp State Park

Originally settled in the 1860s, China Camp was one of thirty fishing villages dotting the shore of San Francisco Bay. Most of its residents were Chinese from the maritime province of Kwangtung who needed new employment when the gold mines played out and work on the transcontinental railroad was completed.

Over 90 percent of the shrimp that these villages produced was dried on the hillsides around the Bay to be shipped to China. In the 1880s and '90s increasing pressure from competing fishermen led to legislation restricting use of bag nets similar to those used in China's Pearl River Delta, and seasonal fishing limitations were also imposed. Finally, in 1905, export of dried shrimp was banned. Despite all this, a few Chinese fishermen managed to hang on.

Today, the village that in the 1880s accommodated nearly five hundred people and boasted three general stores, a marine supply store, and a barber shop is reduced to a few ramshackle buildings along the water's edge, with only fragments of foundations to show where homes and shops once stood.

In 1977 the state acquired China Camp State Park, fifteen hundred acres of the most completely natural watershed remaining along the shores of San Francisco Bay. Hikers and equestrians can visit extensive intertidal, salt marsh, meadow, and oak habitats—even three small redwood groves—that are home to deer, squirrels, and many kinds of shore and water birds. At fishing access spots along North San Pedro Road, anglers can find striped bass, flounder, silver and rubberlip perch, and even an occasional sturgeon. Check the tide tables—at low tide the water may be too shallow for fishing, which is generally at its peak when large amounts of fresh water are flowing into the Bay.

The ridges to the west protect China Camp so that often when San Francisco is shrouded by fog, the park is sunny and warm. There are several picnic areas with tables, along the shore of China Camp Cove and China Camp Point. At Weber and Buckeye Points, barbecues are available. Many people enjoy picnicking and sunbathing on China Camp Cove's sandy beach.

### CAMPING

A small primitive walk-in camp is situated at Back-anch Meadow. It is available on a first come-first served sis.

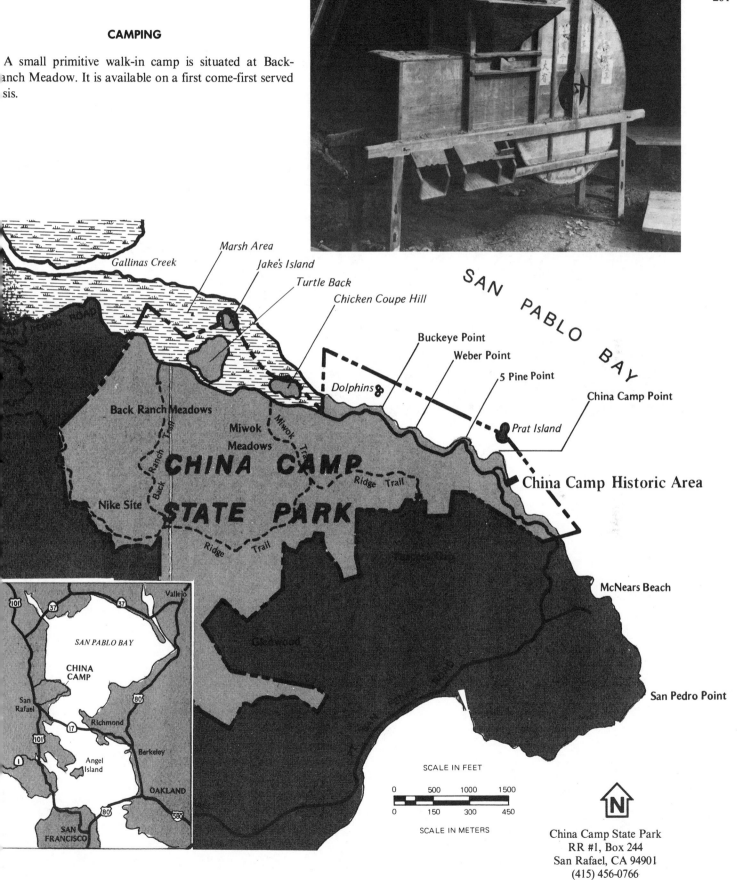

# Dry Lagoon State Park

Dry Lagoon State Park includes a low spit of sand between Stone Lagoon and the ocean, Dry (marshy actually) Lagoon itself, and the sandspit between Big Lagoon and the ocean. Its location provides a dramatic setting for the hikers and fishermen who walk out on the sandspit.

Migratory waterfowl feed at the lagoon and steelhead enter the waters when the sandspit is flooded over during heavy rains.

Nearby Henry A. Merlo State Recreation Area provides parking and access for fishing and hunting at Big Lagoon.

**CAMPING**

Stone Lagoon is the camping area for the state park. From the north end of the lagoon, a short road leads over a ridge to a spit separating the lagoon from the ocean. Thirty primitive campsites are located here; trailers and motorhomes are permitted. No water is available.

Environmental campsites can be reached by boat from the east shore of the lagoon. Parking and a boat ramp is located adjacent to the old Little Red Hen building. Rental boats are available.

Dry Lagoon State Park
C/O Klamath District
3431 Fort Avenue
Eureka, CA 95501
(707) 443-4588

Fort Humbolt 1864.

To early settlers of the isolated Humboldt Bay region Fort Humboldt was a symbol of civilization. Before troops under the command of Lt. Colonel Robert Buchanan arrived with his men in 1853, skirmishes with the Indians were frequent. By the summer of 1854 Buchanan's men had constructed 14 buildings on a barren bluff adjacent to the town of Bucksport. Among the structures was a barrack, commissary, hospital, officer's quarters, guardhouse, and blacksmith's shop.

For the soldiers stationed at this remote outpost life was lonely and depressing. One unhappy soldier was a young officer by the name of Ulysses S. Grant, who wrote to his wife, whom he hadn't seen in two years: "You don't know how forsaken I feel here." Grant took long solitary rides into the surrounding wilderness and drank heavily.

The park features a museum and a logging exhibit. A self-guided trail helps you trace the history of redwood logging from its beginnings in the 1850s to the present.

A picnic area and a fine view of Humboldt Bay are two more park highlights.

SECTION OF REDWOOD TREE

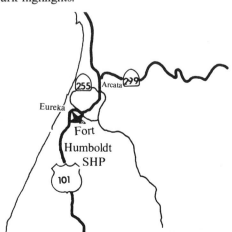

Fort Humboldt State Historic Park
3431 Fort Avenue
Eureka, Ca 95501
(707) 443-7952

# Fort Ross State Historic Park

Here in 1812, ninety-five Russians and forty native Alaskans (Aleuts and Kodiak Islanders) came ashore and built several houses and a sturdy wooden fort—the village and fortress of Ross. They came for a number of reasons: to hunt for sea otter, to grow wheat and other crops for the Russian settlements in Alaska, and to trade with Spanish California. Moreover, though they were careful not to say so, they came with an eye toward continuing the epic saga of Russian eastward expansion—a seemingly irresistible process that had begun some 250 years earlier in the time of Ivan-the-Terrible, Russia's first Tsar.

The presence of Russian fur hunters in the North Pacific had induced Spain to occupy Alta California nearly half a century earlier (1769), but as of 1812, San Francisco Bay still marked the northern limit of Spanish settlement. Moreover, that summer while the fort was being built, Spain, France, Russia and the other great colonial powers of the day were preoccupied with a major European war. Napoleon's army was deep inside Russia—driving toward Moscow. Great Britain was at war with its upstart ex-colony, the small but restless United States of America. No one was ready to block the Russian move. In fact, it was several months before the Spanish Californians were even aware of the development at Ross, and by then it was too late. The fort was complete and though it was made of wood, it was sturdy and well armed and vigilantly manned.

Of special interest to today's visitor is the commandant's house built by Alexander Rotchev, the last commandant of Fort Ross. Rotchev was a well-known poet, writer, traveller, and translator—a master of five languages. His wife, the former Princess Helena Gagarin, was widely known for her beauty, charm, and wit. A favorite with everyone who knew her, she had given up her place in high society and accepted financial disinheritance in order to marry Rotchev. Visitors were delighted by the Rotchevs' choice library, their hospitality, and the excellent piano on which the Princess Helena played Mozart.

Perhaps the most interesting building at Ross, from an architectural point of view, is the small, wooden Russian Orthodox chapel that was originally built about 1824. Sparsely furnished, and used only occasionally—there was no regular priest at Ross—the building remained standing long after the Russians left California. It was completely destroyed by fire in 1970, but has since been reconstructed. One of the original Russian bells, completely melted by the fire, was recast for display.

Made entirely of hand-hewn redwood timbers, the 12-foot high stockade was defended by brass and iron cannons. The seven-sided north blockhouse and the eight-sided south blockhouse contain exhibits covering various aspects of the Fort Ross story.

A number of publications about the history and natural history of the Fort Ross area are available in the park office, and guided tours of the parks are given on the weekends and during the summer.

*Original Redwood Chapel at Fort Ross.*

Fort Ross State Historic Park
19005 Coast Hwy. 1
Jenner, CA 95460
(707) 847-3286

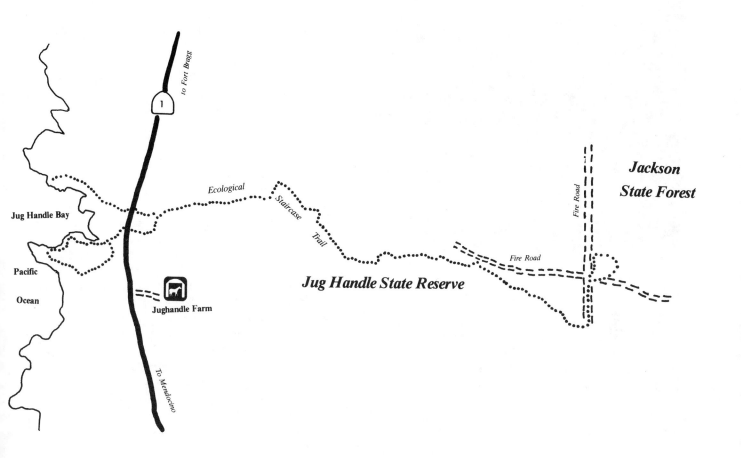

For half a million years or more this part of the Mendocino coast has been rising, jolting upward in response to the tremendous forces that have been building the Coast Range. The sea, rising as a warmer climate melted glaciers, cut into the emerging land to create bluffs and beaches that grew larger as sand and gravel were washed down onto them; then renewed tectonic activity lifted the beaches to form seaside terraces.

The result of this interaction of climate and geology is the five wave-cut terraces you can see at Jug Handle State Reserve, each about a hundred feet higher and a hundred thousand years older than the next. The youngest terrace, where you start your hike, emerged from the sea around a hundred thousand years ago; the highest terrace is over five hundred thousand years old.

As you hike to the second and third terraces, you will see how plants and soils change each other, from the grassy prairie around you to the redwood and pygmy forests on the higher levels.

It will take you about three hours to make the 5-mile roundtrip. Most of the trail is nearly level, but there are some steep slopes. Brochures, available at the rangers headquarters off Highway 1 and at the picnic area next to the parking lot, describe the "ecological staircase" trail.

Adjoining the reserve is privately owned Jug Handle Farm and Nature Center. A small campground and overnight accommodations in a renovated farm house are offered. Facilities are wheelchair accessible. Overnight fee: minor contribution of work requested. Reservations recommended: (707) 964-4630.

Jug Handle State Reserve
C/O Mendocino District
P.O. Box 440
Mendocino, CA 95460
(707) 937-5804

# MacKerricher State Park

*Cleone Lake*

MacKerricher State Park, three miles north of Fort Bragg on the scenic Mendocino coast, preserves its animals, birds, and plants in a wide variety of habitats—beach, bluff, headland, sand dune, forest and wetland.

A herd of harbor seals lives in the rocks off the park's coast, and the California gray whale can occasionally be seen making its annual 6,000-mile migration between Baja California and Alaska. The shoreline is dotted with tidepools.

The mild climate—summer days are cool and sometimes foggy, and winter temperatures seldom fall below freezing—encourages the luxuriant growth of plants and trees found in the park. Though the headlands are nearly bare of trees, they are covered with a thick mat of grass and wildflowers including sea pinks, wild onion, paint brush, lupine, California poppy, and monkey flower.

Further back from the ocean, beneath a forest of Bishop and shore pine, tanoak, and lowland fir, grow wax myrtle, cascara, salal, twinberry, California blackberry, salmonberry, and huckleberry. On the dunes in the north part of the park you can find franseria, sand verbena, sea-rocket, artemesia, sand primrose, and beach morning-glory. Cleone Lake, a former tidal lagoon, has willows, alders, sedges, and cattails along its margins.

Check with the park office for the schedule of nature hikes and campfire programs. Hikers can also take the six-mile (roundtrip) trail down the headlands toward Fort Bragg, or the one-and-a-third-mile trail around Cleone Lake, or explore the six miles of beach and dune in the northern portion of the park, between the campgrounds and Ten Mile River.

## HISTORY

This area, originally occupied by the Yuki and Pomo Indians, became known as El Rancho de la Laguna. It was purchased by Duncan MacKerricher in 1868 and was operated by his family until 1949, when it was gift-deeded to the state.

Anchor pins and holes used to hold pier pilings for ship-loading equipment can still be seen in the rocks of Laguna Point; they and the logging road through the park, which is still in use, are reminders of the area's extensive lumbering industry.

## FISHING

The visitor can take abalone; net surf smelt, fish the ocean for surf fish, several species of rock fish, ling cod, cabazone, blue and black rock cod, and smelt; or rent a boat at Noyo harbor and seek salmon. Cleone Lake, where there is a boat launching ramp (though no power boats are permitted), is stocked with rainbow trout, and in season nearby rivers can be fished for steelhead trout and salmon. A California fishing license is required.

Though visitors enjoy the 500-yard black-sand Cleone Beach and the other, smaller beaches along the headlands, swimming is not advised because of the cold water, rip currents, and rough surf. Skin divers, however, dive for abalone in a few of the coves.

## CAMPING

Each of the park's 143 campsites has a fireplace, table, and cupboard, with piped water and restrooms nearby; hot showers are available in the Pinewood and Cleone campgrounds. Supplies can be purchased at two grocery stores near the park entrance or at Fort Bragg. While there are no trailer hookups, the park has a trailer sanitation station, and campsites will accommodate trailers up to 27 feet in length or housecars up to 35 feet long.

MacKerricher State Park
C/O Mendocino District
P.O. Box 440
Mendocino, CA 95460
(707) 937-5804

# Mount Tamalpais State Park

*Mount Tam*

Mount Tamalpais State Park is located in Marin County just north of San Francisco and the Golden Gate, with the broad expanse of the Pacific Ocean on one side and San Francisco Bay on the other. With its dramatic combination of urban and natural scenery, the view from the top of the mountain is among the most exciting of its kind in the world. Often one can see the Farallon Islands some 25 miles out to sea, beyond the edge of the continent.

To the south lies the city of San Francisco. To the east, beyond the rolling hills of Marin County, is San Francisco Bay with its many arms and inlets. Mount Diablo dominates the eastern horizon. When conditions are right, it's possible to see clear across the great central valley to where the Sierra Nevada and Cascade Ranges loom up grandly against the sky—some two hundred miles away.

# Mount Tamalpais State Park

Within the park, climatic and geologic factors have produced a wonderful diversity of fascinating environments. Deep canyons filled with solemn redwood groves alternate with sun-drenched ridge tops. Stretches of grassland, chaparral, and oak savannah are complemented by wind-sculptured groves of cypress trees, and in some of the more protected areas there are luxurious stands of Douglas fir and California laurel. Adding to this diversity are the many trees, principally Bishop, Coulter, knobcone, and Monterey pine, that were planted in the 1920s and '30s by the Marin Municipal Water District.

This array of spectacular panoramas and delightful natural landscape made "Mount Tam" a popular recreational center long before the mountain was protected by park status. Even before the turn of the century, visitors to the area were so numerous that a passenger railroad—"the crookedest railroad in the world"—and later a toll road up the mountain were profitable ventures.

There are two picnic areas in the park. The one at Bootjack is complete with tables, stoves, piped drinking water, and modern restrooms. Because of the extreme fire hazard, the picnic area at East Peak does not have stoves, and fires are not permitted. For day use, the park opens half an hour before sunrise and closes half an hour before sunset.

## MOUNTAIN THEATER

Mountain Theater is a natural amphitheater with good acoustics and an impressive scenic backdrop two thousand feet above sea level on the eastern slope of Mount Tamalpais. Seating for more than 5,000 people is provided by massive tiers of serpentine and peridotite rock that were set in place by the Civilian Conservation Corps in the 1930s.

## HIKING

Walking for pleasure along the trails on Mount Tamalpais is a tradition that reaches well back into the 19th century. Trail construction was first undertaken by individual volunteers, but soon became an important function of the Tamalpais Conservation Club. During the 1930s the CCC greatly extended and improved the trail system, so that today there are about 42 miles of trail within the park boundaries. Trails within the park, however, are really just the heart of a far more extensive, 200-mile long trail network that extends through Muir Woods National Monument, the Golden Gate National Recreation Area, and watershed lands held by the Marin Municipal Water District.

## CAMPING

Campsites at Pantoll are open the year around and are complete with tables, stoves, piped drinking water, and restrooms. Only walk-in, tent-style camping is permitted—there are no spaces available for vehicular camping and automobile parking is restricted to an area about 100 yards from the campsites. Fires are permitted only in the stone fireplaces. Use of campsites is on a first-come, first-served basis.

The group campground at Camp Alice Eastwood is open to the public use between April 15 and November 15, and can accommodate up to forty people. Facilities include tables, piped drinking water, and pit toilets. Reservations are required.

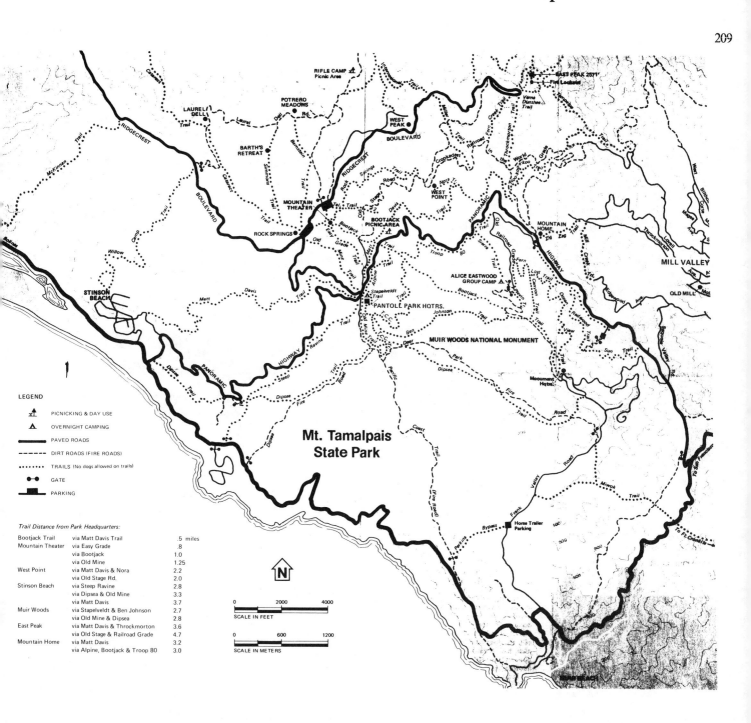

**Mt. Tamalpais State Park**

LEGEND

⛺ PICNICKING & DAY USE

▲ OVERNIGHT CAMPING

PAVED ROADS

DIRT ROADS (FIRE ROADS)

TRAILS (No dogs allowed on trails)

GATE

PARKING

*Trail Distance from Park Headquarters:*

| | | |
|---|---|---|
| Bootjack Trail | via Matt Davis Trail | .5 miles |
| Mountain Theater | via Easy Grade | .8 |
| | via Bootjack | 1.0 |
| | via Old Mine | 1.25 |
| West Point | via Matt Davis & Nora | 2.2 |
| | via Old Stage Rd. | 2.0 |
| Stinson Beach | via Steep Ravine | 2.8 |
| | via Dipsea & Old Mine | 3.3 |
| | via Matt Davis | 3.7 |
| Muir Woods | via Stapelveldt & Ben Johnson | 2.7 |
| | via Old Mine & Dipsea | 2.8 |
| East Peak | via Matt Davis & Throckmorton | 3.6 |
| | via Old Stage & Railroad Grade | 4.7 |
| Mountain Home | via Matt Davis | 3.2 |
| | via Alpine, Bootjack & Troop 80 | 3.0 |

N

| SCALE IN FEET | | |
|---|---|---|
| 0 | 2000 | 4000 |

| SCALE IN METERS | | |
|---|---|---|
| 0 | 600 | 1200 |

Ten rustic cabins, the Steep Ravine Cabins, are located on a coastal bluff overlooking the Pacific Ocean. Each cabin has a wood stove, table, benches, several sleeping platforms and an outdoor barbecue. Primitive toilets and water faucets are nearby. Cabin #1 and its facilities are wheelchair accessible.

Reservations may be made only by mail through the Reservations Office, Department of Parks and Recreation, P.O. Box 2390, Sacramento, CA 95811. For reservation forms and information in California call 1-800-952-5580.

Mount Tamalpais State Park
801 Panoramic Highway
Mill Valley, CA 94941
(415) 388-2070

# Patrick's Point State Park

Patrick's Point State Park is a tree- and meadow-covered headland with a broad sandy beach that juts into the Pacific Ocean thirty miles north of Eureka. Though the 630-acre park is in the heart of California's coast redwood forest, spruce, hemlock, pine, fir, and red alder are its principal trees.

Yurok Indians recognized the importance of the rocky promontory when they selected Abalone Point for their summer site hundreds of years ago. Nearby Penn Creek was a source of fresh water and the forest was rich with game.

The sea also provided the tribe with food. Sea lion meat was a main item in their diet and shell mounds show that the Indians were fond of the marine mussels as well.

Patrick's Point State Park offers a variety of outdoor activities and a wealth of natural beauty. There are thick patches of huckleberry, salal, blackberry, azalea, and rhododendron. In some parts of the forest the plant life is so abundant that it is nearly impossible to penetrate the areas. Some of the park's 12 trails are tightly hemmed in with walls of vegetation that isolate and shelter the hiker from the sounds of other human life.

The shoreline ranges from a broad sand beach to high precipitous cliffs. Sea stacks that were once part of the mainland rock stand offshore like pickets, surrounded by a surging ocean. Because the steep bluffs are constantly being eroded by wind, sea, and rain they are very hazardous. Avoid walking too close to the edge and do not cross barriers.

## AGATE BEACH

This gently curving sand strip, which extends for two miles north of the park boundary, can be reached by a short but steep trail from Agate Beach Campground. Driftwood of an infinite number of sizes and shapes lies high on the beach where winter storms deposited it. The driving winds and high tides of winter also cause the sea to deposit semiprecious stones on the beach where they are washed and polished by the constant motion of sand and water.

South of the Agate Beach, the park's shoreline changes to steep, craggy inlets and rugged promontories that plunge into the sea. Steep trails wind down the cliffs to ledges where fishermen catch ling cod, greenlings, sea trout, and cabezone.

## HIKING

Rim Trail, a two-mile walk with good views of the ocean and offshore rocks, follows an old Indian trail from Agate Beach Campground to Palmer's Point. This old Indian path is the longest in the park.

A cross section of the park's plant life is presented on a self-guided nature trail that loops through the Octopus Trees Grove. The name "octopus" is deceptive, but its use is more easily understood when you see how the roots of Sitka spruce have been deformed. The roots of young trees sometimes grow over decaying logs to seek out moisture stored in the rotting wood and are frequently left in tentacle-like shapes after the decaying logs have disintegrated.

Black-tailed deer are a common sight along the bluffs and in the meadows at sunup and sundown. The raucous chattering of Steller's jays punctuates the air, and you may see and hear sea lions on the offshore rocks south of the park. Shore birds are plentiful, particularly during spring and fall migrations.

As with all the north coast, Patrick's Point State Park is characterized by year-round moderate temperatures, frequent summer fogs, and sparkling spring and fall days. The ocean is cold and dangerous enough to discourage swimming; children should not be permitted even to wade. There are unexpected holes in the underwater sand and the undertow is strong.

Lady Bird Johnson Grove

Orick

Freshwater Lagoon

Stone Lagoon

HUMBOLDT LAGOONS STATE PARK

Tall Trees Grove

Bald Hills Rd.

Big Lagoon

HARRY A. MERLO STATE RECREATION AREA

PATRICK'S POINT STATE PARK

101

## CAMPING

The Abalone, Penn Creek, and Agate Beach Campgrounds have 123 family campsites. Each is furnished with a stove, table, and cupboard. Hot showers and restrooms are nearby. The park also has two family picnic areas. A group camp with accommodations for 250 visitors and a group picnic area that has room for 200 are available to organizations. The group camp and group picnic area must be reserved beforehand.

Patrick's Point State Park
4150 Patrick's Point Dr.
Trinidad, CA 95570
(707) 677-3570

# Russian Gulch State Park

Just ten miles south of Fort Bragg in the scenic Mendocino County portion of the north coast, Russian Gulch State Park offers both the serenity of redwood groves and the excitement of an ocean shore. Its beach is suitable for swimming and sunbathing, though the water is cold, and is also used as an entry point for skindivers. The headland offers a wonderful view of the coast both north and south, as well as of Russian Gulch itself.

Out on the headland is a spectacular point of interest, the Devil's Punch Bowl—a sea-cut tunnel about two hundred feet long that has collapsed at its inland end to make a hole a hundred feet across and sixty feet deep. Its steep walls are lined with wildflowers and other small plants. This is one of the Mendocino coast's "blow-holes." Waves can be seen coming in through the tunnel, but the bowl is too broad and open for any "blowing" effect to be noticeable except under storm conditions.

Inland, the park includes nearly three miles of the heavily forested Russian Gulch Creek Canyon. There are picnic sites on the headland and the beach, and campsites in the protected canyon. A scenic bicycle path makes it easy to see the lower part of the canyon, and a hiking trail continues inland past a beautiful waterfall and up onto the surrounding ridges.

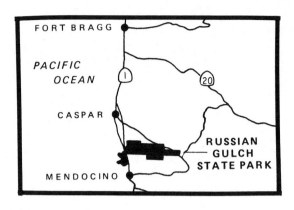

*Highway 1 bridge over Russian Gulch*

If you like to walk in the woods, there are several trails of varying lengths you can try. You may even wish to take a longer hike by connecting up some of these trails—for instance, you can take the South Trail from the group camp, then continue up the Canyon Bike Trail and around the Falls Loop Trail, and finally return to camp via the North Trail. In this three-to-four-hour hike, which covers over nine miles (14 km.), you will pass through six different biotic communities.

The canyon is filled with second-growth coast redwoods, *Sequoia sempervirens,* mixed with Douglas fir, western hemlock, tanoak, and California laurel; alders and big-leaf maples can be found along the creek. Inside this forest there are rhododendrons, azaleas, and many kinds of ferns, along with thimbleberry, salmonberry, blackberry, and many other small, shade-loving plants. Higher up on the slopes are Bishop pine, grand fir, and Mendocino cypress; some of the trees on the headland have been carved and twisted into fascinating shapes by the prevailing onshore winds.

Raccoons, rabbits, chipmunks, and deer are the animals most frequently seen by park visitors, but skunks and an occasional bobcat or fox are also seen. Birdlife is plentiful and varied. Steller jays, quail, and band-tailed pigeons are numerous, and there are also red-tailed hawks, ospreys, and ravens to be seen. Right along the coast are a great many kinds of shorebirds. Kingfishers can occasionally be found plying their trade along the creekbed, and sometimes in the fall a great blue heron with six-foot wingspan will make its home back in the most protected part of the canyon.

## FISHING

Fishing for rainbow trout is allowed in the park during the normal fishing season. However, steelhead trout that come up the creek to spawn during the late fall and winter are protected by various regulations. They may *not* be caught.

Rock fishing is excellent, and salmon fishing in the ocean is good during the summer months. The salmon do not come close enough to shore to be caught from the park's beach or headland, however, so a boat is needed. Small boats can be hand carried over the beach and out to the water; larger boats can be launched at Noyo, a nearby fishing village where party boats are also available.

Skindiving for abalone and other fish is also quite popular here. Most divers enter the water in the shelter of the main cove and do most of their diving either just offshore or in adjoining coves.

## CAMPING

In a creekside setting well inside the forested area of the canyon there are 30 family campsites, each with table, stove, and food locker. Nearby are restrooms complete with hot showers and laundry tubs. Trailers up to 20 feet in length can be parked in some of the campsites, although trailer hookups are not available. There is also a group campground suitable for up to 40 people.

Russian Gulch State Park
C/O Mendocino District
P.O. Box 440
Mendocino, CA 95460
(707) 937-5804

# Salt Point State Park

Salt Point is located in Sonoma County about 90 miles north of San Francisco on State Highway 1. Its rugged northern coastline varies dramatically from protected, sandy beach coves such as Stump Beach on the northern end of the park to the sharp bluffs and sheer sandstone cliffs that plunge straight down to the sea at Salt Point and Gerstle Cove. The park includes one of the first underwater parks to be established in California; except for areas posted as natural preserves it is open for fishing.

The park's 6,000 acres of forest and grassland offer camping, picnicking, fishing, skin diving, and trails for horseback riding and hiking.

As the terrain rises northeast of Highway 1, coastal brush and grasslands blend into lush growths of bishop pine, Douglas fir, madrone, tanoak, redwoods, and quiet meadows. At the top of the coastal ridge, about 1,000 feet elevation, is a large open "prairie" and pygmy forest where stands of cypress, pine, and even the normally gigantic redwood grow in stunted profusion. The pygmy forest is an extension of similar forests found in Mendocino County.

Animal life is abundant. Blacktail deer, raccoon, coyote, bobcat, gray fox, badger, striped skunk, wild pig, and dozens of rodents such as squirrel, chipmunk, and field mouse are native. Many types of birds are found here, including the brown pelican, osprey, and other water birds. Between December and May, park visitors may sight gray whales on their annual migration between Baja California and the Bering Sea.

Divers enjoy exploring Salt Point's tide pools and the rich offshore flora and fauna; beginning divers find Gerstle Cove a good place to gain experience.

## CAMPING

A little upland but still easily accessible to the shore is a 109-unit campground, which includes a group site, walk-in sites, hiker-biker sites, plus five special environmental campsites. Each site has a table and stove, and a central water supply and restrooms are nearby.

Park picnic areas include Gerstle Cove, Stump Beach Cove and Fisk Mill Cove.

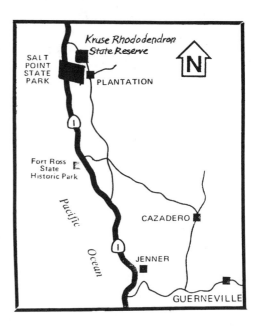

*Bird watchers and admirers of wildflowers are delighted by the bluffs above Salt Point.*

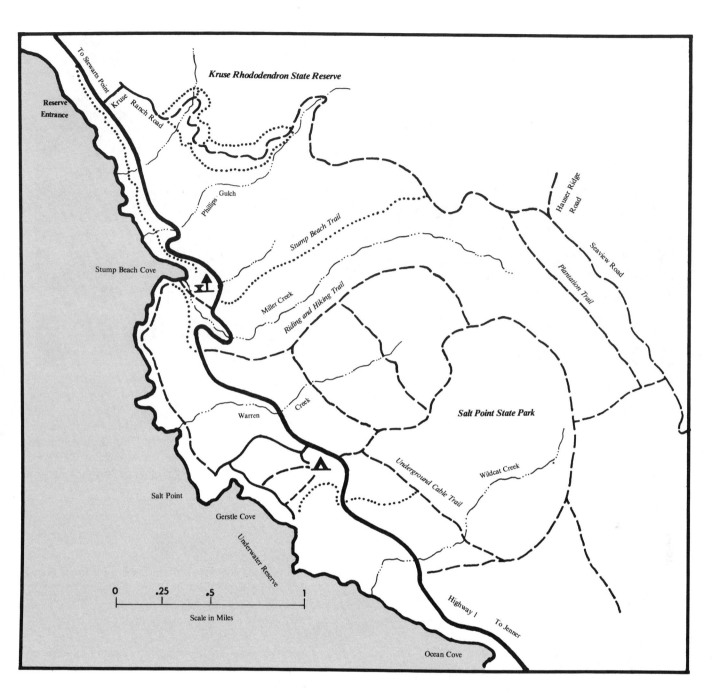

## Kruse Rhododendron State Reserve

Next to Salt Point State Park, Kruse Rhododendron State Reserve contains 317 beautiful acres of second-growth redwood, Douglasfir, tanoak, and, of course, rhododendron. As the rhododendron growth was the result of an early burn, the regenerating forest is jeopardizing the floral display. There are five miles of hiking trails through the quiet forest and picturesque bridges over wintertime streams in fern-filled canyons.

Edward P.E. Kruse donated the land to the State in 1933 as a living memorial to his father, a founder of San Francisco's German Bank, later the First Western Bank. It was a part of a larger ranch established in 1880 where the Kruses raised sheep and carried on lumbering and tanbark harvesting.

Salt Point State Park
25050 Coast Hwy. 1
Jenner, CA 95450
(707) 847-3221

# Sinkyone Wilderness State Park

Sinkyone Wilderness is on California's Lost Coast—an area of unstable earth and fast-rising mountains. The famed San Andreas fault lies just offshore of the Wilderness; it touches land a short distance to the north, at Shelter Cove. So rugged is this country, highway engineers were forced to route Highway 1 a dozen miles inland from the Sinkyone—and the region has remained sparsely settled and unspoiled. Its magnificent vistas and varied terrain—dense forests, prairies, coastal bluffs, beaches—reward the hardy explorer.

The sea is an overwhelming presence here, and its rhythmic sounds provide a thunderous background for a walk along land's end. The sky is filled with gulls and pelicans, sea lions and harbor seals gather at Little Jackass Cove, and the California gray whale migration passes near shore during winter and early spring.

But this aptly named "Lost Coast" is in dispute. Only a small part of the Sinkyone Wilderness, about 3600 acres, has been set aside in the state park. For more than a decade it has been the hope of conservationists and the State Park and Recreation Commission to expand the park southward to include more of the spectacular coastal bluffs and primeval forest. With the old growth forest just outside park boundaries threatened by timber interests and with increased pressure for more vehicular access, plans to expand the Sinkyone Wilderness face an uncertain future.

One of the last surviving old growth redwood groves, the Sally Bell Grove, was named in honor of one of the last full-blooded Sinkyone living on the Lost Coast. She survived a massacre of her people by marauding white men to become a legend, a woman of strong will and strong medicine. She was given the name "Sally Bell" by white settlers who took her in.

Based on artifacts found in the old growth redwood groves, archaeologists speculate that humans may have occupied this area as early as 6,000 B.C. Forest and sea provided an abundant food supply. Until the last century, the richness of the land made this stretch of California coast one of the most heavily populated Native American regions of North America.

## CAMPING

At Sinkyone Wilderness State Park two dozen backcountry campsites are located in protected areas, each with stream water and easy access to secluded black sand beaches. A network of 15 miles of hiking and horse trails leads through the wilderness.

The park's visitor center, located in a turn-of-the-century ranch house at Needle Rock, provides a good staging point with displays, publications, maps and registration for the hike-in campsites.

General information on the park and road conditions are available at Humboldt Redwoods State Park, at Weott, on U.S. Highway 101 (phone 707-946-2311). Check-in/out time is 2 P.M., but you may move into your site earlier if it is not occupied. Plan to leave yourself at least an hour of daylight to find your site.

To reach the park, take the Briceland-Whitehorn Road (Count Road 435) from Redway, 2.5 miles west of Garberville; the access roads are rugged and unpaved for the last 9 miles, but they are passable for passenger cars in summer; in winter, four-wheel-drive may be required. The roads are not negotiable for large RVs or trailers. Six miles south of Whitethorn, the unpaved two-lane road becomes one lane.

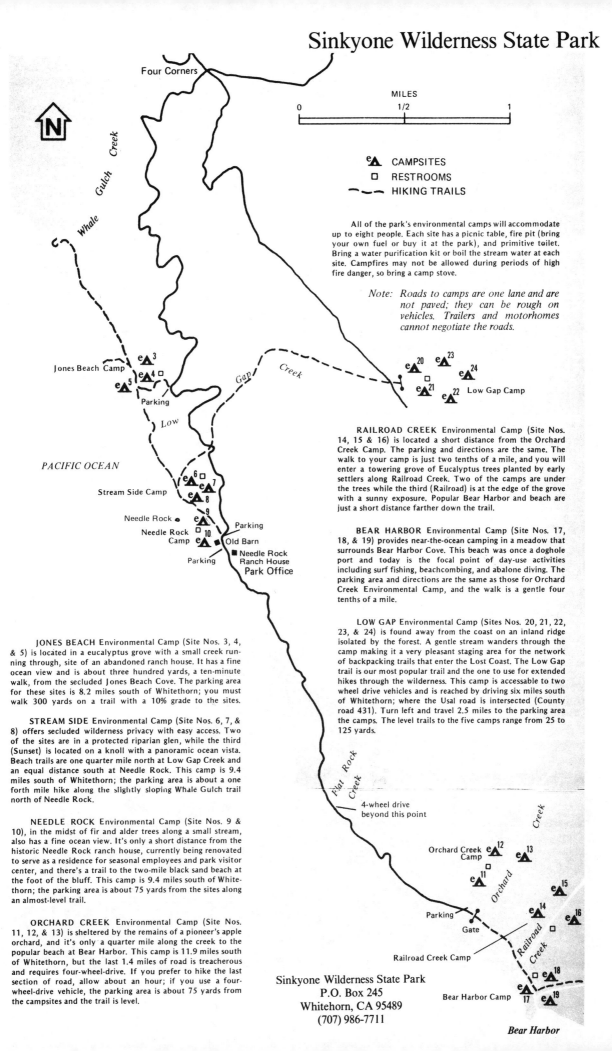

Four Corners

MILES
0    1/2    1

e**A**  CAMPSITES
▫  RESTROOMS
--_--  HIKING TRAILS

All of the park's environmental camps will accommodate up to eight people. Each site has a picnic table, fire pit (bring your own fuel or buy it at the park), and primitive toilet. Bring a water purification kit or boil the stream water at each site. Campfires may not be allowed during periods of high fire danger, so bring a camp stove.

*Note: Roads to camps are one lane and are not paved; they can be rough on vehicles. Trailers and motorhomes cannot negotiate the roads.*

Whale Gulch Creek

Gap Creek

Jones Beach Camp
e**A**³
e**A**⁴ ▫
e**A**⁵
Parking

Low

PACIFIC OCEAN

Stream Side Camp
e**A**⁶ ▫
e**A**⁷
e**A**⁸

Needle Rock ●
e**A**⁹
Needle Rock ▫ ¹⁰
Camp e**A**
Parking
Old Barn
■ Needle Rock
Ranch House
Parking
**Park Office**

e**A**²⁰ e**A**²³
▫          e**A**²⁴
e**A**²¹ e**A**²²  Low Gap Camp

**RAILROAD CREEK** Environmental Camp (Site Nos. 14, 15 & 16) is located a short distance from the Orchard Creek Camp. The parking and directions are the same. The walk to your camp is just two tenths of a mile, and you will enter a towering grove of Eucalyptus trees planted by early settlers along Railroad Creek. Two of the camps are under the trees while the third (Railroad) is at the edge of the grove with a sunny exposure. Popular Bear Harbor and beach are just a short distance farther down the trail.

**BEAR HARBOR** Environmental Camp (Site Nos. 17, 18, & 19) provides near-the-ocean camping in a meadow that surrounds Bear Harbor Cove. This beach was once a doghole port and today is the focal point of day-use activities including surf fishing, beachcombing, and abalone diving. The parking area and directions are the same as those for Orchard Creek Environmental Camp, and the walk is a gentle four tenths of a mile.

**LOW GAP** Environmental Camp (Sites Nos. 20, 21, 22, 23, & 24) is found away from the coast on an inland ridge isolated by the forest. A gentle stream wanders through the camp making it a very pleasant staging area for the network of backpacking trails that enter the Lost Coast. The Low Gap trail is our most popular trail and the one to use for extended hikes through the wilderness. This camp is accessible to two wheel drive vehicles and is reached by driving six miles south of Whitethorn; where the Usal road is intersected (County road 431). Turn left and travel 2.5 miles to the parking area the camps. The level trails to the five camps range from 25 to 125 yards.

**JONES BEACH** Environmental Camp (Site Nos. 3, 4, & 5) is located in a eucalyptus grove with a small creek running through, site of an abandoned ranch house. It has a fine ocean view and is about three hundred yards, a ten-minute walk, from the secluded Jones Beach Cove. The parking area for these sites is 8.2 miles south of Whitethorn; you must walk 300 yards on a trail with a 10% grade to the sites.

**STREAM SIDE** Environmental Camp (Site Nos. 6, 7, & 8) offers secluded wilderness privacy with easy access. Two of the sites are in a protected riparian glen, while the third (Sunset) is located on a knoll with a panoramic ocean vista. Beach trails are one quarter mile north at Low Gap Creek and an equal distance south at Needle Rock. This camp is 9.4 miles south of Whitethorn; the parking area is about a one forth mile hike along the slightly sloping Whale Gulch trail north of Needle Rock.

**NEEDLE ROCK** Environmental Camp (Site Nos. 9 & 10), in the midst of fir and alder trees along a small stream, also has a fine ocean view. It's only a short distance from the historic Needle Rock ranch house, currently being renovated to serve as a residence for seasonal employees and park visitor center, and there's a trail to the two-mile black sand beach at the foot of the bluff. This camp is 9.4 miles south of Whitethorn; the parking area is about 75 yards from the sites along an almost-level trail.

**ORCHARD CREEK** Environmental Camp (Site Nos. 11, 12, & 13) is sheltered by the remains of a pioneer's apple orchard, and it's only a quarter mile along the creek to the popular beach at Bear Harbor. This camp is 11.9 miles south of Whitethorn, but the last 1.4 miles of road is treacherous and requires four-wheel-drive. If you prefer to hike the last section of road, allow about an hour; if you use a four-wheel-drive vehicle, the parking area is about 75 yards from the campsites and the trail is level.

Flat Rock Creek

4-wheel drive
beyond this point

Orchard Creek e**A**¹² e**A**¹³
Camp
e**A**¹¹

Orchard Creek

e**A**¹⁵

Parking
Gate
e**A**¹⁴ ▫
e**A**¹⁶

Railroad Creek

Railroad Creek Camp

▫ e**A**¹⁸
Bear Harbor Camp e**A**¹⁷ e**A**¹⁹

Sinkyone Wilderness State Park
P.O. Box 245
Whitehorn, CA 95489
(707) 986-7711

*Bear Harbor*

# Sonoma Coast State Beach

Broad, shining beaches and secluded coves, rugged headlands and natural arches, and a craggy coastline with tidal pools and reefs characterize one of California's most scenic attractions—Sonoma Coast State Beach.

The Beach, actually a series of beaches separated by rocky bluffs, extends 13 miles between Bodega Head and the Russian River in Sonoma County. It is accessible to beachcombers, fishermen, sunbathers, and picnickers from more than a dozen points along coast Highway 1.

Generally, the weather is ideal. There is some fog during the summer, but it usually burns off by midday, and the cool ocean breezes make Sonoma Coast a haven for visitors seeking to escape the inland heat.

## PICNICKING AND CAMPING

Picnicking is a popular pastime. There are some picnic tables at a few of the beach access points such as Wright's Beach and Rock Point, but generally people like to settle down directly on the sand and use the fire rings provided for cooking.

There are 30 developed campsites (no showers) around the edge of Wright's Beach. Cypress Dunes, a hundred-site developed campground with hot showers, restrooms, a trailer sanitation station, and a campfire center is located half a mile south of Salmon Creek. The campgrounds are very popular, and it is a good idea to make a reservation in advance, especially in summer.

The bluffs, slopes, and dunes of the beach support a hardy ground cover of native shrubs, grasses, and wildflowers. The area is unusually beautiful in the spring when the yellow and blue lupine, sea pink, Indian paintbrush, western wallflower, sea fig, sand verbena, western iris, wild strawberry, monkey flower, and dozens of other varieties of wildflowers all bloom at once.

Animal life is just as varied. There is the raccoon, gray fox, rabbit, blacktail deer, skunk, ground squirrel, and, of course, birds. Shorebirds and waterfowl include gulls, cormorants, pelicans, coots, and most species of ducks; valley quail, ravens, wrens, hawks, swallows, and other land birds also abound. Altogether, some 300 species of birds have been listed for the area.

## FISHING

Sonoma Coast is a fisherman's paradise. The ocean, bay, and river frontage offer many opportunities for the sport fisherman. Species include rock fish, perch, salmon, steelhead, and smelt. There are also red abalone, mussels and cockles to be found. A valid sportfishing license is required.

You'll enjoy visiting GOAT ROCK, at the northern end of the park near the mouth of the Russian River. The scenic shoreline, sandy beach, and fresh and saltwater fishing make this one of the more popular day-use areas.

SHELL BEACH, a favorite of the beachcomber and stroller. It is used by schools as an outdoor classroom for the study of tidal pool marine life, and enjoys a reputation as a prime fishing spot.

DUNCAN'S LANDING, also called Death Rock, is famous for two things: it was used as an early-day landing for loading small coastal ships with lumber and food products; and its rocky headland is the most dangerous point along the beach.

ROCK POINT is on a headland overlooking the scenic shoreline. There are several picnic tables available.

PORTUGUESE BEACH is a sandy beach surrounded by rocky headlands. Rock fishing and surf fishing are popular.

SALMON CREEK BEACH. Salmon Creek forms a lagoon when sand closes the mouth of the stream. This is a well-used area, with surf fishing and beachcombing the most popular activities. Park headquarters are located at the north side of Salmon Creek, beside Highway 1.

SAND DUNE STABILIZATION AREA. In 1951, a program was begun to control drifting sand and keep it from filling in the bay. The dunes between Bodega Bay and Salmon Creek were planted with various specialized grasses including European beach grass, used to protect dykes in the Netherlands. Fire hazard in this area is high.

RIDING AND HIKING TRAIL. For the horseman and the hiker, the park has established a five-mile trail system in the dunes area. Access is at the north end of Bodega Bay at West Bay Road.

Sonoma Coast State Beach
Bodega Bay, CA 94923
(707) 875-3483

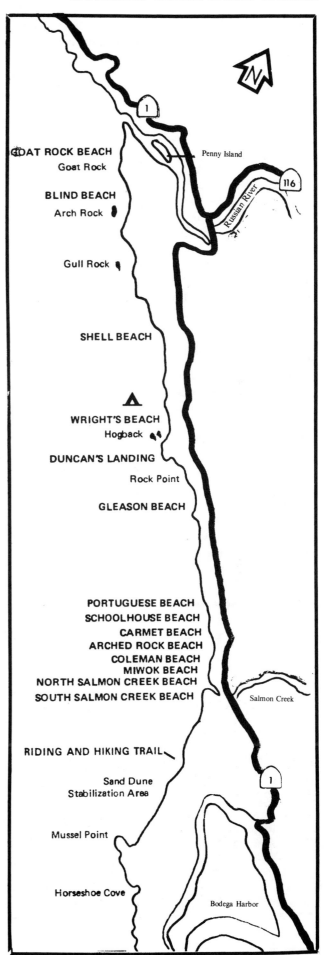

# Tomales Bay State Park

Located on the Point Reyes peninsula, Tomales Bay State Park in Marin County, about 40 miles north of the Golden Gate Bridge, is a recreation haven bounded by the sheltered waters of Tomales Bay on the northeast and protected on the west and south by the rolling hills of the Point Reyes National Seashore. Rich in history and possessing a unique geology, Tomales Bay has attractions for the recreationist, botanist, geologist, ornithologist, and historian.

The region presents a great diversity of climate and geography. Point Reyes Lighthouse area is one of the windiest and foggiest spots on the California coast and yet, a few miles east, in Tomales Bay State Park, the sunny beaches are noted for their warmth and relative freedom from wind and fog. Although much of California's landscape has been greatly altered by development, the Tomales Bay landscape is much the same as it was back in 1542, when Cabrillo sailed nearby.

Russian and German scientists explored the region in 1816. A. von Chamisso and Johann Friedrich Eschscholtz (for whom *Eschscholtzia californica,* the California poppy, was named) explored here and discovered many plant species.

The land was part of Spanish land grants in the 1830s and 1840s, then was sold off to a series of owners. By 1880, homesites were being sold and the village of Inverness was established, primarily as a summer vacation spot. For many years the sunny, secluded beaches along Tomales Bay have attracted Bay Area excursionists for daytime outings, and over the years a few summer and beach homes have been built along Tomales Bay. The peninsula itself was used for dairying, after man drove the native elk and deer from the land, and today it remains among the finest dairyland to be found anywhere.

Despite its attractiveness and some development, most of this area lay untouched until the 1940s, when real estate developers began to purchase large tracts of beachfront land. Local residents, who habitually had enjoyed these beaches, feared they would be closed to public use. A small group formed the Tomales Bay Beaches committee for the purpose of securing the land for a park. The Marin Conservation League adopted the project and with the Sierra Club, Alpine Club, Tamalpais Conservation League, Marin Nature Group, garden clubs and other organizations, and help from the state, succeeded in purchasing portions of the area.

The League then collected funds to acquire what became the Willis Linn Jepson Memorial Grove of Bishop Pines, named after the late University of California botanist who founded the Division (now School) of Forestry at the University of California, Berkeley. Finally, on November 8, 1952, Tomales Bay State Park, comprising over a thousand acres, was dedicated.

## WILDLIFE

Wildlife abounds in this type of country. Foxes, raccoons, badgers, weasels, chipmunks, squirrels, rabbits, deer, occasional bobcats, skunks, wood-rats, field-mice, moles and others inhabit the area. It was from this peninsula, legend has it, that the last Marin County band of Roosevelt elk swam across Tomales Bay in a mass migration, in the early 1860s, and headed north. Black bear, too, roamed the area at that time.

Ornithologists come to study the numerous species of land and sea birds. These include the rare spotted owl, band-tailed pigeons, quail, thrush, horned larks, goldfinches, summer warblers, large and small rails, puffins, murres, the great blue heron, sandhill cranes, towhees, ravens, pelicans, pelagic cormorants, ruddy ducks, geese, scoters, grebes, bitterns, flickers and woodpeckers, meadow larks, kingfishers, pigmy nuthatches and many more.

The park is a lush wilderness of forests, beaches, fields, hills, meadows, and swamps, each with its own plant life. Among the most prominent trees are the bishop pine, madrone, California laurel, oaks, red and white alders, chinquapin, willow and buckeye. Shrubs, some of which grow to tree size, include many varieties of ceanothus, toyon, hazel, huckleberry, gooseberries, salmonberries, thimbleberries, varieties of manzanita, purple and red elderberry, honeysuckle, oso berry, mountain mahogany and the rare leatherwood. Fern fronds edge the beaches and grace the wooded areas. Varieties include woodwardia, sword, deer, bracken, five-finger, maidenhair, gold-back, lady, polypodium, lace, grapefern, and waterfern.

The wildflowers which cover the countryside in great carpets in springtime attract botanists and flower lovers from great distances. Some three hundred varieties of flowers have been identified in the spring and many more in other seasons. There are many kinds of lilies, fritillaria with colors from the rare white to bronze and chocolate, poppy, wild strawberry, many varieties of lupine, iris from pure white through deep violet shades and four varieties of mimulus or monkeyflower.

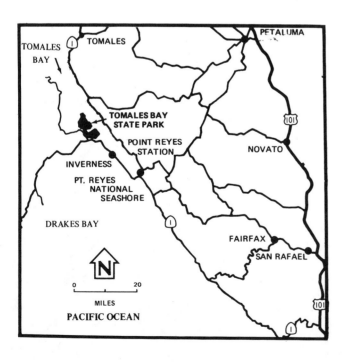

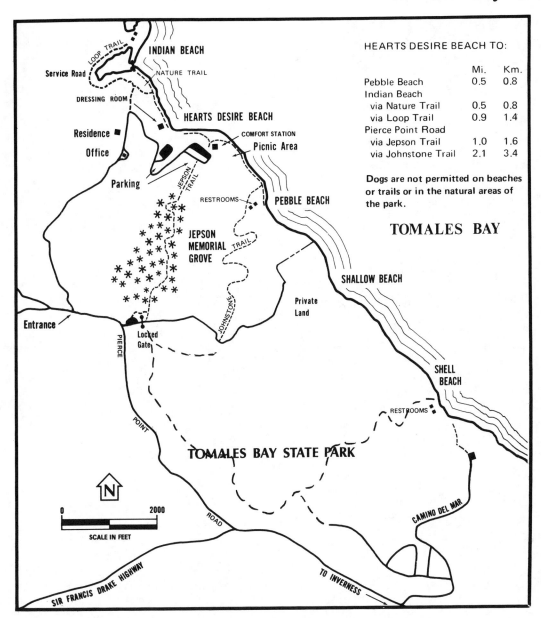

|  | Mi. | Km. |
|---|---|---|
| Pebble Beach | 0.5 | 0.8 |
| Indian Beach |  |  |
| via Nature Trail | 0.5 | 0.8 |
| via Loop Trail | 0.9 | 1.4 |
| Pierce Point Road |  |  |
| via Jepson Trail | 1.0 | 1.6 |
| via Johnstone Trail | 2.1 | 3.4 |

Dogs are not permitted on beaches or trails or in the natural areas of the park.

**TOMALES BAY**

### THE BEACHES

The shallow, gently sloping, surf-free beaches—Indian, Heart's Desire, Pebble, and Shell beaches—are the primary recreation attraction. The first three can be reached in the park, but Shell Beach is separated from the others by a parcel of privately owned land; it can be reached by turning right on Camino Del Mar three-tenths of a mile beyond Inverness.

Picnicking, swimming, hiking, clamming, and boating with small craft are offered in the park. There is water, a picnic area with fire places, dressing rooms, flush toilets and parking at Heart's Desire Beach. The others have only pit toilets and waste disposal facilities. No lifeguard is on duty in the park. All beaches have good populations of horseneck clams and cockles. There are no boat-launching facilities, but hand-carried boats may be put in the water away from the swimming areas. Boaters are welcome to land on the beaches provided they stay clear of the well-marked swimming areas.

### BISHOP PINE

One of the finest remaining virgin groves of bishop pine in California is preserved in the Jepson Memorial Grove. Not as large in stature as some species, craggy in appearance and grotesquely shaped, they are a close relative of the Monterey pine. They belong to a group of "closed cone pines" that have survived from a prehistoric forest. The tight-fisted, prickly cones retain their seeds until opened by heat so seeds are dispersed very rarely—only when the pines are burned or the cones subjected to extreme heat. The grove is reached via a one-mile trail.

Tomales Bay State Park
Star Route
Inverness, CA 94937
(415) 669-1140

# Van Damme State Park

*Little River*

Van Damme State Park is situated in the heart of one of the most scenic areas of Northern California—the Mendocino coast. Its 1,831 acres of beach and upland offer camping, hiking, picnicking fishing, and beachcombing.

Some of the more interesting features of the park are the lush Fern Canyon, where the walls are covered with different varieties of ferns; the Pygmy Forest, where mature, cone-bearing cypress and pine trees stand fully grown at heights from six inches to five feet; and the bog, or Cabbage Patch, where the long-leafed, exotic-looking plant with the not-so-exotic name of Skunk Cabbage grows in abundance.

Van Damme State Park was created in 1934 from a 40-acre parcel of land willed to the State Park System by Charles F. Van Damme, one of the descendants of the original settlers who arrived here in the early 1860s. Subsequent acquisitions over the years increased the park to its present size.

Most of the first settlers came from New England. One of them, lumberman Silas Coombs, found the virgin forests of redwood most appealing. With two partners he built a sawmill at the mouth of Little River. They prospered and before long were having their own schooners built to haul the timber to market.

By 1893 the timber in the area was depleted, so the sawmill was dismantled and the dam forming the millpond was removed. A year later Coombs died.

Charles Van Damme, for whom the park was named, was born in Little River in 1881. He went on to become a wealthy lumberman and a San Francisco businessman and later purchased some of the land around the old sawmill operation. Like Coombs before him, Van Damme left the area open to public enjoyment and camping; upon his death in 1934 it was given to the state to be used as the nucleus for a state park.

## CAMPING

With a sheer bluff rising on its south boundary and the Tuolumne River on the north, a secluded campground offers 65 improved campsites on level ground that, many years ago, served as the river's natural flood plain. Ample shade is provided by native trees, and the heavy growth of native blackberries entices jam and pie fanciers from mid-July into early September. Trails have been cut through the blackberries to the river's edge.

Each campsite has a stove, table, and food locker, and piped drinking water is within a hundred feet of each. Hot showers and restrooms with flush toilets are nearby.

An artesian well, accessible via a footbridge that crosses a small slough, offers drinking water with a special flavor that perhaps you can identify.

Although no trailer hookups are available, trailers up to 18 feet in length can be accommodated in the campsites.

## HIKING

The park's principal trail is the Fern Canyon scenic trail system. Bicyclists can use part of this system, but no motor vehicles of any type are allowed.

The walls of the canyon are covered with millions of ferns, dominated by the western sword fern. There are also five finger, lady, licorice, wood, bird's foot, and deer ferns, and sometimes a few gold back or stamp ferns are seen. In addition, the area is rich with second-growth redwoods and red alders.

Hikers continuing south at the junction of the Old Logging Road Trail, instead of making the small loop, will come upon the Pygmy Forest. There is a short self-guided trail starting at the Pygmy Forest parking lot. The forest can also be reached by car from Airport Road, which is just south of the park entrance on Highway 1.

The cause of these unusual pygmy growths of cypresses and pines is a combination of factors such as highly acidic soil, shallow root penetration, and lack of nutrients. The soil is called a "podsol," and is one of the more extreme examples of this phenomenon to be found anywhere in the world.

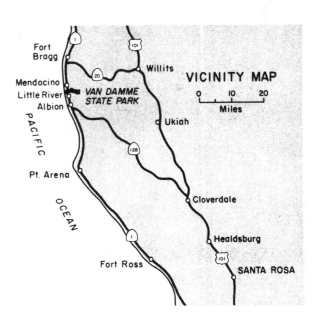

## BEACH

Directly across from the park entrance on Highway 1 is the beach. Since the water temperature along the northern coast seldom reaches higher than 52 degrees, swimming is not recommended and there is no lifeguard service. The beach is excellent for strolling, beachcombing, and informal picnicking (there are several fire rings).

Van Damme State Park
C/O Mendocino District
P.O. Box 440
Mendocino, CA 95460
(707) 937-5804

224

## CAMPING IN THE STATE PARKS

Camping in California's State Park System is very popular—so popular that the Department of Parks and Recreation encourages you to reserve a campsite well in advance of your outing. You can reserve a campsite up to 8 weeks in advance, or as late as 2 days prior to arrival date.

Most of the state park campsites described in the *California State Parks Guide* can be reserved through the **MISTIX** computerized reservation system; all others are available on a first-come, first-served basis. There is a reservation fee in addition to the campsite fee; both must be paid when the reservation is made. Consult the "Reservation Information" chapter in the back of this guide.

For information on the State Park System, the nearest **MISTIX** outlet, or to order reservation forms, call the Department's Information Office at 1-800-952-5580 (or TDD 916-324-1891) between 8:00 a.m. and 5:00 p.m. on business days (recording after hours). Or write to: Department of Parks and Recreation, P.O. Box 942896, Sacramento, CA 94296.

## TO MAKE A CAMPSITE RESERVATION

Fill out the Reservation Application that you requested from the Department's Information Office (that number again is 1-800-952-5580) or make a photocopy of the forms provided in the Reservation Information section of this guide. When you've filled out the forms, you may:

DIAL (1-800) I GO PARK
(1-800-446-7275)

★ PHONE TOLL FREE: 1-800-446-7275 and charge your reservation to your VISA or MASTERCARD.
Reservations for INDIVIDUAL campsites are placed on sale 8 weeks (56 days) in advance at 10:15 daily. Reservations for INDIVIDUAL campsites LESS than 8 weeks in advance are on sale from 8:00 a.m. to 9:00 p.m. each day.

TICKETS PURCHASED BY PHONE: verify that your reservation is for the correct park unit, equipment, starting date and length of stay. Once you hang up the phone, *all* transactions are complete and final. If you wish to change your reservation, you must cancel the previous one, pay the cancellation fee, and make a new reservation.

If you make your reservation more than 10 days in advance of your visit a "ticket" will be mailed to you. If you make your reservation less than 10 days before your trip, you will be given a reservation number. Be sure to take your reservation number with you to the park.

★ MAIL THE COMPLETED FORM: With a check or money order made payable to **MISTIX** or a VISA or MASTERCARD number to **MISTIX**, P.O. Box 85705, San Diego, CA 92138.

Allow 10 days for mailing and processing. Mailed applications received up to a week before the start of the 8-week advance reservation period will be held and processed on the first day of the advance period; applications received more than 9 weeks before the starting dates will be returned. It is suggested tha you include on your application alternate camgrounds or dates, as your application will be returned unfilled if the date(s) and campground(s) you specify are not available. To expedite processing of mail requests, write on lower left-hand corner of envelope the park unit name and date of arrival. Tickets cannot be held at the State Park System unit for your arrival or mailed to a temporary address. All fees must be paid in U.S. dollars.

The Department of Parks and Recreation and **MISTIX** are not responsible for delays in postal service. Plan ahead to allow sufficient time for mail delivery. When you receive your ticket, check to make sure of the park unit, date, and equipment. If there is an error, call **MISTIX** at 1-800-I-GO-PARK

★ GO TO A **MISTIX** OUTLET: They accept CASH, VISA or MASTERCARD as payment. (Outlet hours vary: Call 1-800-952-5580 for information on outlet hours and locations.)
TICKETS PURCHASED AT OUTLETS: must be initialed; when you initial your ticket(s), you are certifying that the outlet sold you a ticket for the correct State Park System unit, date, and equipment. Please inspect and understand what is printed on your ticket before you initial it.

## FAMILY CAMPING FEES

Camping Fees are: $12 per night for sites with hookups. (Electricity, water, and sewer in most campgrounds with flush toilets and hot showers); $6 per night for sites in developed campgrounds (table and barbecue stove at each site, flush toilets, hot showers, and piped drinking water nearby in most); $8 per night for sites in units with developed campgrounds and coastal access in Santa Cruz County and from Santa Barbara County south to San Diego County; $3 per night for sites in primitive campgrounds (sites have tables and water, and chemical or pit toilets are available). Pismo Dunes State Vehicular Recreation Area camping fees are $5 per vehicle, per night. There is a $3.75 reservation fee for *each* campsite reserved.

Other fees (payable at the park in cash) include $3 per night for additional motor vehicles in the park and $1 per night for each dog. Senior Citizen Discount Program *does not* apply when making reservations.

## RESERVATION INFORMATION

Hearst Castle tours are extremely popular and frequently sold out; it's highly recommended that you make your reservations well in advance of your visit. Tickets may be purchased through the **MISTIX** computerized reservation system.

To learn the location of **MISTIX** outlets or to obtain additional reservation information and tour schedules, call 1-800-952-5580 (or TDD 916-324-1891) between 8 A.M. and 5:00 P.M. on business days (recording after hours). Out-of-state residents, dial 916-323-2988.

After you have obtained a reservation application—or photocopied the one in the back of the *California State Parks Guide*—and filled it out, you may make a Hearst Castle tour reservation through the **MISTIX** reservation system by phone, by mail, or by visiting a **MISTIX** outlet in person.

For more information on Hearst State Historic Monument tours, turn to page 121.

## WALK-IN OUTLETS

Hearst tour tickets are available at selected **MISTIX** outlets throughout California. Call 1-800-952-5580 to determine the outlet closest to you. Most outlets *do not* accept checks.

## PHONE-IN RESERVATIONS

Phone Toll Free: 1-800-I-GO-PARK (1-800-446-7275) and charge your reservation to your VISA or MASTER-CARD.

Phone Reservations that do not allow enough time for the tickets to be mailed may be picked up at any **MISTIX** outlet en route to Hearst San Simeon SHM or at the will-call facility at the Visitor Center.

If you plan to pick up your ticket at the will-call facility at the Visitor Center, it is suggested that you arrive at least 20 minutes prior to your scheduled tour to allow enough time to pick up your tickets. The tours leave on schedule and will not wait for people who are in line at the will-call. NO EXCEPTIONS.

## MAIL-IN

Hearst reservations may also be made with **MISTIX** by mail. Photocopy the form on page 227 of this book, and follow the instructions for mail-in park reservations on the preceding page. To expedite processing of mail requests write: HEARST and the date requested in the lower left hand corner of the envelope. Allow at least 10 days for processing.

# Camping Information

### AT THE PARK

Check In/Out Time is 2:00 p.m.; you may be permitted to check into your site earlier if it is vacant. If you do not arrive by 2:00 p.m. of the day following the first day of your reservation, your reservation may be cancelled and the site made available to another camper. Youths under 18 years of age must be accompanied by a parent or guardian. The park supervisor may approve the stay of a youth who presents a written consent from the parent or guardian that includes the full name, address, and telephone number of the parent or guardian, the dates of the authorized stay, and the name of the park.

Campsite assignments are made when you arrive at the State Park System unit based on the type of equipment that must be accommodated. Specific sites cannot be reserved. Every effort will be made to give you the site you wish if it is not already occupied or needed by someone whose equipment cannot be accommodated in any other site.

Dogs must be kept on 6-foot leash during the day and in an enclosed vehicle or tent at night. Except for guide dogs for the blind, dogs are not permitted in park buildings or on traisl, or on most beaches.

Two licensed vehicles (including trailers) are usually permitted in one family campsite; however, the campsite fee allows for the operation of only one motorized vehicle in the park. Additional motor vehicles, when permitted, will be subject to the "extra vehicle" fee. Extra vehicles such as boat trailers or additional cars may have to be parked away from your campsite (if the campsite is too small to accommodate them).

A maximum of eight (8) persons are allowed in a family campsite. If you must reserve more than one site to accommodate your party, the rangers will try to assign you adjacent sites. (Two campsites per customer per campground.)

Only two reservations can be made for the same date and State Park System unit by one person. General occupancy by the same persons, equipment, or vehicles of any camping facility is limited to a total of 30 days in any calendar year in that unit.

### IF YOU MUST CANCEL

Notify **MISTIX** directly by phoning 1-800-I GO PARK. Contact the park if less than 24 hours from your arrival date. If your notification is later than 2 p.m. of the day before you are scheduled to arrive, the first night's camping fee will be deducted from your refund. Retain your ticket until your account has been credited or a refund received from **MISTIX**.

### REFUNDS

Your Entire Camping Fee, less the $3.75 reservation fee and a $2.00 cancellation charge ($3.75 + $2.00 = $5.75), will be refunded if you cancel your reservation. If you leave early, you will receive a refund for the unused nights, less the $2.00 cancellation charge and $3.75 reservation fee ($5.75 total). You will *not* receive a refund for unused days due to late arrival.

Senior Citizen Discount Program *does not* apply for persons making reservations.

## *Equipment Codes*

01   Tent or No Equipment
02   2 Tents
03   Large Tent (over 9'x12')
04   Tent Trailer
05   Van or Bus with Side Tent
06   Camper/Motorhome thru 18' (or van)
07   Camper/Motorhome thru 21'
08   Camper/Motorhome thru 24'
09   Camper/Motorhome thru 27'
10   Camper/Motorhome <u>over</u> 27'
11   Trailer thru 15'
12   Trailer thru 18'
13   Trailer thru 21'
14   Trailer thru 24'
15   Trailer thru 27'
16   Trailer <u>over</u> 27'
17   Site for Disabled

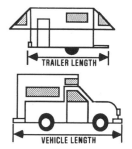

TRAILER LENGTH

VEHICLE LENGTH

TENT (1, 2, 3)

VAN OR BUS WITH SIDE TENT

TENT TRAILER (4)

TRAILER (11-16)

CAMPER (6-10)

MOTORHOME (6-10)

## Tour Reservation Application

### Hearst San Simeon (SHM)

**department of parks & recreation**

**Please Print Clearly**

Last Name | First Name | Initial | Area Code | Telephone

Address

City | State | Zip Code

Mail this form to:
**MISTIX**
P.O. Box 85705
San Diego, CA 92138-5705

| | DATE | TIME | ALTERNATE DATE | ALTERNATE TIME | No. Adults @ 8.00 ea. | No. Youths (6-12) @ 4.00 ea. | Total |
|---|---|---|---|---|---|---|---|
| Tour 1 | | | | | $ | $ | $ |
| Tour 2 | | | | | $ | $ | $ |
| Tour 3 | | | | | $ | $ | $ |
| Tour 4 | | | | | $ | $ | $ |

☐ VISA  ☐ MasterCard  ☐ Check or Money Order Enclosed. Make payable to MISTIX.

**Total Amount Enclosed or To Be Charged . . .** $

X

Authorizing Bank | Account Number | Expiration Date | Authorizing Signature

**ALL FEES MUST BE PAID IN U.S. DOLLARS.**

---

## Family Camping Reservation Application

**department of parks & recreation**

**Please Print Clearly**

Last Name | First Name | Initial | Area Code | Telephone

Address

City | State | Zip Code

Mail this form to:
**MISTIX**
P.O. Box 85705
San Diego, CA 92138-5705

| Equipment Code | State Park Unit Choices | Camp Ground | Starting Date | No. of Nights | $ Fee Per Night (Bottom of Form) | + 3.75 Reserv. Fee/Site | Total |
|---|---|---|---|---|---|---|---|
| | 1. | | | | x $ | + $3.75 | = |
| No. in Party | 2. | | | | x $ | + $3.75 | = |
| | 3. | | | | x $ | + $3.75 | = |

*See Reverse Side For Equipment Codes*

**ALL FEES MUST BE PAID IN U.S. DOLLARS.**

**Total Amount Enclosed or To Be Charged . . .** $

☐ VISA  ☐ MasterCard  ☐ Check or Money Order Enclosed. Make payable to MISTIX.

X

Authorizing Bank | Account Number | Expiration Date | Authorizing Signature

**Hookup Sites $12 per night  /  Coastal Developed Sites $8 per night  /  Developed Sites $6 per night  /  Primitive Sites $3 per night**

---

## Group Camping Reservation Application

**department of parks & recreation**

**Please Print Clearly**

Last Name | First Name | Initial | Area Code | Telephone

Address

City | State | Zip Code

Mail this form to:
**MISTIX**
P.O. Box 85705
San Diego, CA 92138-5705

| Equipment Code | State Park Unit Choices | Camp Ground | Starting Date | No. of Nights | $ Fee Per Night (Back of Form) | + 3.75 Reserv. Fee/Site | Total |
|---|---|---|---|---|---|---|---|
| | 1. | | | | x $ | + $3.75 | = |
| No. in Party | 2. | | | | x $ | + $3.75 | = |
| | 3. | | | | x $ | + $3.75 | = |

*See Reverse Side For Equipment Codes*

**Total Amount Enclosed or To Be Charged . . .** $

☐ VISA  ☐ MasterCard  ☐ Check or Money Order Enclosed. Make payable to MISTIX.

X

Authorizing Bank | Account Number | Expiration Date | Authorizing Signature

**ALL FEES MUST BE PAID IN U.S. DOLLARS.**

# Family Camping

| NAME OF PARK | RESERVATION PERIOD | DAYS LIMIT JUNE-SEPT/OCT-MAY | CAMPSITE CLASSIFICATION | SHOWERS | MAXIMUM LENGTH TRAILER/CAMPER-MOTORHOME | SPECIAL INFORMATION |
|---|---|---|---|---|---|---|
| ANZA-BORREGO DESERT SP* | | | | | | P.O. Box 428, Borrego Springs, CA 92004, (619) 767-5311 |
| • Borrego Palm Canyon (hook-up) | Sep 28-Jun 3 | 30/30 | H | Y | 35' / 35' | No stoves |
| • Tamarisk Grove | Sep 28-Jun 3 | 30/30 | D | Y | 21' / 21' | |
| • Borrego Palm (no hook-up) | Sep 28-Jun 3 | 30/30 | D | Y | 24' / 31' | Lower and upper Borrego Canyon have been combined |
| • Horseman's Camp | Oct 1-May 31 | 30/30 | P | Y | 24' / 24' | Must have at least one horse/site. Maximum 3 horses per corral/site. |
| ATASCADERO SB | May 23-Sep 1 | 7/15 | D | N | 24' / 24' | c/o Morro Bay SP, Morro Bay, CA 93442, (805) 772-2560 |
| BENBOW LAKE SRA | May 23-Sep 8 | 15/15 | D | Y | 30' / 30' | c/o Richardson Grove SP, 1600 S. Hwy. 101, Garberville, CA 95440-0069 (707) 247-3318. Cold Showers |
| BIG BASIN REDWOODS SP* | | | | | | 21600 Big Basin Way, Boulder Creek, CA 95006-9050, (408) 338-6132 |
| • Walk-In (tents only) | All Year | 15/15 | D | Y | —/— | |
| • Drive-In | All Year | 15/15 | D | Y | 27' / 31' | |
| BOTHE-NAPA VALLEY SP** ♿ | All Year | 15/15 | D | Y | 24' / 31' | 3801 St. Helena Hwy., N. Calistoga, CA 94515, (707) 942-4575 |
| BRANNAN ISLAND SRA* ♿ | | | | | | 17645 Highway 160, Rio Vista, CA 94571, (916) 777-6671 |
| • Brannan Island | Feb 23-Oct 27 | 15/30 | D | N | 31' / 31' | |
| • Delta Vista Boat Berths | Feb 23-Oct 27 | 15/30 | D | Y | —/— | Berth 35'x10'—Boats over 10' need 2 berths, includes walk-in site |
| BUTANO SP | | | | | | P.O. Box 9, Pescadero, CA 94060, (415) 879-0173 |
| • Drive-In | Apr 26-Sep 28 | 15/15 | D | N | 24' / 30' | |
| • Walk-In (tents only) | Apr 26-Sep 28 | 15/15 | D | N | —/— | |
| CALAVERAS BIG TREES SP* ♿ | | | | | | P.O. Box 120, Arnold, CA 95223, (209) 795-2334 |
| • North Grove ♿ | May 23-Sep 20 | 15/15 | D | Y | 27' / 27' | Contact park for winter camping info. |
| • Oak Hollow | May 23-Sep 20 | 15/15 | D | Y | 27' / 27' | |
| CARPINTERIA SB ♿ | | | | | | c/o Channel Coast Dist., 24 E. Main St., Ventura, CA 93001 |
| • Anacapa/Santa Cruz ♿ | All Year | 7/15 | CD | Y | —/ 30' | (805) 684-2811 or 654-4611, 2 vehicle maximum all sites |
| • San Miguel | All Year | 7/15 | CD | Y | 30' / 30' | |
| • San Miguel (Beach Row) | All Year | 7/15 | CD | Y | 21' / 21' | |
| • Santa Rosa | All Year | 7/15 | H | Y | 30' / 30' | |
| • Santa Rosa (Beach Row) | All Year | 7/15 | H | Y | 21' / 21' | |
| CASTLE CRAGS SP | All Year | 15/30 | D | Y | 21' / 27' | Castella, CA 96017, (916) 235-2684 |
| CASWELL MEMORIAL SP** | May 15-Sep 15 | 15/15 | D | Y | 21' / 24' | 28000 S. Austin Road, Ripon, CA 95366, (209) 599-3810 |
| CHINA CAMP SP (Walk-in) | All Year | 7/15 | P | N | —/— | East San Pedro Road, San Rafael, CA 94901, (415) 456-1286 or 456-0766 |
| CLEAR LAKE SP** ♿ | | | | | | 5300 Soda Bay Rd., Kelseyville, CA 95451, (707) 279-4293 |
| • Kelsey Creek (nearest lake) | All Year | 15/30 | D | Y | 34' / 34' | |
| • Cole Creek | Mar 1-Sep 30 | 15/30 | D | Y | 21' / 21' | |
| • Lower Bayview | Mar 1-Sep 30 | 15/30 | D | Y | —/— | Tents only. |
| • Upper Bayview | Mar 1-Sep 30 | 15/30 | D | Y | —/— | Tents only. |
| COLUSA-SACRAMENTO RIVER SRA | All Year | 15/30 | D | Y | 24' / 24' | P.O. Box 207, Colusa, CA 95932, (916) 458-4927 |
| CUYAMACA RANCHO SP** | | | | | | 12551 Hwy. 79, Descanso, CA 92016, (619) 765-0755 |
| • Paso (no horses) | Mar 21-Nov 2 | 30/30 | D | Y | 24' / 30' | |
| • Green Valley (no horses) | Mar 21-Nov 2 | 30/30 | D | Y | 27' / 30' | |
| • Los Caballos (horsemen only) | May 16-Nov 2 | 30/30 | D | Y | 24' / 30' | $7.00 per night ($1.00 per horse/night to be paid at park) |
| DEL NORTE COAST REDWOODS SP | May 24-Aug 31 | 15/30 | D | Y | 27' / 31' | P.O. Drawer J, Crescent City, CA 95531, (707) 464-9533. Closed 10/1-3/31. |
| D.L. BLISS SP* | | | | | | P.O. Box 266, Tahoma, CA 95733, (916) 525-7277 |
| • Beach Camp | Jun 14-Sep 1 | 10/Closed | D | Y | 15' / 21' | |
| | Jun 14-Sep 1 | 10/Closed | D | Y | 15' / 21' | Closed mid-Sep to mid-Jun |
| DOHENY SB | All Year | 7/15 | CD | Y | 24' / 28' | 25300 Harbor Drive, Dana Point, CA 92629, (714) 496-6171 |
| • Beach Front | All Year | 7/15 | CD | Y | 24' / 28' | (Two vehicle maximum, including trailer, per site) |
| DONNER MEMORIAL SP | May 21-Sep 30 | 10/Closed | D | Y | 24' / 24' | P.O. Box 9210, Truckee, CA 95734, (916) 587-3841. Closed November to mid-May. (Two vehicle maximum, including trailer, per site) |
| EL CAPITAN SB* | All Year | 7/15 | CD | Y | 27' / 30' | #10 Refugio Beach, Goleta, CA 93117, (805) 968-1411 or 968-0019 |
| EMERALD BAY SP | | | | | | P.O. Box 266, Tahoma, CA 95733, (916) 541-3030. |
| • Eagle Point | Jun 14-Sep 1 | 10/Closed | D | Y | 21' / 21' | Closed mid-Sep to mid-Jun. |
| FOLSOM LAKE SRA* | | | | | | 7806 Folsom-Auburn Rd., Folsom, CA 95630, (916) 988-0205 |
| • Peninsula | May 23-Sep 3 | 30/30 | D | N | 31' / 31' | |
| • Negro Bar ♿ | May 23-Sep 3 | 7/30 | D | N | 31' / 31' | |
| • Beals Point ♿ | May 23-Sep 3 | 7/30 | D | Y | 31' / 31' | |
| GAVIOTA SP | All Year | 7/15 | CD | Y | 24' / 30' | #10 Refugio Beach, Goleta, CA 93117, (805) 968-0019 or 567-5013 |
| GEORGE J. HATFIELD SRA** | May 15-Sep 15 | 7/7 | D | N | —/18' | 4394 N. Kelly Road, Hilmar, CA 95324, (209) 632-1852 |
| GRIZZLY CREEK REDWOODS SP | May 23-Sep 8 | 15/30 | D | Y | 24' / 30' | 16949 Hwy. 36, Carlotta, CA 95528, (707) 777-3683 |
| GROVER HOT SPRINGS SP | May 16-Sep 15 | 15/30 | D | Y | 24' / 27' | P.O. Box 188, Markleeville, CA 96120, (916) 694-2248 |
| HALF MOON BAY SB* ♿ | May 20-Sep 30 | 7/15 | D | N | 36' / 36' | 95 Kelley Avenue, Half Moon Bay, CA 94019, (415) 726-6238 |
| HENDY WOODS SP | May 16-Sep 30 | 15/30 | D | Y | 35' / 35' | c/o Mendocino District, P.O. Box 440, Mendocino, CA 95460. (707) 937-5804 |
| HENRY COWELL REDWOODS SP ♿ | All Year | 7/7 | D | Y | 18' / 35' | 101 N. Big Trees Park Rd., Felton, CA 95018, (408) 335-4598 or 438-2396 |
| HUMBOLDT REDWOODS SP*/** | | | | | | P.O. Box 100, Weott, CA 95571-0100, (707) 946-2311 |
| • Burlington | Apr 25-Oct 27 | 15/30 | D | Y | 18' / 27' | |
| • Hidden Springs | May 23-Sep 1 | 15/Closed | D | Y | 24' / 30' | Closed Sep 23-May 20 (approximately) |
| • Albee Creek | May 23-Sep 1 | 15/Closed | D | Y | 24' / 30' | Closed Sep 30-May 15 (approximately). Solar showers |
| INDIAN GRINDING ROCK SHP | All Year | 30/30 | D | N | 27' / 27' | 14881 Pine Grove-Volcano Road, Pine Grove, CA 95665, (209) 296-7488 |
| JEDEDIAH SMITH REDWOODS SP | May 24-Aug 31 | 15/30 | D | Y | 30' / 30' | 4241 Kings Valley Road, Crescent City, CA 95531, (707) 464-9533 or 458-3310 |
| LAKE OROVILLE SRA* | | | | | | 400 Glen Drive, Oroville, CA 95965 (916) 534-2409 |
| • Bidwell Canyon | Mar 20-Oct 27 | 30/30 | H | Y | 31' / 31' | Include boat trailer in total RV length for both |
| • Loafer Creek ♿ | Mar 20-Oct 27 | 30/Closed | D | Y | 31' / 31' | campgrounds |
| LAKE PERRIS SRA* | | | | | | 17801 Lake Perris Drive, Perris, CA 92370. (714) 657-0676 (M-F) |
| • Luiseno ♿ | Mar 28-Sep 30 | 15/30 | D/H | Y | 31' / 31' | (After hours enter via Moreno Beach Drive) HC site-hook-ups only. |
| LEO CARRILLO SB* | Mar 1-Oct 3 | 7/15 | CD | Y | 31' / 31' | c/o Santa Monica Mtns. District, 2860A Camino Dos Rios, Newbury Park, CA 91320 (818) 706-1310 or (805) 987-3303 |
| MacKERRICHER SP ♿ | Mar 21-Oct 19 | 15/30 | D | Y | 35' / 35' | c/o Mendocino Dist., P.O. Box 440, Mendocino, CA 95460, (707) 937-5804 |
| MALAKOFF DIGGINS SHP* | May 1-Sep 9 | 30/30 | D | N | 18' / 24' | 23579 N. Bloomfield Road, Nevada City, CA 95959, (916) 265-2740 |
| MANCHESTER SB* | May 16-Sep 2 | 15/30 | P | N | 35' / 35' | c/o Mendocino Dist., P.O. Box 440, Mendocino, CA 95460, (707) 937-5804 |
| McARTHUR-BURNEY FALLS MEMORIAL SP | All Year | 15/30 | D | Y | 32' / 40' | Rt. 1, Box 1260, Burney, CA 96013, (916) 335-2777 |

**P**  Primitive Sites $3 per night        **CD**  Coastal Developed Sites $8 per night

**D**  Developed Sites $6 per night        **H**  Hookup Sites $12 per night

| NAME OF PARK | RESERVATION PERIOD | DAYS LIMIT JUNE-SEPT/OCT-MAY | CAMPSITE CLASSIFICATION | SHOWERS | MAXIMUM LENGTH TRAILER/CAMPER-MOTORHOME | SPECIAL INFORMATION |
|---|---|---|---|---|---|---|
| McCONNELL SRA** | May 15-Sep 15 | 15/30 | D | N | 27' / 24' | McConnell Road, Ballico, CA 95303, (209) 394-7755 |
| McGRATH SB | All Year | 7/15 | CD | Y | 30' / 34' | c/o Channel Coast District, 24 E. Main St., Ventura, CA 93001 (805) 985-1188 or 654-4611 |
| MILLERTON LAKE SRA* | Mar 21-Sep 7 | 15/30 | D | Y | 31' / 31' | P.O. Box 205, Friant, CA 93626, (209) 822-2332 |
| MONTANA DE ORO SP | May 23-Sep 1 | 7/15 | P | N | 24' / 31' | c/o Morro Bay SP, Morro Bay, CA 93442, (805) 772-2560 or 772-8812 |
| MORRO BAY SP* | All Year | 7/15 | D | Y | 31' / 31' | c/o Morro Bay SP, Morro Bay, CA 93442, (805) 772-2560 |
| | All Year | 7/15 | H | Y | 31' / 35' | (Handicapped developed sites only) (Hook-ups electricity/water only) |
| MT. DIABLO SP*/** | Oct 1-May 31 | 30/30 | D | N | 27' / 31' | P.O. Box 250, Diablo, CA 94528, (415) 837-2525. Fire restrictions 6/1 to 9/30. Contact park for information. Park entrance gates closed from one hour after sunset to 8:00 A.M. Winding mountain roads. Trailers over 20' not advised. |
| MT. SAN JACINTO SP | | | | | | 25905 Hwy. 243, P.O. Box 308, Idyllwild, CA 92349, (714) 659-2607 |
| • Idyllwild | May 1-Sep 30 | 15/30 | D | Y | 24' / 24' | (North end of town near fire station on Hwy. 243) |
| • Stone Creek | May 1-Sep 30 | 15/30 | P | N | 24' / 24' | (5-1/2 mi. north of Idyllwild on Hwy. 243) |
| NEW BRIGHTON SB | | | | | | 1500 Park Avenue, Hwy. 1, Capitola, CA 95010, (408) 475-4850 |
| • Drive-in | May 16-Sep 15 | 7/15 | CD | Y | 31' / 31' | |
| • Walk-in | May 16-Sep 15 | 7/15 | CD | Y | —/— | Tents only |
| PALOMAR MOUNTAIN SP | | | | | | Palomar Mountain, CA 92060, (619) 742-3462 |
| • Doane Valley | Mar 21-Nov 2 | 30/30 | D | Y | 21' / 21' | |
| PATRICK'S POINT SP* | May 15-Sep 15 | 15/30 | D | Y | 31' / 31' | Trinidad, CA 95570, (707) 677-3570 |
| PFEIFFER BIG SUR SP** | All Year | 7/15 | D | Y | 27' / 32' | Big Sur, CA 93920, (408) 667-2315 |
| PISMO DUNES SVRA | | | | | | Pier Avenue, Oceano, CA 93445, (805) 549-3433. |
| • Pismo Dunes OHV-Beach | All Year | 7/7 | P | N | 40' / 40' | Beach camping (soft sand) Each vehicle entering under own power needs separate reservation |
| PISMO SB | | | | | | Pier Avenue, Oceano, CA 93445, (805) 489-2684 |
| • North Beach | May 23-Sep 1 | 7/15 | D | Y | 31' / 36' | |
| • Oceano | All Year | 7/15 | D | Y | 18' / 31' | |
| • Oceano | All Year | 7/15 | H | Y | 31' / 36' | (Hook-up electricity/water only) |
| PLUMAS-EUREKA SP | | | | | | 310 Johnsville Road, Blairsden, CA 96103, (916) 836-2380 |
| • Upper Jamison | Jun 20-Sep 4 | 15/15 | D | Y | 24' / 30' | |
| • Upper Jamison (walk in) | Jun 20-Sep 4 | 15/15 | D | Y | —/— | Parking for only one vehicle per walk in site |
| POINT MUGU SP | | | | | | c/o Santa Monica Mtns. District, 2860A Camino Dos Rios, Newbury Park, CA 91320, (818) 706-1310 or (805) 987-3303 |
| • Big Sycamore Canyon | Mar 1-Oct 3 | 7/15 | CD | Y | 31' / 31' | |
| • La Jolla Beach | Mar 1-Oct 3 | 7/15 | P | N | 31' / 31' | |
| PORTOLA SP* | All Year | 15/30 | D | Y | 21' / 27' | Star Rt. 2, La Honda, CA 94020, (415) 948-9098 |
| PRAIRIE CREEK REDWOODS SP | | | | | | Orick, CA 95555, (707) 488-2171 |
| • Elk Prairie | May 23-Aug 31 | 15/30 | D | Y | 24' / 27' | |
| REFUGIO SB* | All Year | 7/15 | CD | Y | 27' / 30' | #10 Refugio Beach, Goleta, CA 93117, (805) 968-1350 or 968-0019 |
| RICHARDSON GROVE SP | | | | | | 1600 S. Hwy 101, Garberville, CA 95440, (707) 247-3318 |
| • Huckleberry & Madrone | May 2-Sep 28 | 15/30 | D | Y | 24' / 30' | |
| • Oak Flat | Jun 13-Sep 14 | 15/30 | D | Y | 24' / 30' | |
| RUSSIAN GULCH SP* | Mar 21-Oct 19 | 15/30 | D | Y | 24' / 27' | c/o Mendocino Dist. P.O. Box 440, Mendocino, CA 95460, (707) 937-5804 |
| SALTON SEA SRA** | | | | | | P.O. Box 3166, North Shore, CA 92254, (619) 393-3052 |
| • Headquarters | Oct 3-May 26 | 30/30 | D | Y | 30' / 30' | |
| • Headquarters (no tent) | Oct 3-May 26 | 30/30 | H | N | 30' / 30' | |
| SALT POINT SP* | | | | | | 25050 Coast Hwy. 1, Jenner, CA 95450, (707) 847-3221 |
| • Woodside | Mar 15-Sep 30 | 10/10 | D | N | 31' / 31' | |
| • Walk in (tents only) | Mar 15-Sep 30 | 10/10 | D | N | —/— | .3 to .4 mi. walk from parking area. No dogs. May be closed due to rains |
| SAMUEL P. TAYLOR SP* | Apr 25-Sep 27 | 7/15 | D | Y | 18' / 24' | P.O. Box 251, Lagunitas, CA 94938, (415) 488-9897 |
| SAN CLEMENTE SB* | All Year | 7/15 | CD | Y | 24' / 28' | 3030 Avenida del Presidente, San Clemente, CA 92672, |
| | All Year | 7/15 | H | Y | 30' / 30' | (714) 492-3156 |
| SAN ELIJO SB | Mar 21-Dec 31 | 7/15 | CD | Y | 35' / 35' | 2680 Carlsbad Blvd., Carlsbad, CA 92008, (619) 753-5091 |
| SAN LUIS RESERVOIR SRA | Mar 21-Sep 15 | 15/30 | D | Y | 37' / 37' | 31426 W. Hwy. 152, Santa Nella, CA 95322, (209) 826-1196 |
| SAN ONOFRE SB* | Mar 23-Sep 10 | 15/30 | CD | Y | 30' / 30' | c/o Pendleton Coast District, 3030 Avenida del Presidente, San Clemente, CA 92672, (714) 492-4872. Outdoor/cold showers |
| SAN SIMEON SB | | | | | | P.O. Box 8, San Simeon, CA 93452, (805) 927-4509 or 927-4621 |
| • San Simeon Creek | — | — | — | — | —/— | San Simeon Creek closed for construction |
| • Washburn | Mar 19-Sep 30 | 10/30 | P | N | 21' / 30' | |
| SEACLIFF SB | All Year | 7/7 | H | Y | 30' / 30' | 1500 Park Avenue, Capitola, CA 95010, (408) 688-3222 or 475-4850 |
| SILVERWOOD LAKE SRA* | All Year | 10/30 | D | Y | 31' / 31' | Star Route 7A, Hesperia, CA 92345, (619) 389-2303 |
| SONOMA COAST SB | | | | | | Bodega Bay, CA 94923, (707) 875-3483 or 865-2391 |
| • Bodega Dunes | All Year | 10/30 | D | Y | 31' / 31' | |
| • Wrights Beach | All Year | 10/30 | D | N | 27' / 27' | |
| SOUTH CARLSBAD SB | Jan 1-Nov 30 | 7/15 | CD | Y | 35' / 35' | 2680 Carlsbad Blvd., Carlsbad, CA 92008, (619) 438-3143 |
| STANDISH-HICKEY SRA | | | | | | P.O. Box 208, Leggett, CA 95455, (707) 925-6482 |
| • Hickey Rock Creek | May 2-Sep 28 | 14/30 | D | Y | 24' / 27' | |
| • Redwood | Jun 13-Sep 14 | 14/30 | D | N | —/18' | No trailers |
| SUGARLOAF RIDGE SP* | Mar 14-Oct 25 | 15/15 | D | Y | 24' / 27' | 2605 Adobe Canyon Road, Kenwood, CA 95452, (707) 833-5712 |
| SUGAR PINE POINT SP* | Jun 13-Sep 8 | 10/30 | D | Y | 24' / 30' | P.O. Drawer D, Tahoma, CA 95733, (916) 525-7982, showers closed during winter |
| SUNSET SB* | May 16-Sep 15 | 7/15 | CD | Y | 31' / 31' | 201 Sunset Beach Road, Watsonville, CA 95076, (408) 724-1266 |
| TAHOE SRA | | | | | | P.O. Box 583, Tahoe City, CA 95730, (916) 583-3074 |
| • Lakeside | May 23-Sep 1 | 10/30 | D | Y | 21' / 30' | 2 veh. limit/site (including trailers). Closed mid-Sep to mid-May |
| • Hillside (tents only) | May 23-Sep 1 | 10/30 | D | Y | —/— | 2 veh. limit/site (no trailers). Closed mid-Sep to mid-May |
| TURLOCK LAKE SRA | May 15-Sep 15 | 15/30 | D | Y | 24' / 27' | 22600 Lake Road, La Grange, CA 95329, (209) 874-2008 or 874-2056 |
| VAN DAMME SP* | Mar 21-Oct 19 | 15/30 | D | Y | 35' / 35' | c/o Mendocino Dist., P.O. Box 440, Mendocino, CA 95460, (707) 937-5804 |
| WOODSON BRIDGE SRA* | All Year | 15/30 | D | Y | 31' / 31' | 25340 South Avenue, Corning, CA 96021, (916) 839-2112 |

**Abbreviations**

| | |
|---|---|
| SP | State Park |
| SHP | State Historic Park |
| SB | State Beach |
| SRA | State Recreation Area |
| SVRA | State Vehicular Recreation Area |

* — Group campsites on MISTIX reservation system
** — Group campsites reservable through park unit
 — Handicapped sites available
Y — Yes
N — No

| NAME OF PARK | RESERVATION PERIOD | CAMPSITE CLASS | ADULT FEE PER NIGHT | YOUTH FEE PER NIGHT | MAXIMUM NO. OF PEOPLE | MAXIMUM TRAILER/RV LENGTH | MAXIMUM NO. VEHICLES | SHOWERS | SPECIAL INFORMATION |
|---|---|---|---|---|---|---|---|---|---|
| **ANZA-BORREGO DESERT SP**/P.O. Box 428, Borrego Springs, CA 92004, (619) 767-5311 | | | | | | | | | |
| • Borrego Palm Canyon Group (5 group camps each) | Sep 28-May 31 | D | $24 | $12 | 24 | — | 6 | Y | No trailers/RVs/campers. 6 vehicles per site, limited parking. Solar showers. |
| **BIG BASIN REDWOODS SP**/21600 Big Basin Way, Boulder Creek, CA 95006-9050, (408) 338-6132 | | | | | | | | | |
| • Sequoia (3 group camps each) | All Year | D | $50 | $25 | 50 | — | 12 | Y | Tent camping only; camps may be reserved together for larger groups but campgrounds located 2-1/2 miles apart should not be reserved by one large group; Sky meadow walk-in camping 50-150 yards from parking. |
| • Sky Meadow (2 group camps each) | All Year | P | $50 | $25 | 50 | — | 12 | N | |
| **BRANNAN ISLAND SRA**/17645 Highway 160, Rio Vista, CA 94515 (916) 777-6671 | | | | | | | | | |
| • 6 Group Camps each | All Year | P | $30 | $15 | 30 | 31' | 15 | N | May be reserved together for larger groups. |
| **CALAVERAS BIG TREES SP**/P.O. Box 120, Arnold, CA 95223, (209) 975-2334 | May 23-Sep 20 | D | $100 | $50 | 100 | 16' | 25 | Y | Contact park prior to May 23. Best suited for tent camping. Central cooking and eating area. |
| **D.L. BLISS SP**/P.O. Box 266, Tahoma, CA 95733, (916) 525-7277 | June 14-Sep 1 | D | $50 | $25 | 50 | — | 10 | N | Limited parking; No RVs/buses. Closed Sept-June. |
| **EL CAPITAN SB**/#10 Refugio Beach Road, Goleta, CA 93117, (805) 968-1411 or 968-0019 | | | | | | | | | |
| • Cabrillo | All Year | D | $75 | $37.50 | 75 | — | 15 | Y | Tent camping only—walk in 50-100 yards |
| • Drake | All Year | D | $100 | $50 | 125 | — | 25 | Y | Tent camping only—walk-in 50-100 yards |
| • Ortega | All Year | D | $50 | $25 | 50 | — | 10 | Y | Tent camping only—walk-in 50-100 yards |
| **EMMA WOOD SB**/c/o Channel Coast District, 24 Main Street, Ventura, CA 93001 (805) 643-7532 | | | | | | | | | |
| • 4 Group Camps (each) | All Year | D | $30 | $15 | 50 | — | 5 | Y | Very limited parking. |
| **FOLSOM LAKE SRA**/7806 Folsom-Auburn Road, Folsom, CA 95630, (916) 988-0205 | | | | | | | | | |
| • Negro Bar—A | All Year | D | $50 | $25 | 50 | 31' | 25 | N | May be reserved together for group up to 100. |
| • Negro Bar—B | All Year | D | $50 | $25 | 50 | 31' | 25 | N | Bus parking available. |
| **HALF MOON BAY SP**/93 Kelley Avenue, Half Moon Bay, CA 94019, (415) 726-6238 | | | | | | | | | |
| • Sweetwood | All Year | P | $50 | $25 | 50 | 21' | 12 | N | Check-in at park office prior to occupying camp. No trailers. |
| **HUMBOLDT REDWOODS SP**/P.O. Box 100, Weott, CA 95571, (707) 946-2311 | | | | | | | | | |
| • Williams Grove—A | May 23-Sep 1 | D | $50 | $25 | 50 | 30' | 25 | N | A & B can be reserved together for group up to 125. |
| • Williams Grove—B | May 23-Sep 1 | D | $75 | $37.50 | 75 | 30' | 30 | N | Maximum trailer length 24'. — |
| **LAKE OROVILLE SRA**/400 Glen Drive, Oroville, CA 95965. (916) 534-2409 | | | | | | | | | |
| • 6 Group Camps each | Mar 20-Oct 27 | D | $25 | $12.50 | 25 | 20' | 8 | Y | Very limited RV parking; no trailers. Can be reserved for group up to 150. Limit 5 tents per camp. |
| Boat-in camps: | | | | | | | | | |
| • Bloomer—A | Mar 20-Oct 27 | P | $45 | $22.50 | 45 | — | — | N | Register at Bidwell Canyon Campground. No drinking water. |
| • Bloomer—B | Mar 20-Oct 27 | P | $30 | $15 | 30 | — | — | N | Access by boat only. Long walk to sites due to low water during summer. |
| **LAKE PERRIS SRA**/17801 Lake Perris Drive, Perris, CA 92370, (714) 657-0676 (M-F) | | | | | | | | | |
| • 6 Group Camps each | All Year | D | $100 | $50 | 100 | 31' | 15 | Y | Enter via Moreno Beach Drive. Campsites may be reserved together for group up to 1000. |
| **LEO CARRILLO SB**/2860-A Camino Dos Rios, Newbury Park, CA 91320, (805) 987-3303 or (818) 706-1310 | | | | | | | | | |
| • Walk-in camp | All Year | D | $50 | $25 | 50 | — | 18 | N | Tent camping only; campsites 100 yds. from parking. No camping in parking lot. |
| **MALAKOFF DIGGINS SHP**/23579 North Bloomfield Road, Nevada City, CA 95959, (916) 265-2740 | Mar 15-Sep 9 | P | $50 | $25 | 50 | — | 20 | N | Tent camping only. |
| **MANCHESTER SB**/c/o Mendocino District, P.O. Box 440, Mendocino, CA 95460 (707) 937-5804 | May 16-Sep 2 | P | $20 | $10 | 40 | 21' | 12 | N | |
| **MILLERTON LAKE SRA**/P.O. Box 205, Friant, CA 93626, (209) 822-2332 | | | | | | | | | |
| • Large group | Mar 21-Sep 7 | D | $75 | $37.50 | 75 | 31' | 25 | Y | Can be reserved together for group up to 115. |
| • Small group | Mar 21-Sep 7 | D | $40 | $20 | 40 | 31' | 15 | Y | Bus parking. |
| **MORRO BAY SP**/Morro Bay, Morro Bay, CA 93442, (805) 772-2560 | | | | | | | | | |
| • Group—A | All Year | D | $50 | $25 | 50 | 36' | 25 | Y | Campsites may be reserved together. |
| • Group—B | All Year | D | $25 | $12.50 | 30 | 27' | 30 | Y | Shower facilities in nearby campground. Group 'B' best suited for tent/no equipment camping. |
| **MT. DIABLO SP**/P.O. Box 250, Diablo, CA 94528, (415) 837-2525 | | | | | | | | | |
| • Boundary | Oct 1-May 31 | P | $20 | $10 | 20 | — | 5 | N | Fire restriction Jun 1 to Sep 30. Contact park for information. Park entrance gates closed from one hour after sunset to 8:00 a.m. |
| • Buckeye | Oct 1-May 31 | P | $30 | $15 | 30 | — | 5 | N | |
| • Stagecoach | Oct 1-May 31 | P | $20 | $10 | 20 | — | 5 | N | |
| • Wildcat | Oct 1-May 31 | P | $30 | $15 | 30 | — | 5 | N | |
| **PATRICK'S POINT SP**/Trinidad, CA 95570, (707) 677-3570 | All Year | D | $100 | $50 | 150 | 24' | 30 | Y | Cook shelter w/gas stove. Parking for 2 buses. Summer fog |
| **PORTOLA SP**/Star Route 2, La Honda, CA 94020, (415) 948-9098 | | | | | | | | | |
| • Group #1 | All Year | D | $50 | $25 | 50 | — | 12 | N | Tent camping only. Can be reserved together for group up to 100. Walk 100 yards to campsite. |
| • Group #2 | All Year | D | $50 | $25 | 50 | — | 12 | N | |
| **REFUGIO SB**/#10 Refugio Beach, Goleta, CA 93117, (805) 968-1350 or 968-0019 | All Year | P | $60 | $30 | 60 | 21' | 20 | N | 20 vehicles including trailers. Camp store. May be closed by spring and fall rains. |
| **RUSSIAN GULCH SP**/c/o Mendocino District, P.O. Box 440, Mendocino, CA 95460 (707) 937-5804 | Mar 21-Nov 30 | D | $40 | $20 | 40 | — | 10 | N | Tent camping only. |
| **SADDLEBACK BUTTE SP**/17102 East Avenue J, Lancaster, CA 93534, (805) 942-0662 | | | | | | | | | |
| • Joshua Tree | All Year | P | $30 | $15 | 30 | 24' | 12 | N | Limit 2 RVs; no trailers. Very limited parking. |
| **SALT POINT SP**/25050 Coast Highway 1, Jenner, CA 95450, (707) 847-3221 | Mar 15-Sep 30 | D | $40 | $20 | 40 | 21' | 10 | N | No trailers/no dogs. Maximum 5 RVs. |
| **SAMUEL P. TAYLOR SP**/P.O. Box 251, Lagunitas, CA 94938, (415) 488-9897 | | | | | | | | | |
| • Madrone No. 1 | All Year | P | $50 | $25 | 50 | — | 20 | N | Tent camping only. Can be reserved for group up to 75. Bus parking available. No RVs. |
| • Madrone No. 2 | All Year | P | $25 | $12.50 | 25 | — | 10 | N | |
| **SAN CLEMENTE SB**/3030 Avenida Del Presidente, San Clemente, CA 92672, (714) 492-3156 | | | | | | | | | |
| • South Camp | All Year | D | $50 | $25 | 50 | 30' | 20 | Y | On bluff overlooking ocean. |
| **SAN ONOFRE SB**/c/o Pendleton Coast District, 3030 Avenida Del Presidente, San Clemente, CA 92672, (714) 492-4872 | All Year | D | $50 | $25 | 50 | 18' | 12 | Y | Primarily tent camping. Cold/outdoor showers. |
| **SILVERWOOD LAKE SRA** &/Star Route 7A, Hesperia, CA 92345, (619) 389-2281 | | | | | | | | | |
| • Valle | Mar 1-Oct 31 | D | $100 | $50 | 100 | 31' | 30 | Y | Limited RV parking. Camps can be reserved together for group up to 360. |
| • Barranca | Mar 1-Oct 31 | D | $100 | $50 | 100 | 31' | 30 | Y | Phone park prior to arrival. |
| • Rio | Mar 1-Oct 31 | D | $100 | $50 | 100 | 31' | 30 | Y | |
| **SUGARLOAF RIDGE SP**/2605 Adobe Canyon Road, Kenwood, CA 95452, (707) 833-5712 | All Year | P | $50 | $25 | 50 | 27' | 30 | N | Limit 15 RV/trailer combinations. 8-horse corral available. |
| **SUGAR PINE POINT SP**/c/o Sierra District, P.O. Drawer D, Tahoma, CA 95733, (916) 525-7982 | | | | | | | | | |
| • General Creek (10 group camps each) | Jun 13-Sep 8 | D | $40 | $20 | 40 | 30' | 10 | Y | Limit 6 RVs over 15' per camp. Can be reserved together for group up to 400. |
| **SUNSET SB**/201 Sunset Beach Road, Watsonville, CA 95076, (408) 724-1266 | All Year | D | $50 | $25 | 50 | 18' | 10 | Y | Limit 2 RVs per group, rest of parking for conventional vehicles. |
| **VAN DAMME SP**/c/o Mendocino District, P.O. Box 440, Mendocino, CA 95460 (707) 937-5804 | Mar 21-Nov 30 | D | $40 | $20 | 40 | 30' | 15 | Y | Maximum trailer length 27' |
| **WOODSON BRIDGE SRA**/25340 South Avenue, Corning, CA 96021, (916) 839-2112 | All Year | D | $25 | $12.50 | 50 | 31' | 20 | Y | Maximum of 10 RVs over 30' |

**P** PRIMITIVE
**D** DEVELOPED

**Abbreviations**

| | | |
|---|---|---|
| SP | State Park | & — Handicapped |
| SHP | State Historic Park | Y — Yes |
| SB | State Beach | N — No |
| SRA | State Recreation Area | |
| SVRA | State Vehicular Recreation Area | |

You may reserve group campsites in the following parks directly with the park.

**Benbow Lake SRA** (200)—(707) 946-2311
**Bothe-Napa Valley SP** (50)—(707) 942-5370
**Caswell Memorial SP** (50)—(209) 599-3810
**Clear Lake SP** (50)—(707) 279-4293
**Cuyamaca Rancho SP** (60)—(619) 765-0755
**Fremont Peak SP** (50)—(408) 623-4255
**George H. Hatfield SRA** (200)—(209) 632-2311
**Henry W. Coe SP** (500)—(408) 779-2728
**Hollister Hills SVRA** (100)—(408) 637-4874
**Lake Elsinore SRA** (350)—(714) 674-3005
**McConnell SRA** (35)—(209) 394-7755
**Mount Diablo SP** (horse camp) (84)—(415) 837-2525
**Mount Tamalpais SP** (50)—(415) 388-2070
**Pfeiffer Big Sur SP** (100)—(408) 667-2315
**Salton Sea SRA** (125)—(619) 393-3052

Youth groups under 18 years of age must have at least one adult for every 15 youths. Conduct of your group must be in accordance with park rules and consideration for others. Any group that has been notified in writing by the district superintendent that its behavior has been unacceptable will be denied further use of the camp, even with reservations.

Maximum number of people, vehicles, and allowable camping equipment will be strictly enforced. Travel-, boat-, and utility-trailers are counted as licensed vehicles.

## GROUP CAMPING FEES

You Pay a minimum fee (½ the Maximum × number of nights) plus a reservation charge of $3.75 per group campsite when you make your reservation. An additional fee of $1.00 per adult and $.50 per youth (for all over the minimum) will be collected at the State park System unit when you register. Other fees (payable at the park) include $3 per night for additional motor vehicles used in the park and $1 per night for each dog.

*"Anyone into tent or RV camping amid beautiful scenery, special trails or wilderness will enjoy the 'California State Parks Guide.' It's a large-size compendium of 250 parks with 150 maps, 125 photos and lots of information that includes historical data, facilities and reservation details."*
**—Los Angeles Times**

*"A guide that will prove useful to anyone who likes to step outdoors. With this wish book you can armchair browse for the site of your next outing or vacation."*
**—Santa Barbara Magazine**

*"Guidebooks are everywhere, but this one is both specific and accurate. What more can you ask of a guidebook?"*
**—San Luis Obispo Telegram Tribune**